Down and Out in Los Angeles and Berlin

DOWN AND OUT IN LOS ANGELES AND BERLIN

The Sociospatial Exclusion of Homeless People

JÜRGEN VON MAHS

TEMPLE UNIVERSITY PRESS
Philadelphia

TEMPLE UNIVERSITY PRESS
Philadelphia, Pennsylvania 19122
www.temple.edu/tempress

Published 2013
Paperback edition published 2015

Library of Congress Cataloging-in-Publication Data

Von Mahs, Jürgen, 1967–
Down and out in Los Angeles and Berlin : the sociospatial exclusion of homeless people / Jürgen von Mahs.
p. cm.
Includes bibliographical references and index.
ISBN 978-1-4399-0826-6 (cloth : alk. paper)
ISBN 978-1-4399-0828-0 (e-book)
1. Homelessness—California—Los Angeles. 2. Homelessness—Germany—Berlin. 3. Homelessness—Government policy—California—Los Angeles. 4. Homelessness—Government policy—Germany—Berlin. 5. Homeless persons—California—Los Angeles.
6. Homeless persons—Germany—Berlin. I. Title.

HV4506.L67V66 2013
305.5'6920943155—dc23

2012025890

ISBN 978-1-4399-0827-3 (paper : alk. paper)

∞The paper used in this publication meets the requirements of the American National Standard for Information Sciences—Permanence of Paper for Printed Library Materials, ANSI Z39.48-1992

Printed in the United States of America

2 4 6 8 9 7 5 3 1

Contents

Preface

At the time, I had no idea that a bright Saturday morning in October 1993 in Los Angeles would forever change the course of my life. A Fulbright student from Germany studying at the University of Southern California (USC), I was taking a course on "Los Angeles and the American Dream," taught by Professor Jennifer Wolch of USC's geography department. On this delightful day, twenty-five undergraduate students embarked on a class field trip to downtown L.A., where Professor Wolch showed us the area's impressive international business center, some amazing architecture, the charming yet kitschy historic pueblo, and then, to everyone's utter disbelief, Skid Row. I can still feel the anguish and utter shock I experienced when we entered the outskirts of this infamous district, to this day home to an estimated eleven thousand homeless people who live contained within a seven-by-five-block area just a few streets east of Los Angeles's thriving commercial downtown. Makeshift cardboard-box homes lined many of the sidewalks, and primarily older black males were roaming the streets. A sense of despair and hopelessness filled the air, and I remember vividly how out of place, helpless, and overwhelmed I felt at that moment. That same day, I went to a bookstore and picked up Professor Wolch's most recent book, *Malign Neglect: Homelessness in an American City,* which she had co-written with her colleague and husband, Michael Dear (Wolch and Dear 1993). I read the book—which I still consider one of the best studies on homelessness ever conducted—in one sitting and, from that moment on, was hooked on the topic and determined to help find a way to aid people in overcoming this disempowering social condition.

Little did I know at the time that this field trip and my subsequent conversations with my professors and peers were the beginning of a working relationship with Professors Wolch and Dear, who recruited me to be their principal assistant in a research project on an innovative grassroots organization in Los Angeles (Dear and von Mahs 1997). I eventually entered USC's master's program in geography and became involved in a research project examining the controversial siting of homeless service facilities and the frequently ensuing "not in my backyard" (NIMBY) battles that prevent equitable service distributions and reinforce the containment of homeless people in Skid Row areas and service-dependent ghettos (Dear and von Mahs 1995). I had the opportunity to learn about the subject matter and benefited from a slew of critical studies on homelessness in North America that were published during this time. I remember reading, with great interest, Neil Smith's *The New Urban Frontier* (1996), Talmadge Wright's *Out of Place* (1997), and Don Mitchell's "The Annihilation of Space by Law" (1997), studies that provided me with clear-eyed assessments of the deliberate exclusion of homeless people in U.S. cities. During this time, I also studied with great fascination qualitative studies employing ethnographic approaches, such as David Snow and Leon Anderson's *Down on Their Luck* (1993); Sue Ruddick's *Young and Homeless in Hollywood* (1996), focusing on homeless youth; and Stacy Rowe and Jennifer Wolch's (1990) ethnographic study of homeless women in Skid Row, all of which I found to be particularly helpful in understanding the nuances that ultimately explain why and how some people overcome homelessness while others do not. These studies, alongside the relatively few international comparative studies at the time (G. Daly 1996; Heilman and Dear 1988; Huth and Wright 1997), provided me with the theoretical, epistemological, and methodological backing to undertake and legitimize further research on homelessness and homeless policy from an international comparative perspective.

Being German, I immediately thought about undertaking a transatlantic urban comparison of public policy's impact on homeless people, something that had not been done before. I felt emboldened to make such a comparison upon reading Margit Mayer's (1995, 1997) poignant articles on what postunification Berlin could learn from the recent, postmodern development of Los Angeles, alongside discussions about the potential "Americanization" of cities in Germany more generally (Albrecht 1994; Häußermann 1998). Such theoretical backup seemed necessary, simply because Los Angeles, in many ways, is quite different from most U.S. cities, let alone European or German cities. Knowing that the economic restructuring processes underlying povertization and homelessness were similar, with relatively similar outcomes in both places, was important to legitimize a comparison of cities that differ tremendously in terms of size, governance, population, and economic activity. At the same time, I also knew from a variety of comparative social-policy studies that the German welfare system is much more developed and comprehensive than that of the United States, including its provisions for poor and homeless people (Esping-Andersen 1990, 1996; van Kersbergen 1995). This comparison, I thought, would make for a good case to advocate for more and better welfare and social-service provision in the United States.

Equipped with my new understanding of homelessness in Los Angeles and a rationale for a comparative analysis, I returned to Germany to start my Ph.D. studies in geography on the previously unexplored impact of public policy from the comparative international perspective. My intentions, at the time, were twofold: Using the example of homelessness, I wanted to show a German audience that any flirtation with U.S.-style neoliberal policy—hotly debated at the time—was counterproductive and damaging. At the same time, I wanted to show a U.S. audience that an alternative—better provision of welfare, as in Germany—was possible and desirable. Yet when I started doing secondary research on homelessness in Germany in the mid-1990s, I came across a finding that truly surprised me. As I discuss in more detail in Chapter 1, despite Germany's more extensive and better integrated set of homeless policies, the numbers and characteristics of homeless people were similar in the two countries, and the average durations of homelessness were longer in Germany during the mid-1990s. Understanding this contradiction—different welfare systems yielding similar outcomes—subsequently became my main objective in writing this book.

Acknowledgments

Considering that my research project and the attempt to write this story unfolded over the better part of fifteen years, many people were directly or indirectly involved in the research and the making of this book, and they deserve my heartfelt gratitude.

This book and the work that went into it would not have been possible without the generous support of a number of organizations that allowed me to conduct research, travel, obtain materials, or hire assistants, including, in chronological order, the Fulbright Commission, the Friedrich Ebert Foundation, the German Marshall Fund, the Andrew Mellon Foundation, and Project Pericles, as well as internal grants and student support from the New School. At the New School, a most amazing place to work, I owe thanks to all my wonderful students, colleagues, chairs, and mentors who offered encouragement and support or provided invaluable feedback on components and drafts of this book, including Julia Foulkes, Joseph Heathcott, Miodrag Mitrasinovic, Gustav Peebles, Scott Salmon, and Gina Walker. I also drew a lot of support and encouragement from the brave group of faculty and students at Eugene Lang College, the New School for Public Engagement, and Parsons, who constitute the Urban Studies/Urban Design community at the New School and provided me with a most inspiring intellectual, social, and political environment. Thanks also to the administrators at the deans' and provost's offices of the New School, who provided me with financial support, a much-needed sabbatical, and the opportunity to hire amazing research and teaching assistants, including Jennie Kaufman, Kelly McMahon, and Caroline Wilson. Jennie, in particular, deserves a lot of credit for helping me complete this book. Without her tremendous editorial skills, attention to detail, and smarts, I would not have been able to move this project from draft to final product so smoothly. The timely completion of the book was also facilitated by the wonderful staff at Temple University Press and, above all, my editor, Mick

Gusinde-Duffy, who did a fantastic job of helping me navigate the process and always provided me with excellent advice.

I was fortunate to have numerous mentors and advisors who helped me along the way. Instrumental to my progress were my two fabulous dissertation advisors, Susan Halford and Traute Meyer at the Department of Sociology and Social Policy at the University of Southampton in England. Their support, guidance, and intellectual stimulation allowed me to situate this project theoretically and empirically and helped me write a persuasive dissertation. Even more, Susan and Traute taught me how to be a good advisor, and I hope I can repay their tremendous effort by doing well by my current students. I would also like to thank former advisors and mentors, including Jennifer Wolch and Michael Dear at USC (both now at UC Berkeley), for their support over the years. I am also grateful for the many ways in which colleagues, friends, and peers have helped me constantly rethink and refine my scholarship or have helped in an editorial capacity, including Melissa Gilbert, Don Mitchell, Laura Pulido, Lois Takahashi, Rob Wilton, Peter Wissocker, and Jim Wright in the United States; Geoff DeVerteuil and Jon May in the United Kingdom; and Volker Busch-Geertsema, Volker Eick, Susanne Gerull, Margit Mayer, and Franz Schaffer in Germany, as well as the countless anonymous reviewers who have commented on various publications that came out of this research, including the three external reviewers of this book. Over the years, I was also lucky to receive tremendous support from staff and administrators at every place I worked—Verna de La Mothe, Yvonne Garrett, Marlene Petlick, Billie Shotlove, Monika Stöcker, and Linda Tribune are among the countless staff members whose diligence, brains, and organizational skills made and continue to make my work and that of my colleagues possible. All aforementioned individuals surely taught me a thing or two about collegiality, reliability, attention to detail, and friendship.

A great number of people have contributed to this research directly by lending their time and expertise, thus helping me gather information and refine my research. In Berlin, I owe thanks to Jens Sambale and Dominik Veith, who helped me establish contact with other key informants; to Klaus Breitfeld, Stefan Schneider, and Uta Sternal, who as facility operators granted me access to my study locations and spent countless hours talking with me; and to Helga Burkert, Sigi Deiß, Jürgen Demmer, Ralf Gruber, Michael Haberkorn, Karlheinz Kramer, Anneliese Leps, Sybille Paetow-Spinosa, Matthias Schulz, Uwe Spacek, Ingo Thederan, Carola von Braun, and Reiner Wild, who met with me. In Los Angeles, Harrold Adams, Richard Bonneau, Mark Casanova, Deborah Davenport, Maya Dunne, Merryl Edelstein, Bob Erlenbusch, Ted Hayes, Arthur Jones, Gregg Kawczynski, Dale Lowery, George Malone, Ruth Schwarz, and Judy Weddle deserve thanks for their willingness to talk with me. They gave me a great opportunity to learn about local policy initiatives, as did, at the national level, Steven Berg, Laura DeKoven-Waxman, Barbara Duffield, John Heinberg, Tanesha P. Hembrey, Fred Karnas Jr., Marsha Martin, Shawn A. Mussington, Nan Roman, and Laurel Weir in Washington, D.C. Their insights clearly helped me develop a more nuanced understanding of the subject matter, and I continue to be impressed by the tremendous dedication and commitment these key informants bring to their jobs on a daily basis.

To be able to write, I needed balance in my life, and I owe a great deal of thanks for the support and love I continue to receive from family and friends in Germany, the United Kingdom, and the United States. Many wonderful people have opened their homes, hearts, and minds to accommodate me, my research, and my antics, including Amos Bransford, Gudrun Frommherz, Ray Hendrickson, and Leon and Carol Rippy in Los Angeles; Stan Deutsch and Marilyn Wender in New York; Susan Halford and Dave Laughlin in Chichester, United Kingdom; my lifelong friends Holger Flügel and family, Christian Schubert, and Christian Wolf back in Franconia; and my friend Alexander Kühl, who provided me with shelter, friendship, and Glenfiddich during my many research travels to Berlin (*Prost!*). I extend my heartfelt thanks and gratitude to my parents, Greta and Jürgen von Mahs, and my brother Christian and his lovely family in Franconia, and to my in-laws, Michael and Gloria Gilbert, and entire extended family in Maryland. I can surely consider myself lucky to have such a wonderful international network of family and friends. Most important, my wife, Melissa, and my two amazing sons, Sam and Ben, deserve my biggest thanks and apologies, as it was often family time that was sacrificed to facilitate writing this book. Melissa has helped me in so many ways by keeping me grounded, supported, assured, and sane, and my boys continue to provide me with hope for the future and tremendous gratitude for the present. I firmly believe that we can and must do better for their future and that of other generations.

Envisioning a better future, ultimately, also implies that we must do better vis-à-vis the least fortunate and perhaps most disenfranchised and disempowered among our fellow citizens—the homeless. My last and perhaps most important thank-you goes to the twenty-eight homeless individuals who shared their life stories and their experiences with me in 1998–1999. I have provided short biographical sketches in Appendix 1 that introduce the respondents and detail how they became homeless. Without these individuals, I could not have told this story, and I hope I have done justice to the openness, honesty, and trust my respondents invested in me. I am humbled by their experiences and extremely grateful for the generosity they have so kindly shown toward me. Their trust has become my obligation, and I hope I have represented them accurately, fairly, and well. I certainly owe it to them!

Commonly Used Abbreviations

AFDC	Aid to Families with Dependent Children (federal welfare program for impoverished families until 1996, United States)
AK	Arbeitskreis (working group), as in AK Wohnungsnot (Berlin)
ALG	Arbeitslosengeld (unemployment compensation prior to 2005, Germany)
ALG I	Arbeitslosengeld I (unemployment compensation since 2005 Hartz Reforms, 63 percent of previous income, Germany)
ALG II	Arbeitslosengeld II (unemployment compensation since 2005 Hartz Reforms, fixed benefit amount, Germany)
ALH	Arbeitslosenhilfe (unemployment assistance prior to 2005, Germany)
ALMP	Active labor market policies
BSHG	Bundessozialhilfegesetz (federal social code, Germany)
BVG	Berliner Verkehrsgemeinschaft (public transportation authority, Berlin)
CDU	Christlich Demokratische Partei Deutschlands (Christian Democrats, Germany)
DPSS	Department of Public and Social Services (Los Angeles)
FEANTSA	European Observatory on Homelessness (Brussels, Belgium)
FRG	Federal Republic of Germany (former West Germany)
GA	General Assistance (local welfare program for single adults, United States)
GDR	German Democratic Republic (former East Germany)
GG	Grundgesetz (basic law, German constitution)

GR	General Relief (local welfare program for single adults, California variant of GA)
GROW	General Relief Opportunities to Work (local job training program, Los Angeles)
HSMIS	Homeless Service Management Information Systems
HUD	U.S. Department of Housing and Urban Development
IT	Information Technology
LACEHH	Los Angeles Coalition to End Hunger and Homelessness
LAHP	Los Angeles Homelessness Project
LAHSA	Los Angeles Homeless Services Authority
NAEHP	National Alliance to End Hunger and Poverty (Washington, D.C.)
NCH	National Coalition for the Homeless (Washington, D.C.)
NLCHP	National Law Center on Homelessness and Poverty (Washington, D.C.)
PRWORA	Personal Responsibility and Work Opportunity Reconciliation Act (federal welfare reform, United States)
SenVer	Senatsverwaltung (district administration, Berlin)
SPD	Sozialdemokratische Partei Deutschlands (Social Democratic Party, Germany)
SSI	Social Security Supplemental Income (federal welfare program for poor people with disabilities, United States)
SSMIS	Social Service Management Information System
TANF	Temporary Aid for Needy Families (federal welfare program for impoverished families since 1996, United States)

1

Different Welfare Regimes, Similar Outcomes?

The Impact of Public Policy on Homeless People's Exit Chances in Berlin and Los Angeles

Homelessness is a complex societal condition that has proliferated over the past three decades in most industrialized nation-states of the global north. Moreover, nations' homeless populations have become increasingly diverse, more closely reflecting the poverty populations inhabiting these countries. It is commonly understood that homelessness in industrialized nation-states is a function of the complicated interplay between individual risk factors and broader structural root causes, including economic restructuring and ensuing marginality, demographic changes, and a shortage of affordable housing. Such factors, experts agree, also function as substantial barriers toward overcoming homelessness, because highly stigmatized homeless people face particular obstacles in overcoming market barriers.

There is less consensus, however, on the impact of government intervention on homelessness and attempts to overcome it, simply because the nature and extent of government intervention varies greatly among industrialized countries. The United States, for instance, provides little assistance to poor and homeless people, and neoliberal welfare-state restructuring is often identified as a major structural root cause of homelessness as well as an exit barrier.[1] Germany, on the other hand, has a much more comprehensive national welfare system that includes specific service options for homeless people, resulting in more extensive benefits covering income, shelter, health care, and other needs.

Considering the differences in the nature and extent of welfare systems, it is rather perplexing that the prevalence rates of homelessness were almost as high in Germany as in the United States in the late 1990s, affecting close to 1 percent of the total population.[2] Not only that, but the extent of long-term homelessness (homeless spells lasting more than one year) was almost twice as high in Germany, affecting approximately two-thirds of all homeless people nationwide. As if this statistic were not surprising enough, the implementation of neoliberal welfare reforms in Germany in 2005 should have increased the numbers of homeless people, if the U.S. experiences with neoliberal policy were any indication, yet the numbers across the country continued to decline. Why did homelessness in Germany increase despite a more comprehensive welfare system, and why did it decline upon the enactment of neoliberal reforms? More precisely, what role does government intervention play in helping homeless people secure income and shelter and, ideally, move on to employment and housing?

To provide answers to these questions, I decided to focus this comparative analysis on Berlin and Los Angeles, both dubbed "homeless capitals" for having the largest homeless populations of their respective countries (Mayer 1997). An urban focus is further warranted, because Germany and the United States are federal systems, giving state and local authorities a great deal of discretion regarding how, in compliance with federal welfare legislation, they organize their social welfare and homeless service systems, including the ways in which they incorporate the "third sector" of voluntary service providers. The two cities are good test cases for assessing the impact of public policy on homeless people and their chances to overcome homelessness, simply because they do, at first sight, seem to confirm the assertion that Germany's welfare approach is superior. As I explain in more detail later in this chapter, homeless people in Berlin are provided with substantially more service options than their peers in Los Angeles. Yet, as elsewhere in Germany, the numbers of homeless people in Berlin continued to rise throughout the 1990s, homeless populations became more diverse in terms of gender and ethnicity, and long durations were common—homeless spells lasted longer in Berlin than in Los Angeles.[3] Furthermore, the number of homeless people eventually declined despite the implementation of neoliberal policies and workfarist[4] practices in Germany after 2005.

To understand why homelessness has risen in Germany despite the existence of a comprehensive national welfare system and why local service and shelter options did not help reduce homelessness or decrease durations during the late 1990s, I conducted original empirical research in Berlin, which I compared to existing data from Los Angeles, where homelessness has been more extensively studied over the past twenty-five years.[5] Specifically, I employed ethnographic research methods of participant observation and in-depth interviewing in three case studies in Berlin over the course of one year (1998–1999). This approach allowed me to document success and failure among twenty-eight single adult homeless people, including four women and four foreign nationals, and to assess the role government intervention played in the process. I complemented such field research with more than thirty key-informant interviews, secondary sources, and public-opinion surveys (see Chapter 2). This "multiperspectival," multimethod approach allowed me to generate an abundance of information on homeless people's experiences with various forms of government and nongovernmental intervention as well as with other institutions and actors over an extended period of time and thus gain a more nuanced understanding of the impact of public policy on homeless people's immediate life circumstances and long-term chances to overcome homelessness.

Ultimately, this comparison at the urban scale and the scale of lived experiences has allowed me to answer these questions and explain that a malfunctioning interchange between homeless people, homeless service provision, and broader welfare policies at the local level needlessly delays an exit from homelessness and forecloses the long-term chances of many homeless people to overcome this state, even when more welfare provisions are provided and more social rights exist. Specifically, I demonstrate that homeless people in both Germany and the United States experience "sociospatial exclusion" in that their behaviors are criminalized, their services are located in service ghettos, and their chances in the marketplace are impeded by their lack of resources and employability.

Sociospatial exclusion consists of three interrelated trajectories—namely, legal exclusion (i.e., the criminalization of homeless people and their survival strategies), service exclusion (i.e., the warehousing of homeless people in decrepit shelter facilities and the containment of homeless shelter and service facilities in impoverished parts of town), and market exclusion (i.e., the barriers to accessing both labor and housing markets and the inability of local welfare to facilitate reintegration). Individual homeless people experience such exclusion differently, depending on their life courses. Moreover, Berlin and Los Angeles have different configurations of exclusion. In Berlin, market exclusion is more pronounced, because the city's more regulated and exclusionary labor market results in higher rates of long-term unemployment and thus often chronic or long-term homelessness. Homeless people in Los Angeles, on the other hand, find work more easily and thus temporarily escape homelessness. Yet the jobs are likely to be low wage and temporary, so homeless people often cycle in and out of homelessness. Additionally, both legal and social exclusion tend to be more prevalent in Los Angeles, simply because impoverished urban areas in Berlin are not as deprived and neglected as North American ghettos, and Berlin's antihomeless regulations are not as sweeping.[6] Regardless of local configurations, sociospatial exclusion and its inherent trajectories of legal, service, and market exclusion constitute formidable barriers to both overcoming homelessness and achieving social and economic stability. This exclusion often has devastating personal consequences for individuals' life chances by reinforcing a downward spiral of defeatism, regardless of the nature and extent of the welfare system.

The concept of sociospatial exclusion expands our understanding of the impact of public policy on homeless people's exit chances for a number of reasons. First, the model allows for recasting dominant assumptions about what constitutes "successful" welfare-state performance. Specifically, I argue that although the German welfare system is, as demonstrated by existing research, de jure more comprehensive and extensive at the *national* level, de facto policy and service delivery deficiencies exist at the *local* level due to sociospatial exclusion. Although the trajectories of sociospatial exclusion and its related policy deficiencies are configured differently in Berlin and Los Angeles, they affect homeless people's long-term chances to permanently overcome homelessness in surprisingly similar ways. This finding warrants paying more attention to processes occurring at the urban and community levels—the levels of policy implementation and actual service provision—and at the level of lived experience in comparative social policy analyses.

Second, homeless people's individual experiences with public policy and service provision vary substantially, as does the outcome of such efforts. The Berlin research clearly demonstrates that the extent to which homeless people are affected by the three trajectories of exclusion is largely dependent on their life-course experiences, particularly whether they had previously been integrated into the societal "mainstream."

Third, homeless people's exit and life chances are strongly affected by fundamental reconfigurations of urban space, impeded by diminishing public spaces (legal exclusion), the geography of homeless service provision (service exclusion), and a spatial mismatch in the geography of labor and housing markets (market exclusion).

Finally, I argue that sociospatial exclusion must be accounted for to maximize the effectiveness of homeless policy and service provision. Accordingly, I propose universal policy recommendations to improve local policy practice and service delivery and to overcome sociospatial exclusion, thus facilitating a more rapid and lasting exit from homelessness. In this context, I also reflect on the most recent changes to the German welfare system—the 2005 Hartz IV reforms—and the question of whether these reforms are likely to improve homeless people's exit chances.

Conceptualizing Exit in Comparative Perspective

Finding out why a more interventionist and comprehensive welfare system, such as Germany's, does not seem to produce better outcomes than the comparatively more residual U.S. welfare state in reducing both the extent and the duration of homelessness is a difficult challenge. Not only do we need to find a way to compare the dissimilar policy and administrative frameworks of Germany and the United States, but we also have to come to terms with distinct local contexts of homelessness and inherently different urban economies, plus their implications for labor and housing markets. In addition, homeless people are a heterogeneous group of people who are difficult to identify, track, and therefore research. Because of such difficulties, few international comparative studies exist, few studies specifically focus on exit from homelessness, and no studies to date explore policy effects on homeless people's exit chances from the international comparative perspective.[7] To be able to compare homelessness and homeless policy responses in different places, I have devised a conceptual model of exit that has been inspired by four theoretical frameworks: welfare regime theory, deconstruction, internal and external determinants of exit, and life-course theory.

First, I use Gøsta Esping-Andersen's (1990) *welfare regime theory* to provide a well-established framework through which to compare the dissimilar systems of Germany and the United States. Welfare regime theory posits that a nation-state's approach to alleviating social risks (e.g., illness, lack of education and job training, poverty, old age) depends on the interplay between the family (i.e., social or communal networks), the market (i.e., employment), and the state (i.e., welfare system). The goal of the modern welfare state is therefore to "decommodify" and "defamilialize" social risks (i.e., to protect individuals from market risks and to reduce family burdens and risks, respectively) and to provide or finance a range of services over the course of a person's lifetime, literally from the cradle to the grave (for discussion of concepts, see Esping-Andersen 1990). The ways in which individual nation-states attempt to do so are subject to considerable variation. Still, upon studying a broad range of variables, including a "decommodification index," Esping-Andersen identifies three worlds of welfare capitalism, each of which emphasizes particular aspects of the welfare mix: the "liberal" (emphasizing the market; e.g., the United States and the UK), the "conservative/corporatist" (emphasizing the family and the state; e.g., Germany and France), and the "social-democratic/universalist" (emphasizing the state; e.g., Sweden and Denmark). His findings and a number of studies that use this typology agree that the German conservative/corporatist system achieves a better balance among the family, the market, and the state than the U.S. system.[8] Direct comparisons of the United States and Germany provided by Robert Goodin et al. (1999) and Lutz Leisering and Stephan Leibfried (1999) also suggest that Germany's system performs significantly better than that of the liberal United States in terms of welfare-state outcomes, such as advancing economic efficiency, reducing poverty, and promoting social equality, stability, autonomy, and social integration (for overall results, see Goodin et al. 1999, 240–245 and 253–258). This broader conceptualization of welfare is important, because policy effects cannot be understood without recognizing their relationship to both the sphere of the market (which homeless people commonly wish to access) and the personal dimensions associated with family and thus social networks (which homeless people commonly wish to establish, extend, or repair).

Second, an important aspect of understanding homelessness and the various personal, structural, and institutional manifestations of this social condition involves using *deconstruction* as a means to find out why—and, more precisely, where—people become homeless and how geographic processes determine, constrain, and mediate people's attempts to overcome homelessness for good. Perhaps the most persuasive account as to how various restructuring processes affect the geography of homelessness and thus the contained spaces in which the homeless must exist has been provided by Jennifer Wolch and Michael Dear's (1993) comprehensive account of homelessness in Los Angeles. Aptly titled *Malign Neglect,* their book is the result of a multiyear study by the Los Angeles Homelessness Project, and it provides an important reference point for this volume. In their book, the authors deconstruct urban homelessness, showing how it is the product of broader structural economic, social, and political root causes and their geographic embeddedness. They show how homeless people and the services that cater to their needs are deliberately contained in ghettos excluded from more promising urban spaces, a practice that itself adversely affects homeless people's activity space and options. The importance of geographic processes for a more nuanced understanding of homelessness can be considered one of the most important omissions in research on homelessness in Germany to date.[9]

Third, Bradley Wright's (1996) conceptualization of *internal and external determinants of exit* allows me to link specific broader structural factors associated with the three welfare regime dimensions with corresponding internal determinants, such as human capital (linked to the market), social capital (the family), and social-welfare capital (the state).[10] After all, it has been well established that homelessness is not just an unfortunate confluence of personal vulnerabilities, traumatic events, choices, and behaviors but rather is in large part determined by external structural root causes, which, in both countries, have been associated with economic restructuring processes and their impact on labor and housing markets, simultaneously increasing the demand for and diminishing the supply of affordable housing. In the United States—much more so than in Germany—welfare-state restructuring has also been associated with increasing homelessness, a particularly strong emphasis of Wolch and Dear's study (1993). Differentiating between and exploring the relationships among these factors also emphasize homeless people's agency in that doing so recognizes homeless people as conscientious actors who try to make the best out of adverse circumstances using whatever human, social, and social-welfare capital they have at their disposal.

Finally, an emphasis on poor people's agency is also inherent in Leisering and Leibfried's (1999) *life-course approach,* which they devised to understand the effects of welfare on recipients over time. Focusing on welfare recipients' specific poverty management over a ten-year period in Bremen, Germany, the authors examine recipients' ability to overcome whatever hardship caused their poverty, paying particular attention to the role of the local welfare state. In doing so, the study further explores the question of whether the German welfare state, like that of the United States, results in welfare dependence and entrenchment. Their longitudinal analysis of (nonhomeless) welfare recipients clearly reveals that, contrary to the popular assumption, the German welfare system is rather successful in ensuring fairly quick and successful poverty management by either optimizing or stabilizing recipients' life courses—that is, either helping them overcome poverty or at least preventing further economic descent. As a result, fewer welfare recipients than in the United States become truly entrenched in the welfare system and thus dependent on assistance for extended periods of time (224–236). Whether this positive assessment also holds up in the context of homelessness and whether the homeless, too, manage to optimize their poverty management has remained unknown and thus is an important objective of this study.

To show how I am combining insights from these theoretical frameworks for understanding homeless people's attempts to overcome homelessness in comparative perspective, I have developed a graphic conceptualization of exit from homelessness, with particular emphasis on the role of the state (Fig. 1.1). Specifically, I propose that homeless people's exit chances depend on the interplay

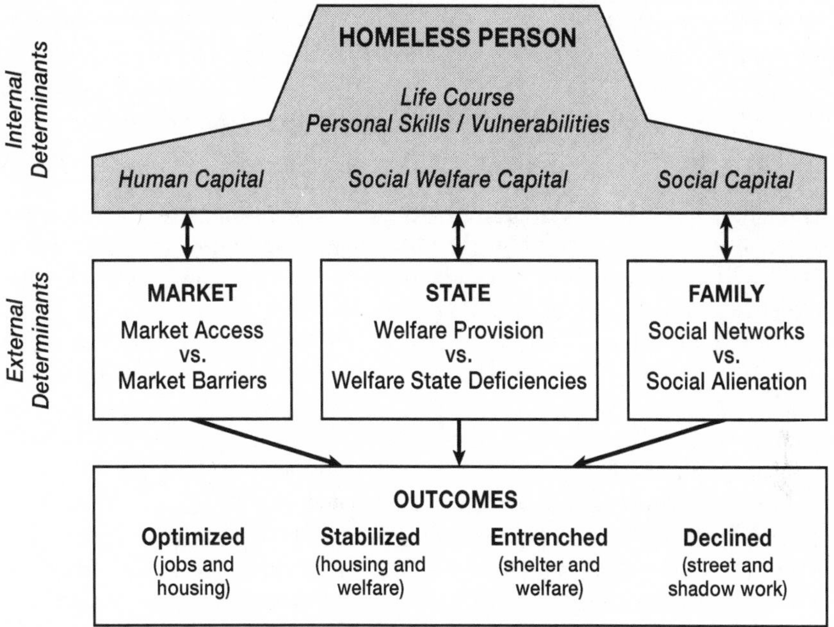

FIGURE 1.1 Internal and External Determinants of Exit from Homelessness

between internal factors (the individuals themselves) and external factors (the institutional and structural context in which homeless people operate), which, over time, may or may not lead to exit from homelessness—outcomes may include optimization, stabilization, entrenchment, or the complete exclusion of homeless people. The internal determinants consist of individual homeless people's distinct characteristics, which may either help or hinder exit, including personal vulnerabilities (e.g., gender, race, age, or social problems, including substance abuse and mental illness), human capital (education, job skills, and work experience), social capital (existence of social networks and extent of social integration), and social-welfare capital (awareness of, access to, and use of welfare and other social services). The extent to which such personal factors matter in facilitating exit, in turn, depends on the institutional and structural context in which homeless people operate, including local housing and labor markets, homeless service provision, and the local social networks homeless people may or may not possess (B. Wright 1996). Although these specific internal and external determinants have not been explicitly linked to welfare regime theory by Wright or other existing studies, they broadly correspond with the three dimensions of a welfare regime that are commonly used in comparative social policy analyses—namely, the market, the state, and the family.

In the following review of the literature on homelessness, I address the various components of the aforementioned theoretical framework separately and, in so doing, provide further evidence for the apparent contradiction of different welfare regimes yet similar outcomes at the federal and local levels.

Determinants of Exit in Comparative Perspective: A Review of the Literature

Any library or Internet search on the topic of homelessness in postindustrial societies reveals rather quickly that homelessness is a much-studied subject, encompassing a vast array of literature spanning almost the entirety of academic disciplines. There are also scores of government reports, data, and policy briefs, alongside an abundance of "gray literature" compiled by think tanks, advocacy organizations, and grassroots organizations, providing information about homelessness and homeless people. Almost every study is quick to point out that homelessness is a tremendously difficult condition to study and comprehend, a problem that starts with the rather difficult task of properly defining homelessness and its multiple meanings.[11] Because of inconsistent definitions and substantial obstacles to counting homeless people, we do not even know precisely how many people are homeless at any given time; consequently, great inconsistencies exist in the data on homelessness, regardless of country (Corday and Pion 1997).

To provide a coherent account of the determinants of exit along the lines of the previously identified dimensions, I am giving a rather cursory, interdisciplinary overview, because any of these factors in and of themselves warrant further analysis that could fill entire volumes (and in many cases already has). Still, through this discussion, I demonstrate that serious gaps remain in our understanding of exit barriers in Germany in general and in Berlin in particular. I also wish to establish a rationale as to why Berlin and Los Angeles, despite their obvious differences in size, structure, population, and local economy, are particularly good case studies to explore the paradox of different welfare regimes yielding similar outcomes. I begin with a brief discussion of internal determinants, which, despite being difficult to quantify, play an important role in a person's path into homelessness, her or his life under the condition of homelessness, and the path out of homelessness. This complexity of personal circumstances makes proactively addressing homelessness a difficult undertaking.

Internal Determinants: Life Course, Identity, and Social Risks

Considering that we generally lack reliable and representative data on homelessness in the first place, resulting in tremendous variations between high and low estimates as well as between and among urban jurisdictions, it is difficult to quantify internal dimensions, especially considering the fact that no homeless person's life story is completely identical to another's. Countless intersecting circumstances contribute to a person's loss of a residence and, conceivably, delay or even foreclose his or her lasting exit from homelessness. Still, from a quite extensive range of literature on homelessness and the empirical base these studies supply, we can isolate a number of internal determinants that tend to be overrepresented among the homeless in both countries and within their respective cities. Such determinants include certain variations in gender, race/ethnicity/nationality, life course, and associated personal problems. Many of the underlying social risks, in theory at least, ought to be addressed by public policy and the welfare system in its function to "defamilialize" such risks. In the following section, I provide a cursory overview of the key factors that demonstrate why homelessness is such a difficult social problem to address.

Identity: Race, Class, and Gender

It is commonly accepted that the formation of one's identity and the subsequent acquisition of human and social capital are in large part determined by one's gender as well as one's race or ethnicity and class standing. Although homelessness is a condition that could conceivably affect any person regardless of his or her previous standing in society—and I have met Ph.D.'s, former executives, lawyers, and other educated folks among the homeless—most homeless people hail from more marginal economic backgrounds and, as a result, often lack the human capital necessary to succeed in a competitive capitalist economy (U.S. Department of Housing and Urban Development 2010). Marginality may also imply that people cannot as easily rely on their social capital, as their social networks are also likely to be low income.

Similarly important is the notion of gender, given the general trend toward a feminization of poverty in most industrial nation-states, Germany and the United States included (Klodawsky 2006; Rosenke 2006; Passaro 1996). Although homelessness largely remains a problem that primarily affects disaffiliated and marginalized single adult males in both countries, the proportion of women has been rising steadily; some 15 percent of single homeless are women (U.S. Department of Housing and Urban Development 2010; BAG Wohnungslosenhilfe 2009). In the United States, much more so than in Germany, the percentage of homeless families is steadily growing, the overwhelming majority of which are headed by single mothers (Haber and Toro 2004). In this context, we can already surmise that lower extents of family homelessness in Germany (including Berlin) are the primary result of welfare intervention, which, compared with the United States, is substantially more comprehensive in that cash assistance (DM 2,160/ $1,200[12] for a family of four, compared with a maximum Temporary Aid for Needy Families [TANF] benefit in the United States of $744 in 2010) can be relatively easily bundled with additional programs (e.g., housing subsidies, public housing). A gendered analysis, however, also requires us to look at masculinity and stereotypes, as most homeless are still stigmatized single men who, in most cultural contexts, are often considered less deserving of help (Passaro 1996).

Finally, ethnicity and citizenship may be among the most persistent, overarching factors in rising homelessness. Although homelessness traditionally was a problem affecting disaffiliated white/native males in both countries (the so-called old homeless), the proportion of ethnic minorities and foreign citizens has been increasing steadily in both places, and ethnic minorities now constitute the majority of homeless people in Los Angeles (LAHSA 2011).[13] Both welfare systems have been accused of discriminatory practices, although foreign nationals in Berlin have, de jure, the same rights and access to the same public resources as native Germans, provided they are legal residents (Neubeck and Cazenave 2001).

Risk Factors Associated with the Life Courses of Homeless People

According to empirical research in both countries, a number of additional risk factors and personal vulnerabilities are associated with the likelihood of a person's becoming and perhaps even remaining homeless. It is generally difficult to find statistically significant relationships because of the tremendous variability of individual circumstances; moreover, many of these variables are not static and are constantly changing over time and space to create quite differently configured trajectories into, during, and ideally out of homelessness. Nonetheless, the following overview provides a brief description of each of these, showing that such individual factors matter regardless of country or city and thus pose tremendous challenges for local welfare systems.

A great number of risk factors are associated with biographical aspects, the most obvious being age. In this regard, we notice slight clusters among younger (ages 15–30) and older (ages 40–65) people in Berlin, thus comprising people with disproportionately high exposure to long-term unemployment (Senatsverwaltung für Gesundheit und Soziales 2004; LAHSA 2011). The proportion of homeless people over 40 is bigger in Berlin than in Los Angeles, where homeless people tend to be younger and typically in their prime working age. Age is also important, because each phase in a person's life course involves its own set of risks. We know, for instance, that disproportionate numbers of homeless people have had previous experience with foster care, violence, or residential instability and frequent, often involuntary moves. We also know, as I describe shortly, that homeless people by and large tend to be less successful in building human and social capital and are at a disadvantage vis-à-vis other people seeking jobs and housing, a problem that worsens over their lifetimes. Such factors, in the United States at least, have also been associated with longer durations of homelessness and lower extents of exit among homeless people. Similarly, sudden, often traumatic events throughout life, such as accidents, deaths in the family, domestic violence, or sudden and debilitating illnesses, can cause people to become indigent and, as a result, eventually homeless.

Acute or chronic health problems and disability in particular are further overrepresented among homeless people. Although estimates vary, up to one-third of all homeless people in both countries may have mental health problems ranging from depression to psychosis. In this area, however, government intervention can make a big difference, in that people with documented disabilities, if they qualify, have access to more service options and higher benefits and thus tend to exit more rapidly. In this context, homeless people in the United States might even have an advantage in that they may qualify for Social Security Supplemental Income (SSI), a work-related cash-assistance program for people with documented physical or mental disabilities that pays a maximum benefit of about $700 per month, which is almost double the German social-assistance payments. Unfortunately, however, only about 2 percent of the homeless in Los Angeles and in the United States overall receive such benefits.

Another factor, and one frequently associated with homelessness in the public eye, is a disproportionate prevalence of substance abuse, particularly alcohol problems. Although estimates vary, Jan Podschus and Peter Dufeu (1995) found that almost two-thirds of homeless street people they examined in Berlin had alcohol or other substance-abuse problems. In Los Angeles, we notice greater variations depending on population group and location, but studies from Skid Row—home to some eleven thousand homeless people—reveal high rates similar to those in Berlin (Cousineau 1993). It comes as no surprise, then, that high alcohol and drug use among the homeless contributes to the stigmatization and often negative perception of homeless people.

Finally—and this may be a phenomenon particular to the United States—almost one-third of all U.S. homeless are veterans, many of whom have had combat experience and suffer from mental illness (e.g., post-traumatic stress disorder [PTSD]), frequently dual or triple diagnoses (LAHSA 2011, 18). Although specific services are available for veterans, many do not utilize them because they were dishonorably discharged, are ineligible for procedural reasons, or simply cannot or refuse to seek help. And although many German homeless men also served in the military (German men were, until 2010, subject to military draft or social service), they were not in combat and thus did not suffer war-related trauma.

Yet perhaps the most important internal determinants of homelessness and the paths out of it are associated with the nature and extent of a person's human and social capital, because both ideally function to prevent homelessness in the first place, stabilize the life course and prevent further descent if home loss cannot be averted, and allow a person to reenter the regular job and housing markets. Through such economic integration, people also wish to establish the continuity and stability necessary to create, reestablish, or repair social relationships. These goals and the principal steps to achieve them are clearly the most common objectives of homeless people, according to studies on the subject from both countries (Acosta and Toro 2000; Busch-Geertsema 2002). In the following three sections, I therefore provide a differentiated discussion regarding how the internal dimensions of social, human, and social-welfare capital correspond to broader societal changes associated with the three key dimensions of the welfare regime: the family, the market, and the state.

The Social Capital–Family Nexus

One aspect that most studies on homelessness agree upon is that a lack of social capital and, therein, place-based social networks to kin and other nonhomeless people is a major contributor to the onset of homelessness and a barrier to its exit.[14] Social networks are also main ingredients of the welfare regime dimension of "family," invoking the concept of familial, tribal, and communal ties that, before the industrial age, used to be the primary constituent of a person's welfare. To this day, social networks are typically the first recourse in case of a financial or housing emergency, particularly when government resources are scarce or have not been accessed or the person facing homelessness is unaware of other options. Therefore, it is not surprising that a lack of kinship or other social ties is a major risk factor for becoming homeless. If a person does not have social networks, if a person's social contacts are poor or precariously housed themselves, or if a person has exceeded his or her social networks (e.g., couch surfing beyond the point of welcome), homelessness is often the logical outcome.

U.S. research further suggests that social networks change over the course of homelessness. According to Stacy Rowe and Jennifer Wolch (1990), losing their homes and often social contacts constitutes a time-space discontinuity, which, over time, requires homeless people to establish a new time-space continuity in the context of homelessness, often including the creation of new social networks. Such networks, as Wolch and Dear's (1993) Los Angeles study shows, can have both positive and negative outcomes. If and to what extent this also applies to Germany and Berlin remain relatively understudied.

Further understudied are the geography and the nature of the changes in homeless people's social networks. In Los Angeles, deliberate containment and ghettoization of homeless people and the services that cater to their needs into deprived urban communities are major detriments to their ability to maintain external social networks, further reinforcing their social and spatial isolation (Rowe and Wolch 1990; Dear and Wolch 1987). What's more, researchers from Los Angeles have further suggested that the deliberate containment of homeless people in impoverished communities constitutes a spatial mismatch between the locations in which homeless people live (or are permitted to live) and the location of potentially better housing and job opportunities (Wolch and Dear 1993; DeVerteuil 2003a). Whether homeless people were similarly entrapped in Berlin has remained unknown, but I attempt to provide an answer in Chapter 4. If anything, the U.S. data suggest that overcoming homelessness from within a ghetto and in a highly contested urban labor market is an uphill battle, especially if an individual's human capital is low.

The Human Capital–Market Nexus

Perhaps the single-most-important reason why people become homeless is income poverty and the associated inability to afford regular rental housing due to lack of employment.[15] It is commonly understood that low human capital (defined as a person's ability to perform in a market economy to secure material survival) constitutes a competitive disadvantage, which can be a major root cause of homelessness, especially in tight urban housing and labor markets. In this context, we notice a substantial welfare regime difference in that the U.S. economy and its urban labor markets are much less regulated, thus allowing for low-wage employment, which gives homeless people a greater chance to enter the service sector but hardly any chance for upward mobility (Burns, Flaming, and Haydamack 2004; U.S. Department of Housing and Urban Development 2010). The German system, by contrast, is more highly regulated through its compulsory social-insurance system and complex labor legislation, which, until recently, disallowed employment below union-negotiated wages. As a result, homeless people are less likely to find jobs than their U.S. counterparts, instead becoming and often remaining long-term unemployed. Yet the results of underemployment in the United States and persistent unemployment in Germany are the same—increasing and increasingly relentless urban poverty and, in combination with tight urban housing markets, homelessness. And, as with the social capital–family nexus, a question arises: Why did the German system with all its labor market policies fail to ensure homeless people's more rapid reentry into the labor market? Before discussing these questions, let us first look at the U.S. system and the case of Los Angeles and how economic restructuring has facilitated the rapid growth of homelessness since the 1980s.

Los Angeles: Globalization, Economic Restructuring, and Low-Wage Employment

That a lack of human capital increases one's chances to be impoverished and entrapped in precarious low-income employment should come as no surprise, especially in the case of a liberal welfare regime with limited government intervention, such as that of the United States. It consequently also comes as no surprise that, according to U.S. research on exit from homelessness, a positive correlation exists between lack of education, job training, and work experience and lack of success in overcoming homelessness. Although the U.S. homeless population is, by most accounts, slightly more educated than the nation's overall poor population, it still has disproportionate numbers of people who never finished high school and, as a result, never received formal job training (Burt et al. 2001). That primarily people with low educational attainment and low human capital become adversely affected by economic restructuring processes has been well established in scores of literature discussing the new urban poverty in the United States. The perhaps inevitable consequence is extreme marginalization and, consequently, often homelessness. How economic restructuring has affected urban homelessness is superbly demonstrated in Wolch and Dear's 1993 book, *Malign Neglect*. The authors show persuasively how the combination of rising marginality and a lack of affordable housing result in a massive proliferation of people threatened by impending homelessness (proto-homelessness), which, depending on quite different individual circumstances, may result in episodic (one-time), chronic (long-term), or cyclical (repeated) forms of homelessness. Not only has economic restructuring facilitated a massive rise in homelessness, but it is also a reason why people remain entrapped in chronic poverty and as a result often experience repeated bouts of homelessness.

Perhaps more alarmingly, even finding a regular job does not necessarily help one achieve economic stability or upward mobility in Los Angeles. According to a longitudinal study of 1,250 homeless adults who participated in a job-training program in Los Angeles in the early 1990s, 40 percent managed to find jobs within one year and used such income to pay for housing (Burns, Flaming, and Haydamack 2004, 37–39; Einbinder et al. 1995, 2). The primary reason for such rapid escape was access to low-income work, which is readily available in Los Angeles's comparatively unregulated labor market (Burns, Flaming, and Haydamack 2004, 46; Schoeni and Koegel 1998; Tepper and Simpson 2003). Yet this economic study also demonstrates that few homeless people overcome homelessness for good, because they become entrapped in the low-income, low-security, and low-gratification formal labor market, or the informal economy.[16] The primary reason for this stagnation is that most jobs are unstable, are temporary, and provide very low income—the average hourly wage of a job a homeless person was able to find was $6.61 in 1992, whereas an hourly wage of $11 was needed to afford a studio apartment under fair market conditions (Burns, Flaming, and Haydamack 2004, 39–41). Therefore most newly found housing arrangements are overcrowded, shared accommodations that are easily lost should one roommate become unemployed again and thus unable to contribute to rent payments (40–41). The ultimate result is recurrent or cyclical homelessness; almost three-quarters of the homeless from the Course of Homelessness Study who exited became homeless again (Koegel 2004; Wolf et al. 2001).[17]

Berlin: Unification, Deindustrialization, and Long-Term Unemployment

Economic restructuring undoubtedly has also played a major role in the dramatic increase in the number of homeless people in Germany, especially in the aftermath of Germany's costly unification in 1990. But although unification played a major role—it fundamentally changed housing and labor markets, particularly in the newly unified national capital of Berlin—it alone cannot explain the increase, which raises the question of why and how the local welfare system appeared unable to prevent homelessness or to at least reduce its duration.[18]

German unification immediately tightened affordable housing segments and, in so doing, surely accelerated the growth of homelessness to its peak of more than eleven thousand officially registered homeless people in 1997 (Senatsverwaltung für Gesundheit und Soziales 1997, 41). The numbers have since declined and, according to most estimates, have remained fairly stable at around six thousand since 2004 (Abgeordnetenhaus von Berlin 2008). This trend indicates that market forces and consequent fluctuations in local housing and labor markets play important roles in causing homelessness and in preventing people from overcoming it. The consolidation of administrative entities and real estate markets in Berlin, along with the move of the federal government from Bonn, clearly accelerated pressures on the housing market, setting in motion a wave of speculation and housing conversions during the early 1990s (Schnur 1999). Rental prices soared, and many landlords sought opportunities to renovate units for more upscale customers. Some 150,000 people were looking for housing in Berlin in the 1990s, resulting in a housing squeeze. New residential-housing construction, especially affordable units, lagged the demand. Demographic changes—most notably immigration and the proliferation of single-person and single-parent households—put further pressures on the low-income housing market, which became more expensive and increasingly concentrated in the city's most impoverished and ethnically diverse parts of town, most notably in Wedding, Mitte, and Kreuzberg. More recently, former blue-collar districts, such as Spandau and Neukölln, joined the most impoverished districts.

The reason people are ultimately unable to maintain their homes is most often associated with income poverty. Economic restructuring after unification resulted in deindustrialization and massive job losses in manufacturing, which could not be offset by the growth of service-sector employment. Between 1993 and 2007, Berlin lost 21 percent of its employment opportunities. Many elderly homeless have dated skills and lack experience compared with graduates and low-wage immigrants. Younger homeless, in turn, find it difficult to find apprenticeships and entry-level jobs, especially in the declining manufacturing sector and, in the wake of the construction boom, the building and construction sectors. This situation further tightened the labor-market opportunities of the long-term unemployed and excluded.

So although it would certainly be convenient to blame the surge of homelessness during the 1990s solely on the economic aftermath of unification, this explanation falls short for two reasons. First, homelessness had already reached crisis proportions before unification, as almost six thousand people—about the same level as today—were registered as homeless in West Berlin alone. Although homelessness grew disproportionately quickly in the eastern parts of town after unification, urban homelessness remains primarily a Western phenomenon that occurred under a presumably functioning West German welfare system (East Germany did not have or need a homeless service infrastructure). But, more important, we know very little about the specifics of homeless people's difficulties breaking into the formal labor and housing markets. How much do they rely on public assistance, how much on nonprofits, and how much on self-initiative? What strategies do they employ, and how do those strategies change? How successful are their efforts, and which factors contribute to success or failure? Such questions need to be asked before we can feel confident in an explanation.

Although economic restructuring processes undeniably contributed to increasing poverty and homelessness in Berlin and Los Angeles, the reasons why Germany's regulatory welfare system and its much more tightly woven social safety net seemed to fail in helping homeless people overcome market barriers more rapidly have remained perplexing.

Social-Welfare Capital–State Nexus

In terms of homeless people's social-welfare capital, a category conceived by Wright as an internal determinant of exit (1996), homeless residents of Germany have a tremendous advantage over homeless people in the United States. Compared with the U.S. homeless, who are often excluded from mainstream welfare provisions, homeless people in Germany possess more social rights, with access to the same services as any welfare recipient and thus a right to income support, shelter, housing subsidies, health care, and a host of specialized services. Coverage through the welfare state is consequently much more widespread than in the United States, where, since welfare reform, most cash and housing assistance programs are means tested, and coverage rates are consequently very low. In the United States, social-welfare capital is low not only because of the less-comprehensive public-welfare system but also because of a range of documented qualitative welfare-state deficiencies. To what extent such qualitative deficiencies also exist at the local level in Germany and thus in Berlin remains relatively understudied. To provide evidence that the German system—nationally, and locally in Berlin—provides a substantially more comprehensive social safety net, let me first describe the U.S. approach, with particular reference to Los Angeles, a city that is notorious for its ineffective ways of addressing homelessness.

United States and Los Angeles: The Shadow State within a Residual Welfare System

Any discussion of the inadequacy and frequently counterproductive effects of the U.S. welfare state on homelessness must begin with the understanding that the U.S. welfare state, from the onset, never was and perhaps never will be as comprehensive as European models, which, inevitably perhaps, affects the nation's response to homelessness (Mitchell 2011). Moreover, and as current discourse on welfare in the United States continues to reveal, there is little public consensus behind a comprehensive welfare system, although, according to surveys, most Americans seem to favor more intervention to address homelessness and provide citizens with affordable housing (Toro et al. 2007).

It is clear upon taking an inventory of policies pertaining to homelessness that the United States lags other industrialized nations when it comes to the nature and extent of public-welfare intervention (except for, ironically perhaps, public expenditures associated with health care and Social Security). To make matters worse, neoliberal welfare-state restructuring—the defunding, devolution, and privatization of actual service provision—has been attributed by many as a key reason for the proliferation of U.S. homelessness since the 1980s (for an overview, see Mitchell 2011).[19] Programs important for ensuring housing support have been cut or defunded, and other mainstream social programs, especially those providing cash assistance, remain inaccessible to homeless people—less than half of homeless families and less than 17 percent of single homeless adults receive cash assistance in Los Angeles. The nation also fails in providing people in need with shelter—the shelter-applicant ratio in Los Angeles, as in most U.S. cities, is abysmally low, five applicants per bed. The annual survey conducted by the U.S. Conference of Mayors on hunger and homelessness in American cities (2011) has continued to report an increase in demand for services and shelter almost every year since 1986, an inability to meet such demand, and even instances of families having to break up to obtain shelter.

In light of this crisis, the U.S. federal government began to take action in 1987 by passing the Stuart B. McKinney Act, which established the Interagency Council on Homelessness to distribute up to $1.4 billion to twenty-two programs across eight federal agencies. Since then, the program, annually reauthorized, has undergone a number of programmatic changes, including a laudable change in policy orientation from the initial, primarily emergency, concerns to a more longitudinal approach (such as the Continuum of Care programs adopted by the U.S. Department of Housing and Urban Development [HUD]) and, most recently, "Housing First" approaches and the Homelessness Prevention and Rapid Re-Housing Program (part of the American Recovery Act legislation in 2008; see U.S. Department of Housing and Urban Development 2010). Although many of these recent developments are positive departures, as with previous McKinney outlays, it is questionable how much these temporary interventions can accomplish. Fred Karnas, deputy secretary at HUD, has remarked rather cautiously, "The McKinney funds are merely a drop in the ocean, perhaps enough to effectively address homelessness in three major American cities, certainly not more" (interview, September 3, 1997).

In light of the increasing retreat of the federal government, it is up to the "third sector" of secular and nonsecular nonprofit service providers to pick up the slack at the local level. Local homeless service industries have clearly proliferated over the past few decades, as Burt et al.'s 2001 analysis of the development of the U.S. homeless service industry reveals. Most service options pertaining to shelter, food, and social support, especially in urban areas, have expanded dramatically, whereas public funding has noticeably diminished. Although the localized homeless service industry has found creative ways to obtain other (primarily philanthropic and corporate) sources of funding, these efforts have resulted in predictably uneven outcomes—people deemed more deserving (e.g., families, children) receive more and often better assistance and shelter options than presumably undeserving ones, most notably able-bodied single minority males. Another outcome is that the local service infrastructure is highly fragmented, in large part because of pressure to compete for funding. Although numerous coordination efforts have been made at the federal and state levels, and laudable ten-year action plans have surfaced in virtually every American city, the third sector remains fragmented, selective, and largely separate from mainstream social welfare.

Los Angeles is a good example of how the retreat of the formal welfare system and the simultaneous proliferation of the third sector affect homeless people, their life circumstances, and, consequently, their ability to overcome homelessness in negative and sometimes positive ways (DeVerteuil 2006; DeVerteuil, Lee, and Wolch 2002). As in most U.S. cities, it was primarily Los Angeles's nonprofit sector of secular and religious organizations that expanded to serve heightened demand over the past three decades, increasing the extent and in many cases (assisted by competitive pressures) raising the quality of homeless shelter and service provision. The problem was that much of the improved service provision catered to clientele perceived as more deserving and more likely to evoke interest and empathy—and therefore charitable funding. Some of the most vulnerable groups among the homeless, in the meantime, continue to be affected by minimal and often low-quality service provision that does little to improve their lot. Largely ineligible for federal and local cash-assistance programs and often labeled "unemployable," a huge portion of homeless individuals remain unserved or underserved by the local homeless service industry. Ex-convicts, able-bodied male adults, people with severe substance-abuse problems, and people with two or three mental-health diagnoses are among those who do not benefit much from the privatized welfare system.

In addition, although it is spatially contained, the local shadow state, as Dear and Wolch (1987) have come to call it, is highly fragmented and despite laudable local efforts remains rather incoherent. Part of the problem is that the acquisition of governmental and philanthropic grants is primarily competitive, favoring providers who are established or can provide evidence for success. Those serving clients with particularly debilitating personal vulnerabilities or stigmata inevitably have a competitive disadvantage even if proactive solutions are provided.

The inadequacy of the U.S. public policy and service approach is reinforced by the geographic distribution of homeless shelter and service facilities across urban space, which, as I argue earlier, has implications for market access and social relations. Like most U.S. cities, Los Angeles shows distinctive clusters of service facilities located in the most impoverished parts of town, where homeless people become reconcentrated upon being deconcentrated (i.e., displaced) elsewhere (Wolch and Dear 1993; Reese, DeVerteuil, and Thach 2010). Such clusters, although clearly important, then ironically fail even to meet the growing demand that exists in surrounding "service dependent ghettos" (Dear and Wolch 1987). Because of such containment within the most impoverished parts of town, a spatial mismatch develops between the location of shelters and services and the location of more promising job and housing opportunities in suburban areas, which, in the absence of a reasonable public-transit system, are inaccessible to homeless people seeking to improve their situation. The reason that facilities are concentrated and contained in ghettos and hardly ever located in presumably more promising areas is associated with NIMBYism (protests and resistance from residents of the desirable areas); the deliberate spatial exclusion of homeless service facilities from more affluent areas puts an unfair burden on already impoverished communities (Lyon-Callo 2001; Dear 1992; Dear and von Mahs 1995).

But it is not only homeless services that are being excluded; more recently, homeless people themselves, their survival strategies, the behaviors associated with them, and essentially their sheer existence are being excluded. Using punitive policies—a vast array of antihomeless ordinances alongside existing public order and safety laws—more promising places successfully displace and oftentimes criminalize homeless people (Marr, DeVerteuil, and Snow 2009; Amster 2008; Mitchell 1997, 2003; Davis 1990). Although courts more often than not side with the homeless on the issue of deliberate displacement, suggesting that the deliberate targeting and exclusion of homeless people and their services is illegal—unconstitutional, in fact—homeless people, homeless service providers, advocates, and supporters seem to be relatively powerless (Mitchell 1998a, 1998b). This clear injustice—and perhaps the most blatant expression of the harshness of neoliberal local governance—has resulted in an avalanche of literature from a range of disciplines theorizing how the deliberate, unjust exclusion of the homeless is financially driven and associated with a general commodification and redefinition of previously public spaces. As a result, homeless people become stripped of their citizenship, deliberately herded into ghettos, and voided of any chance to achieve lasting exit from homelessness, let alone poverty. Interestingly, however, few of these studies are actually based on real empirical evidence as to the extent and consequences of such practices on homeless people (for a critique, see DeVerteuil, May, and von Mahs 2009).

Yet despite this rather scathing testimony about the ineffectiveness of the U.S. public policy approach to homelessness, evidence suggests that the state can and sometimes does play a positive role in alleviating homelessness and decreasing its durations (Burt 2008; DeVerteuil 2005). In all fairness, it must be noted that tens of thousands of dedicated government workers at all administrative levels, diligent caseworkers at nonprofits, and advocates are all tirelessly working on behalf of the homeless, but, with all the public and political backlash against the homeless, they face an uphill battle. And evidence shows that certain types of public policy can be successful. Virtually every existing study on exit from homelessness from U.S. cities, including Los Angeles, suggests that public intervention is positively correlated with exit; all studies imply that receiving housing subsidies and public-income assistance increases exit chances and decreases long-term financial strain for individuals and for the system (Burt 2008; B. Wright 1996; Zlotnick, Robertson, and Lhiff 1999; DeVerteuil 2005). The problem, quite simply, is that there is not enough political and financial commitment to expand potentially positive programs. In this light, it is even more surprising that Germany—a system that de jure is mandated to provide shelter, public cash assistance, and other supportive services—performs so poorly in terms of facilitating rapid and lasting reentry into conventional housing and labor markets.

Germany and Berlin: Social Rights in the Corporatist System

The empirical data most studies using welfare regime theory rely on clearly suggest that the conservative/corporatist German welfare regime outperforms the U.S. liberal or residual welfare state in any category used to assess successful welfare-state performance, such as efficiency, promotion of equality, or reduction of social risks (Goodin et al. 1999). But does this positive comparative assessment hold up in the case of homelessness, a complex social problem that typically involves multiple administrative entities? The following discussion provides evidence that, at face value, the key assertion of welfare regime theory seems to hold: The German system—at any level, whether federal or local—is more interventionist, comprehensive, and inclusive, providing substantially more services to poor and homeless people (see Table 1.1).

However, despite resistance to full-scale welfare-state restructuring in the American mold, there are some indications that Germany may be following the American lead toward the implementation of neoliberal policy, including most notably the deliberate exclusion since unification of homeless people from public spaces and the hotly debated 2005 Hartz IV reforms that introduced workfare to Germany. How does this affect homeless people, and do they possess the human capital necessary to succeed in the new globalized service economy?

Germany's Social Code (*Sozialgesetzbuch*) consists of a comprehensive albeit confusing set of legislation that compels subordinate state and local administrations to provide eligible applicants with a range of services. Unlike most American homeless people, homeless people in Germany have a right to and enjoy access to all social services available to locally registered poor residents, including cash assistance, rental subsidies, health care, and a range of specialized services for the homeless. Because Germany is a federal system, like the United States, actual policy implementation is primarily a state and local responsibility.

Given its particularly high numbers of homeless people, Berlin has a comprehensive approach to addressing homelessness, resulting in substantially higher coverage rates.[20] At the Senate level (Berlin is a city-state), a specific agency within the Senate Administration for Health and Social Affairs is responsible for allocating funds to a broad range of public, nonprofit, and even commercial shelter and service providers. Senate funds are also used to fund prevention programs and specialized services for homeless people with particular needs, such as battered women and people with HIV/AIDS or severe disabilities. At the level of Berlin's twenty-three districts (consolidated into eleven since district reform in 2000), social-welfare offices (*Sozialämter*) provide cash assistance and other services to eligible welfare recipients. They also provide referrals to specialized homeless services and shelters, which receive either a per-diem amount for services rendered or operate from a fixed budget. During the late 1990s, almost two-thirds of shelters were either low-quality shelters operated by the districts themselves or commercial shelters providing temporary low-quality housing for homeless people, asylum seekers, or labor migrants. In addition, homeless people in Berlin are provided with health services; officially registered welfare recipients have free choice of doctors and are exempt from copayments on doctor visits and medication.

Any welfare recipients deemed able to work are required to register with the local labor office (*Arbeitsamt*), attend regular meetings with assigned caseworkers, and pursue any job leads provided. The labor office also provides referrals to educational as well as job-training or retraining programs and

TABLE 1.1 Nature and Extent of Services for Homeless People in Berlin and Los Angeles

	Los Angeles	Berlin
Characteristics of provision of local homeless services	• Conventional welfare—administered by DPSS at the county level—includes no services specifically designed for homeless people • All homeless services are provided by small voluntary organizations; few are associated with larger organizations (e.g., Salvation Army, Catholic Charities) • Most service providers rely on mixed funding from public (federal, state) and private sources; providers typically compete for funding	• Conventional welfare—administered by the Senate and implemented by 23 district welfare offices—includes specific provisions for homeless people • 80% of service providers are voluntary organizations affiliated with the six leading national welfare associations • Services are funded primarily by local revenues, with additional funds coming from welfare associations, membership fees, and donations
Income		
Extent of coverage	16% of homeless people receive welfare	66% of homeless people receive welfare
Benefit levels	$203/month (General Relief)	DM 660 ($365)/month (social assistance/ALGII)
Welfare as % of rent	41%	144%
Housing		
Prevention	None	Eviction prevention, housing assistance
Extent of shelter	Insufficient, primarily emergency	Comprehensive, primarily transitional
Applicants per shelter bed	5	2
Additional services		
Health care	Limited public health coverage (only children and veterans covered), limited voluntary coverage	Universal insurance-based health coverage for welfare recipients, additional publicly funded voluntary services
Day centers	18, spatially concentrated, mixed funding	34, public funding
Food	Food stamps (public funding), soup kitchens (private funding)	Soup kitchens (public funding)
Clothing	None	Clothing vouchers
Transportation	None	Transportation subsidies (50% discount)

Sources: Los Angeles—Shelter Partnership 1994; LACEHH 1997; Berlin—AK Wohnungsnot 1996; Neubarth 1997.

operates a number of active labor-market programs (i.e., publicly subsidized private-sector employment); in the late 1990s, this system made a valiant attempt to help the more than two hundred thousand officially registered unemployed find jobs in a largely stagnating economy (Statistisches Landesamt Berlin 2000).

Finally, Berlin's welfare administration and the nonprofits it funds also provide ample service options for homeless people. Twenty percent of homeless shelters and most of Berlin's thirty-eight day centers in the late 1990s were operated by nonprofit organizations, which, in contrast to the United States, rely almost exclusively on public reimbursements. For people who primarily live on the streets, eleven large emergency shelters and seventeen small "night cafés" (operated by church congregations) provide emergency accommodations and the occasional meal. Nine soup kitchens of various sizes dispense upward of three thousand meals a day. District welfare offices there also sponsor a number of health clinics, including the famous "Doctor's Van" featuring a mobile medical unit of volunteers. Nonprofits are also involved in transitional housing projects, many of which include social services.

Although this inventory of public and nonprofit services is, by any standard, more extensive and comprehensive than that of Los Angeles, Berlin's approach is not without flaws, some of which were already known before I began my investigation, allowing me to further scrutinize the apparent ineffectiveness of Berlin's system.

Critiques of Berlin's Approach: Toward Americanization?

Berlin's approach has a number of critics who have argued that it is overly rigid, uncoordinated, and at times even discriminatory (Gerull, Merckens, and Dubrow 2009). The Senate Administration itself has acknowledged problems en route to proposing a number of reforms and improvements, most notably associated with bureaucratic fragmentation and lack of transparency. Critical accounts have also come from academics (Gerull, Merckens, and Dubrow 2009; Schneider 1998; Schenk 2004) or in regular press statements from advocacy groups working on behalf of the homeless (e.g., AK Wohnungsnot's Web site). The common tenor of these accounts is that, although Berlin has largely satisfied the demand for emergency services, too few services provide transitional support. Some studies have also found that qualitative service deficiencies contribute to people's becoming homeless (e.g., insufficient use of eviction-prevention measures) and exacerbate the situation during their homelessness (e.g., low-quality shelter provision; see Schneider 1998), although none of these studies has related shelter experiences to long-term attempts to overcome homelessness and is thus unable to assess why so many homeless remain unsuccessful in their attempts to exit (Schneider 1998). Yet despite such reports, the city has failed to enact measures to ensure the quality of shelter and service provision and has, to date, failed in its goal to develop a comprehensive action plan (*Obdachlosenrahmenplan,* last discussed in Abgeordnetenhaus von Berlin 1999). Schneider's ethnographic study of homeless street people (1998) also documents how bad experiences in publicly funded shelters caused people to resist further public intervention and pursue informal yet similarly futile strategies. Such critiques are akin to critical accounts from Los Angeles, demonstrating the need to further examine the performance of Berlin's welfare state from a comparative perspective and to pursue the intriguing question of whether circumstances of service delivery are, in fact, Americanizing. This research is also warranted because all the aforementioned studies describe the ways policy and service-delivery problems affect paths into homelessness and life under the condition of homelessness, yet they reveal little about how these deficiencies affect homeless people's ability to overcome homelessness.

Another alarming indication of the potential Americanization of homeless policy is the fact that Berlin, like most U.S. cities, has been removing homeless people and other social fringe groups from the public and semipublic spaces in the city's commercial center since unification, and perhaps even before (Eick 1996). A number of authors have commented on the deliberate and systematic nature of such expulsion from public spaces for purely capitalist reasons, noting that this is ultimately not too different from, if less explicit than, the practice in U.S. cities (Busch-Geertsema 2008; Belina 2003; Eick 1996). Yet conspicuously absent from these debates is a thorough and empirically based discussion of the actual ramifications of such punitive policy. Who among the homeless experiences punitive policy? Why and precisely from which places are people displaced? By whom and how? What are the consequences? Are there long-term effects in terms of criminal records and lack of employability?

Exploring New Terrain

The foregoing review, differentiated by internal and external determinants along the lines of the welfare regime dimensions of family, market, and state, reveals that, although we may possess a reasonable understanding of exit barriers in the United States and Los Angeles to serve as a reference point, we lack a nuanced understanding of such factors in Germany and its new capital, Berlin. Specifically, we lack any comparative studies that focus in sufficient detail on homelessness, homeless policy, and the effects of policy and homeless service provision. Moreover, few studies have to date examined homelessness in the context of welfare regime theory, and few of those and other comparative studies have focused on lived experiences using qualitative, ethnographic data as their basis. Finally, the relevance of geographic processes—most notably, the spatiality of homeless people's containment and exclusion so aptly described for Los Angeles—remains seriously understudied in Germany and in Berlin.

Considering that we possess only a limited understanding of the impact of public policy on homeless people's life chances in Berlin, I begin Chapter 2 by describing how and where I conducted research in Berlin and introducing the homeless people who inform our understanding of exit barriers in Berlin. The chapter starts with a more general discussion about the challenges involved in conducting research on homeless people and the ways in which I addressed those challenges. Next, I introduce the three case studies in which I conducted research and interviewed homeless people. On the basis of my findings, I propose a grounded typology of homeless people based on similarities in their life courses. Specifically, I show that there are substantial differences in terms of respondents' life experiences, their paths into homelessness, their lives under the condition of homelessness, and the outcomes of their efforts to overcome homelessness, depending on whether their life courses had been more "regular" (i.e., higher social and human capital and residential stability) or "irregular" (i.e., lower social and human capital, greater social problems and vulnerabilities). I then use this life-course typology in subsequent chapters to provide a more nuanced discussion of the effects of homeless policy and service delivery on homeless people's exit chances in Berlin and show how these findings compare to results from Los Angeles.

Each of the next three chapters describes one of the types of exclusion that homeless people encounter, focusing first on the more pressing needs of income and shelter and moving on to long-term attempts to find jobs and housing, goals that all respondents shared. Chapter 3 starts this discussion by introducing the concept of "legal exclusion," which ties homeless people's immediate need to generate income by using their human capital and their use of public spaces more generally to the increasing displacement and criminalization of homeless people and their behaviors in public and semipublic spaces. This discussion extends current academic debates in Germany and the United States on punitive policy and reconfigurations of public spaces by providing a more nuanced understanding regarding where and how such displacement occurs, whom it affects, and what the personal short- and long-term consequences are, as differentiated by life-course experiences.

Chapter 4 provides a discussion of "service exclusion" by describing how homeless people's critical need for shelter and safety is met with substandard shelter and service provision, offering few chances for improving their life circumstances. Such warehousing is exacerbated by the broader geography of shelter and service delivery in that facilities for the homeless in Berlin and Los Angeles are contained in the most impoverished parts of town, which thus offer few chances to find sustainable housing and job opportunities. This chapter deepens our understanding of the effects of containment and warehousing by demonstrating that such effects depend on homeless people's distinct life-course experiences.

Chapter 5 then shifts the focus away from homeless people's more immediate attempts to stabilize their lives and examines both their long-term strategies to fulfill their ultimate goals of finding work and housing and the outcome of these efforts. "Market exclusion" thus represents how homeless people's long-term economic goals and exit strategies are met with severe barriers to the labor and housing markets, barriers that are, in large part, reinforced by legal and service exclusion and thus insufficient policy intervention. I demonstrate that although more than half the respondents managed to find housing, especially those with lesser degrees of social problems and more regular life courses, hardly anybody found work. This, in turn, relates to one key problem of the German economic system: It is difficult for "outsiders" to gain entry into the highly regulated formal economy, and thus they remain reliant on welfare. If these experiences and those of U.S. homeless people are any indication, the workfare policies inherent in the 2005 Hartz reforms will likely not increase exit chances, particularly for people with more irregular life courses.

In Chapter 6, I synthesize the three trajectories of exclusion into one coherent theory of sociospatial exclusion, which describes how homeless people's life chances are impeded by policy and service-delivery deficiencies in Berlin and Los Angeles in surprisingly similar fashion, although sociospatial exclusion is configured differently in each place. Despite the fact that market exclusion is more pronounced in Berlin, leading to comparably longer and more persistent spells of homelessness, legal and service exclusions are felt more in Los Angeles, which, alongside frequent underemployment, result in more persistent poverty and cyclical homelessness. Neither situation is advantageous for homeless people, because a host of interrelated problems with the delivery of services and shelter impede homeless people's life chances and further their decline. This, in turn, makes it increasingly difficult for homeless people to exit homelessness for good.

Ultimately, however, despite the local policy deficiencies and potentially negative ramifications of the 2005 reforms, the German approach remains superior—by providing a more coherent safety net, it spares homeless people from the most degrading circumstances of street life and provides them with a better chance to remain housed once they exit. In this sense, the key assertions of welfare regime theory about the superiority of Germany's system hold true, but with qualifications about the scale of analysis. Specifically, substantial qualitative deficits at the local level of policy implementation contribute to the entrenchment that homeless people experience and to the negative ramifications for optimizing their poverty management.

A more nuanced understanding of the policy deficiencies that underlie sociospatial exclusion and how it affects individual homeless people consequently allows me to propose policy recommendations—taking more recent policy changes, such as the 2005 Hartz laws, into account—that make an argument for more case management, communication, and coordination as the three key instruments with which to overcome sociospatial exclusion and provide homeless people with a better chance to overcome homelessness for good.

2

Homeless Spaces, Homeless Lives

Using Ethnography to Assess Homeless People's Life Courses and Exit Chances in Berlin

Having provided a cursory overview of the different contexts of homelessness in Germany and the United States and highlighted some of the weaknesses in our contemporary understanding of the impact of policy on homeless people's lives in Berlin, I continue in this chapter by introducing the methodology that underlay my empirical research in Berlin, the study locations, and the people I met and interviewed in such places. I describe why and how I employed a "multiperspectival" research approach that looks at the issues through both a "top-down" context analysis and a "bottom-up" ethnographic research strategy, and then I introduce the three case studies in which I conducted original empirical research, including a transitional housing project, a day center, and a grassroots organization. In describing these facilities, I provide a rationale for choosing them and explain the spatial setting of such "homeless spaces." I then describe the ways in which I approached and ultimately interviewed thirty-two people, twenty-eight of whom I was able to track over the course of at least one year and thus include in this study. Given the similarities and differences in their biographies, their paths into homelessness, and the nature and extent of personal vulnerabilities and other internal determinants, I propose an innovative grounded, fivefold life-course typology, which I subsequently use in the empirical chapters to differentiate my findings.

I conclude this chapter by discussing the potential implications of this life-course typology for public policy by first examining whether the respondents' service needs can be met by Berlin's homeless service and shelter infrastructure. Encouragingly, I find it to be so, at least theoretically; yet in contrast to this promising theoretical finding, homeless people's actual experiences reveal a completely different story. Despite having rather easy access to the system, the overwhelming majority of respondents were either dissatisfied or very dissatisfied with the nature and extent of services they received. The reason people were so dissatisfied, along with the question of whether public intervention ultimately turned out to be successful, is the subject of the later chapters of this book. For now, let us turn to more general methodological considerations that went into this research.

Approaching Homelessness: A Multiperspectival Approach

Homelessness is a fascinating and challenging topic to examine, and, not surprisingly, perhaps, it has been studied from virtually every theoretical and disciplinary angle with the entire gamut of research methods employed in the social sciences. At the same time, homelessness is a dynamic, multidimensional societal condition that is extremely difficult to study, posing tremendous challenges for researchers. It requires interdisciplinary approaches, mainly because no one methodological angle has been able to fully capture the complexity of homelessness and produce reliable data about it. Regional variations, different courses and durations of individual homeless experiences, and myriad individual circumstances make it virtually impossible to generate "accurate" data, a problem that nearly every serious study on homelessness clearly states up front.

Studies taking a positivist approach, for instance, are frustrated by tremendous variations in data that make strong correlations or time-series difficult to establish. Longitudinal studies suffer from high attrition rates, especially among more "problematic" case studies who, for a variety of reasons, more easily fall out of the data pool. Qualitative research, on the other hand, suffers from its inherent subjectivity and inability to produce generalizable data. No matter how much a researcher may admit to such problems—and all good researchers do—they cannot be negated, and thus they complicate the accuracy of findings, resulting in tremendous variation. If such problems exist even at small community scales, it is not hard to imagine that international comparisons are even more difficult to sustain, as different national definition criteria and completely different institutional, economic, and cultural circumstances apply.[1]

Such awareness is important, because a lack of accurate data affects the ability to make valid projections. Hard data are crucial if we want to make policy decisions regarding allocating budgets and funding services. Still, I feel confident in saying that contemporary data on homelessness in Los Angeles are empirically strong enough to provide us with a baseline from which to investigate the situation and circumstances in Berlin, where the processes surrounding exit from homelessness are not understood as well. Moreover, upon looking at the considerations that went into the analyses of homelessness in Los Angeles and other cities, I was able to devise a methodology for Berlin that employed innovative and proven approaches. Most influential for me was David Snow and Leon Anderson's study (1993), which, by employing a multiperspectival approach,[2] finds a reasonable middle ground for approaching and analyzing urban homelessness. A multiperspectival approach requires "consideration of the voices and experiences of a range of actors of focal concern, of the perspectives and actions of other relevant groups of actors, and of interactions among all of them" (21).

To do this, the authors rely primarily on ethnographic research methods to explore homelessness from a bottom-up perspective and triangulate such findings with a broader sample of service users and economic and social data from a top-down perspective. This approach allows the authors and their research associates to collect ample and fairly reliable data on homeless people's material survival strategies, producing, in my estimation, one of the best studies on homelessness to date. Given the success of this approach, I decided to proceed in similar fashion by exploring homeless people's experiences with public policy from the bottom up as well as analyzing the broader structural context of urban homelessness in Berlin.

Top Down: Analyzing the Context of Urban Homelessness in Comparative Perspective

Exploring the broader context of urban homelessness to provide a comparative analysis required a careful examination of processes occurring at the local, national, and international scales. To examine such different contexts, I relied primarily on secondary sources; I was able to benefit from a number of multiyear research projects undertaken in Los Angeles, whose findings became the basis for the cursory literature review undertaken in Chapter 1.

Upon analyzing such secondary data and learning about the gaps in our understanding, I identified and eventually conducted key-informant interviews with a range of people working for, with, or on behalf of homeless people in Berlin, Los Angeles, and Washington, D.C. (see Appendix 2 for a list of key informants). With the help of gatekeepers in all three places, I was able to identify key informants and eventually arrange interviews that were tailored to meet their areas of expertise, which I taped and transcribed in full. In selecting my key informants, I intended to reach a reasonable cross section of nonhomeless "experts" working with or on behalf of homeless people, including administrators, social workers, local politicians, police and security officers, and activists.

Moreover, I employed a range of additional strategies to explore the societal and geographic context and some of the questions that were inadequately addressed in the existing literature. To examine the geographic distribution of facilities in Berlin, I took an inventory of homeless service and shelter facilities and their basic features (size, approach, funding, staffing), determined the characteristics of the corresponding neighborhoods, and produced a series of maps that allowed me to ascertain whether homeless service facilities in Berlin are clustered and contained in deprived urban quarters, as they are in Los Angeles (and, for that matter, most other U.S. cities).

To explore how community members perceived homeless service facilities and to see whether there was, analogous to U.S. circumstances, community resistance (NIMBYism), I informally talked with neighbors, shopkeepers, and other community gatekeepers and, in the case of one shelter facility, conducted a public-opinion survey in the direct vicinity of the facility, talking briefly with sixty-eight neighbors. Upon learning that Berlin's public-transit authorities target street-newspaper vendors in the belief that their sales activities are viewed as detrimental by *Berliner Verkehrsgemeinschaft* (BVG) passengers, I surveyed 176 passengers to learn about their perceptions of street-newspaper vendors, their experiences with them, and their opinions about the prosecution of vendors in transit facilities that continues to be practiced to this day.

To keep up with developments since the conclusion of the primary empirical phase of my research in 1999, I stayed in touch with a number of informants who, whenever contacted, provided me with further information, clarifications, and assessments of more recent developments. I also revisited the city in 2007 and 2009 and met with a number of informants again on those occasions. This continued research, along with a careful review of recent literature, has allowed me to provide a reasonable, holistic view of developments and changes that have occurred since the late 1990s up until 2011, particularly the potential impact of the much-debated 2005 Hartz IV welfare reforms and the extent to which they herald a potential Americanization of German social policy.

Although this contextual analysis reveals important information, it does not help us understand what any of these processes and changes mean to individual people and their personal life trajectories. The only way to find out is to look at this subject from the perspective of the homeless themselves—that is, from the bottom up.

Bottom Up: Analyzing Homeless People's Lived Experiences in Berlin

The key to ultimately understanding the impact of public policy on homeless people's exit chances lies in learning about homeless people's own personal experiences over time. Rather than simply taking a point-in-time, in-depth view of their experiences during their current spell of homelessness, I employed a more longitudinal, life-course approach. To get such information and thus a lifelong perspective on homeless people's paths into, experience of, and attempts to escape homelessness, I employed ethnographic research methods. I chose this ethnographic research strategy for three primary reasons.

First, I found that ethnographic studies provide in many ways the most insightful accounts of people's paths into and life under the condition of homelessness by showing how various factors intersect to produce and often reinforce homelessness.[3] Surprisingly, though, only two studies, both unpublished dissertations, have applied ethnographic methods to examine exit from homelessness, including the aforementioned excellent study by Bradley Wright (1996) and a much-less-persuasive study by Susan Bennett (1999).[4] Ethnography therefore constitutes a seriously underutilized approach in local studies of exit from homelessness and in comparative studies of social policy and service delivery.

Second, the analysis of scale has been largely absent from quantitative research. It is undeniable that individual experiences with policy vary substantially depending on personal circumstances, and the nature and extent of social problems necessitate focusing on processes occurring on the scale of lived experiences. Focusing analysis on a smaller scale than national or regional is further warranted by the fact that both Germany and the United States are federal systems that grant local communities a great deal of discretion as to how they enact social policy and administer social services. Communities usually delegate service delivery to the nonprofit sector, which results in a wide range of variation and a broad spectrum of service types and approaches (Leisering 2001; Busch-Geertsema 2003). Such an array of variables, in conjunction with the diversity of the homeless population itself, is reason to utilize a qualitative research approach.

The third reason for conducting an ethnographic study is associated with pragmatic reasons: As a graduate student at the time, I simply did not possess the resources or any useful existing data to complement the ethnographic portion with quantitative research.[5] Although I certainly would have liked to triangulate the ethnographic insights with panel data or other survey research in the fashion of Wright (1996), which undoubtedly would have enhanced the persuasiveness of the results with regard to justifying policy recommendations, I was not in the position to conduct such time-consuming, labor-intensive, and expensive research.

Nonetheless, as I show in the remainder of this book, this ethnographic approach proved immensely useful, as it allowed me to generate an abundance of data that ultimately provided a basis for answering the research questions I sought to address. In the following section, I discuss the ethnographic research methods I chose and elaborate on what they allowed me to accomplish in the context of three distinct case studies, which I selected with careful consideration to create a qualitative sample that exemplifies the diversity of Berlin's homeless population. For each case, I tailored my research approach to suit the circumstances that revolved around my personal contact with homeless people in such facilities. Participant observation, as I show, provided me with an opportunity to first inconspicuously observe before initiating contact, and, over time, to create an atmosphere of openness and trust that allowed for more-intimate, in-depth interviews with homeless people about their lives before and since homelessness. It was certainly advantageous that I first had the opportunity to get to know and informally talk with people before inviting them to participate in interviews. To be able to provide a longitudinal perspective on personal experiences, I did my best to stay in touch with respondents via follow-up visits, mail and telephone correspondence, and information from others, including caseworkers at the study sites and the respondents' fellow homeless people. In this way, I was ultimately able to conduct thirty-two in-depth interviews and keep in contact with and remain knowledgeable about twenty-eight people's whereabouts for at least one year—seven of them for even longer, including three people with whom I still maintain contact.

In the following section, I provide a rationale for choosing the three study locations and a descriptive account of the "homeless spaces" I included in my field work in Berlin, then I offer a more detailed account of "homeless lives" in such spaces and how I approached, interviewed, tracked, and analyzed such data. Upon this analysis, I developed a grounded fivefold typology of homeless people based on similarities and differences in their life courses, thus indicating the extent of their human and social capital as well as the nature and extent of their aggravating social problems. My analysis reveals rather quickly that respondents had overwhelmingly negative experiences with welfare, service, and shelter interventions in Berlin.

This analysis then sets the stage for a more nuanced account in the following three empirical chapters of homeless people's experiences with public policy in Berlin and how they compare to circumstances in Los Angeles. For the remainder of this chapter, I focus on the empirical basis of the Berlin study, starting with a description of the "homeless spaces" I selected to learn more about homelessness in Berlin.

Homeless Spaces: Three Case Studies in Berlin

The first step in developing a comprehensive ethnographic approach was to identify suitable study locations that would allow for participant observation of a reasonable cross section of Berlin's diverse homeless population, from which I could identify potential respondents for in-depth interviews. Moreover, the study locations would have to permit sustained long-term observations, which made establishing good working relations with staff and clients paramount. To identify potential case studies, I repeatedly visited Berlin in the fall and winter of 1997. I contacted a number of researchers at the Freie Universität Berlin and, based on their advice, visited a number of potential study locations, including emergency shelters, transitional housing projects, day centers, advocacy organizations, and public spaces that were reportedly frequented by homeless people. These visits provided my first glimpse of homelessness in Berlin, and, sharpened by my experiences and studies in the United States, I began to see some indications that local circumstances often mirrored those I had seen in Los Angeles. Although the extent of visible street homelessness in Berlin was always lower, I began noticing people who "looked" homeless in many commercial and pedestrian areas of the city's commercial center. In such places, I witnessed how potentially homeless people were singled out by police and displaced, and I noticed that some areas where homeless facilities were located were rather impoverished or surrounded by industrial or commercial land use. In visiting emergency shelters, I noticed appallingly poor social and hygienic conditions that clearly resembled those of emergency shelters in Los Angeles. Upon careful consideration, I selected three particularly promising study locations, including a transitional housing project, a day center, and a homeless street-newspaper agency.

Wohnheim Trachenbergring: Transitional Housing for Single Males

The first case study I selected was a transitional homeless shelter surrounded by industrial property and located adjacent to a middle-class residential community in the western district of Tempelhof. The Wohnheim Trachenbergring was a so-called mid-level transitional shelter providing sixty-eight homeless men with single furnished rooms, communal cooking and bath facilities, and in-house social-service provision by three part-time social workers.[6] Operated by the Internationaler Bund and financed through funds provided by the local welfare administration, the main goals of the shelter were to provide homeless people with an opportunity to stabilize their lives and, with the help of social workers, address their problems in individualized fashion in preparation for exit from homelessness. The shelter served a broad range of adult homeless men of different ages, backgrounds, and national origins, most of whom had been homeless for quite some time and thus had experience with other types of homeless services and shelter facilities. The latter was a particularly important selection criterion, because the residents could report in retrospect about their experiences in places that provided little or no support and were reportedly characterized by terrible conditions.[7] The facility manager, Uta Sternal, agreed to let me stay at the shelter for a nominal fee as long as rooms were available and on the condition that I would ensure the anonymity of the residents. I consequently moved into the shelter in February 1998 and stayed for one month. While living at the shelter, my close proximity to homeless residents allowed me to get to know forty people, many of them well enough to establish a basis of trust. I was able to initiate seventeen interviews and track sixteen respondents over the course of one year. In retrospect, living in the shelter, despite a host of ethical problems, proved to be a particularly advantageous strategy in that I was able to more fully immerse myself into the lives of homeless people.[8] The opportunity to carefully establish cordial relationships with fellow residents over time allowed for honesty and openness. It also allowed for easy follow-up conversations and the possibility of interest in maintaining contact, thus keeping attrition to a minimum.

Warmer Otto: A Multiservice Day Center

Upon the recommendation of one of my key informants at the time, the second case study I selected was the day center Warmer Otto, located in Moabit, an impoverished working-class neighborhood in the western central district of Berlin-Tiergarten. The Warmer Otto was a year-round day center for poor and homeless citizens, providing food, a place to stay during the day when most shelters were closed, and on-site social services and referrals.[9] The facility was a nonprofit organization affiliated with a local Lutheran church congregation and relied primarily on public Senate and district funds as well as additional funds generated by the church congregation. This day center had a maximum capacity of 55 visitors and was, especially in the winter months, always crowded, serving up to 120 visitors per day. The facility offered the advantage of being small enough to allow for general observations yet large enough to ensure a certain amount of anonymity and privacy while I was conducting interviews. The facility occupied the first floor of a five-story apartment building. The two front rooms had groupings of tables and chairs for the use of patrons and were sparsely but lovingly decorated, with pictures and posters adorning the walls. The back rooms served as a kitchen, a storage room for clothing and other supplies, and two staff offices.

The atmosphere at the smoke-filled facility was relatively somber, as most patrons sat by themselves in near silence. Some conversation took place among people who seemed to know each other and who turned out to be regular patrons of the facility. Given this atmosphere and my admitted initial discomfort, I had a difficult time initiating conversations during my first few visits. Most patrons were not regulars and were seemingly uninterested in conversation. Over time, I managed to get to know four regular visitors, among them two homeless women, well enough to conduct in-depth interviews. Because coming to the day center was part of their regular routines, I managed to stay in touch with them and documented their progress over the course of one year.

Strassenfeger: Street-Newspaper Agency, Advocacy Organization, and Service Provider

The third case study I selected was a homeless street-newspaper agency, which served as an example of an advocacy/self-help project serving a diverse group of homeless people with particularly severe social problems.[10] Because ongoing privatization is reconfiguring the task of service provision, it is important to also examine alternative service providers that work independently of the leading cartel of welfare organizations.[11] The Mob Obdachlose Machen Mobil e.V. is a nonprofit organization guided by four overarching objectives. Its foremost objective is the production and distribution of the *Strassenfeger*, one of Berlin's two homeless street newspapers, which give homeless people the opportunity to sell newspapers for profit.[12] Other objectives include involving homeless people in the agency's management and operations, providing emergency shelter in the agency's editorial office, and giving homeless vendors an opportunity to engage in grassroots activism. Ultimately, I was able to conduct four in-depth interviews with homeless vendors and through the agency established contact with two unaffiliated homeless women, whom I also interviewed and tracked over the course of one year. Of particular importance in establishing a cordial relationship with street-newspaper vendors was a chance encounter with Sioux, an old acquaintance of mine from my high school days in southern Germany. Through many detours, Sioux became a homeless street-newspaper vendor in Berlin, where he managed to become the elected vendor representative on the organization's governance board and one of the most successful vendors. He introduced me to other vendors and taught me the ins and outs of successful vending. We are still in contact thirteen years later.

Although the three selected case studies, perhaps inevitably, could not cover all elements of the provision of homeless services in Berlin, and some known subpopulations among the homeless remained underrepresented (youth, ethnic minorities and foreign nationals, women, families, senior citizens), the studies allowed me to get to know a diverse set of homeless people: men and women of different ages; East and West Germans and foreign nationals, including two U.S. citizens; people with and without physical or mental health problems; and people with and without previous economic and social integration into "mainstream" society. Therefore, the case studies provided a fairly reasonable cross section of Berlin's overall population of single homeless individuals. Moreover, the choice of these particular case studies provided me with an excellent opportunity to assess homeless people's experiences with and opinions about social policy and to examine their past and present use of homeless services and the long-term effects these services had on their lives and life chances.

Homeless Lives: Using Ethnography to Compare Policy Outcomes across Life-Course Types

Over the course of my investigation, I got to know a broad range of quite remarkable people who all shared the long-term goal of overcoming homelessness by finding appropriate housing and sufficient income through regular jobs, hoping to achieve or regain economic self-sufficiency and residential stability. Over the past eighteen years, I informally talked with hundreds of homeless individuals in an array of settings in Berlin, Los Angeles, New York, and Philadelphia (where I live). In Berlin, I talked with more than a hundred homeless individuals and, with the three case studies selected, developed more in-depth relationships with and interviewed thirty-two homeless individuals, twenty-eight of whom are included in this study. I ultimately included only individuals whose whereabouts I could ascertain one year after the first interview and with whom I had ample opportunity to meet and conduct follow-up interviews. In this way, I was able to conduct thorough, semistructured baseline interviews (average length: 2.5 hours) and, on average, five follow-up interviews that, depending on the nature of the inquiry, lasted between fifteen minutes and one hour each. In addition, I spent countless hours informally interacting with the respondents—some more than others—by hanging out in their rooms; joining them for lunch or dinner; accompanying them on walks, errands, or visits to the local welfare office and service providers; and joining the demonstrations organized by the Mob e.V. Ultimately, it was important to me that in all these cases, I was able to provide a holistic picture of respondents' lives, their paths into homelessness, their experiences under the condition of homelessness, and, whenever possible, their paths out of homelessness. Such observations also included entirely subjective impressions to capture the ambience and atmosphere in homeless places or my personal feelings about people, places, and practices I encountered. I recorded such impressions and other thoughts in a field diary.

One thing that immediately struck me while I conducted the initial interviews with homeless people in Berlin was how, for the lack of a better word, "normal" and inconspicuous most homeless people I met turned out to be. Few resembled the stereotypical picture of a "homeless person" or stood out in any way by appearance, behavior, or attitude. Most people I met, sometimes after initial reservations, were quite outspoken, vocal, and open about their lives and experiences—often regretful and sometimes self-critical about bad choices they had made. I also noted that most homeless people I talked with and all the respondents I include in this study wished to establish residential stability and economic self-sufficiency, including people who had lived on the streets or on the margins of society for extended periods of time. I was amazed by the remarkable diversity of life experiences but noticed rather quickly that a number of similarities and differences characterized the biographies of the respondents, their paths into homelessness, and their extenuating personal circumstances. Such similarities ultimately allowed me to delineate five distinct life-course trajectories, each of which poses different challenges for social policy intervention.

About "Regularity" and "Normalcy" in Homeless People's Life Courses

Looking into a person's past to uncover the reasons for present-day difficulties is a century-old quest and still one of the most effective ways to uncover the source of problems and, in understanding them, provide a solution. Examining homeless people's past life courses turned out to be quite revealing, often defying common stereotypes. Most respondents had, at some point and perhaps for most of their lives, functioned within the parameters of "mainstream" German society, a fact that also held true for the four respondents who immigrated at some point from other countries. Furthermore, they were all socialized—albeit differently in East and West Germany or other countries—by conventional cultural forces and mass media. In conversation, they rarely appeared out of touch with the social and cultural mainstream and its present-day cultural manifestations. Given that most had access to and used some form of media (most read a daily newspaper, and twenty respondents had regular access to TV), all were well informed about contemporary political, economic, and cultural discourses. In fact, many respondents had rather "normal" or "regular" life courses, without standing out in any way. Most took care of themselves, and their attire, demeanors, and appearances made them virtually indistinguishable from the "mainstream" (i.e., other city dwellers).

One might ask, of course, for a definition of "normal" or "regular," let alone the societal "mainstream." Granted, such terms cannot be properly defined, as they are inherently subjective and depend on one's interpretation. What is normal to one person may be immoral, abnormal, and objectionable to another person. And such terms can stigmatize by inadvertently reinforcing stereotypes. The reason why I ultimately resorted to such terminology is that many homeless themselves often used such terms to describe their lives. Helmut echoed many when he said:

> I used to have a stinking normal life (*stinknormales Leben*). Nice apartment, car, wife, dog. Boring, not really fulfilling, but stable, you know? Then, apartment lost, car sold, wife left, dog died. . . . Now I wish I had my stinking normal life back [sighs]. (Helmut, age 37, shelter resident, older regular life course, interview, February 23, 1998)[13]

It was also the homeless themselves who indicated that their present lives were anything but "normal" and were nothing they had expected them to be. Residential instability, social isolation, and often ensuing health and addiction problems were common self-reported phenomena, causing such respondents to describe their life courses as "strange," "fragmented," "unconventional," "broken," or "off track" (*aus der Bahn geworfen*).

This self-awareness allowed me to distinguish between people with comparatively more regular or more irregular life courses. Among the twelve people with more regular life courses, age—and thus life experience and their extent of human capital—was the main differentiating point, allowing me to discuss the experiences of eight older homeless people with regular life courses and of four younger ones (all under thirty) separately. The sixteen homeless people whom I initially placed in the broader category of relatively irregular live courses had different reasons for why and how they became homeless. Most of them became homeless rapidly, few received any form of public assistance at the time, and all had, compared to the "regular" groups, more severe social problems. The nature of such problems, in turn, allowed me to further differentiate circumstances and devise three life-course types, including eight respondents with "transient" and rather unsettled life courses, four younger respondents with comparatively troubled "deviant" life courses, and four people with lifelong or accident-induced "disabilities."

Toward a Life-Course Typology

To provide a more empirically sound basis for the proposed five life-course types, I used the various internal determinants that I outline in Chapter 1 as a guide. This method allowed me to devise variables of which at least some were quantifiable, enabling limited comparisons to other quantitative data and thus either substantiating or putting into question the qualitative data from the Berlin study. For instance, certain variables associated with social problems (psychological evaluations, substance-abuse screenings) and with human capital (years of schooling, grades, years of job training) can be quantified, while others remain ultimately subjective categories that are based on personal judgment. One could measure, for example, the extent of social networks by volume and frequency, but it remains difficult to associate meaning with such numbers. Two really good friends could conceivably be more meaningful and materially and emotionally supportive than a whole range of acquaintances whom a person meets frequently. Therefore, much of the further differentiation, albeit highly insightful, remains on slippery empirical footing, a weakness that conceivably pertains to any ethnographic study on diverse populations, such as the homeless.

Table 2.1 provides an overview of internal determinants, including extent of personal vulnerabilities, human and social capital, and pathways into homelessness. In accounting for small case numbers and the fact that this information is hard to quantify, I simply indicate in the table whether an occurrence is high (affecting more than two-thirds of respondents in that group), moderate, or low (affecting less than one-third).

The table reveals clearly that fundamental differences exist among the five life-course groups, which I describe next. In this context, I refer the reader to Appendix 1, which provides short biographical sketches for all respondents in alphabetical order, differentiated by life-course type.

Older Homeless People with "Regular" Life Courses

For the twelve people with relatively "regular" life courses, age, reasons for homelessness, and the roles of accompanying risk factors were the main differentiating variables. The eight older homeless people (ages 35 or older) with regular life courses had all led relatively inconspicuous lives well into adulthood and consequently had experienced all aspects of a "normal" adult life, including the rewards and challenges it brings. This group comprised seven men (Bernie, Det, Hanno, Hans, Helmut, Kalle, and Sachse) as well as one woman (Maria). For these eight respondents, the loss of employment was a major turning point in their lives, setting in motion a gradual but seemingly unstoppable social and economic decline that was exacerbated by a number of additional emerging social problems. In virtually all these cases, the descent into homelessness was the culmination of problems characterized by numerous unsuccessful attempts to find employment and increasing indebtedness; all eight cases included the breakdown of marital and social relationships, five included increasing alcohol problems, and three included deteriorating mental and physical health. For Maria, domestic violence and abandonment by her partner contributed to her eviction and subsequent homelessness.

All members in this category made it clear that they did not perceive themselves as homeless, nor did they wish to be categorized as such. Rather, they perceived themselves first and foremost as unemployed and, as a result, poor. Each of these respondents had prior insurance-based employment and thus qualified for and received public assistance, which they correctly viewed as an earned right after years of social-insurance contributions. Still, none of them was comfortable being an unemployed welfare recipient, and all hoped to overcome this dependence quickly:

TABLE 2.1 Characteristics of Homeless Respondents in Berlin

Internal determinants	Older homeless people with regular life courses (n = 8)	Younger homeless people with regular life courses (n = 4)	Homeless people with transient life courses (n = 8)	Homeless people with deviant life courses (n = 4)	Homeless people with disabilities (n = 4)
Personal vulnerabilities					
Child abuse	Low	Low	Moderate	High	Low
Mental health problems	Low	Low	Moderate	High	High
Physical health problems	Moderate	Low	Moderate	Moderate	High
Alcohol problems	High	Low	High	Moderate	Low
Drug addiction	Low	Low	Low	High	Low
Family problems	High	High	Moderate	High	High
Residential instability	Low	Low	High	High	Moderate
Incarceration/ criminal record	Low	Low	Moderate	High	Low
Human capital					
Complete schooling	High	High	High	Low	High
Complete job training	High	Low	Moderate	Low	Moderate
Job experience (>5 years)	High	Low	Moderate	Low	Moderate
Excessive debts (>DM 7,200/$4,000)	High	Low	Moderate	Low	Moderate
Social capital					
Social networks: nonhomeless	High	High	Low	Low	Low
Social networks: fringe groups	Low	Moderate	Moderate	High	Moderate
Path into homelessness					
Gradual descent	High	Low	Low	Low	Low
Sudden event	Low	High	High	High	High
Formal eviction	High	Low	Low	Low	Low
Respondents by name*	Helmut, Sachse, Kalle, Hanno, Det, Hans, Bernie, Maria	Mario, Bob, Markus, Radek	Tobias, Dan, Schlöter, Harri, Matze, Martin, Leo, Jens	Oliver, Sioux, FTW, Marita	Andrea, Monika, Paule, Biker

Source: A simplified version of this table first appeared in von Mahs 2005a.

Note: High = more than two-thirds; moderate = one-third to two-thirds; low = less than one-third.

* Short biographies of the respondents are provided in Appendix 1. The respondents listed in the table are male, except for Maria, Marita, Andrea, and Monika.

> I have to admit that I used to view welfare recipients as spongers, and I'm telling you that it's a humiliating situation that you find yourself in the same boat with the people you once despised. (Kalle, age 44, shelter resident, older regular life course, interview, February 28, 1998)

The urge to quickly overcome homelessness was further intensified by their desire to preserve existing social relationships and create new ones. In fact, most respondents in this group had years-long ties to their local community, what Berliners fondly call their *Kiez.* Yet since the beginning of their homelessness, all respondents with local social networks experienced a decline in the frequency of such place-based social contact, which raises the question of why such a decline occurred.

One thing was certain—losing their jobs and then becoming homeless was a major psychological blow to all eight respondents' self-esteem, instilling fears of further social decline. For all eight, work had been a defining element of their lives. Even if such work was hardly ever fulfilling, it had provided stability, security, social contact, and something to do on a regular basis:

> Well, it wasn't precisely a great job or exciting career. You know, I was a construction worker. Hard work. Honest work. But at the end of the day, you knew you got something done. I can show you a whole bunch of buildings I worked on. I am proud of it. Huh, I never knew how great bricklaying is [sarcastic tone] until I had no job. (Hanno, age 35, shelter resident, older regular life course, interview, March 6, 1998)

The painful memory of past stability, meaning, and status was particularly apparent among two East German respondents, Det and Hanno. Both had steady employment in the former German Democratic Republic (GDR) and, in Det's case, some formal standing as a party member and police officer. Both of their lives turned for the worse after unification and the loss of their jobs shortly afterward; they considered themselves "unification losers":

> Sometimes I wish the Wall back. . . . Our GDR was not perfect, but you had a job and a place to live. Simple, but we did not really need that much more. And, more importantly, I had friends. Now? I have Hanno and Barney [fellow shelter residents], three unification losers. (Det, age 48, shelter resident, older regular life course, interview, March 6, 1998)

Rather puzzling was why six of these respondents, who were formally evicted for rent arrears, lost their homes despite existing legal provisions (§15 BSHG) that could have been applied to avert their evictions. It turned out that such preventive measures failed in five of these cases because neither the respondents nor their prospective landlords knew about eviction-prevention options; in the other case (Helmut's), the caseworker at the welfare office was apparently on vacation and thus processed the case too late. In any event, preventive policies designed to deal with formal evictions often miss the target. None of the remaining twenty-two respondents had been formally evicted; some had never established residence in Berlin, while most others had lost their homes for various other reasons and typically in much more rapid fashion than the cases in which preventive policies could have been applied.

Younger Homeless People with "Regular" Life Courses

In contrast, four younger homeless people with regular life courses—Bob, Mario, Markus, and Radek—became homeless in a rather abrupt fashion following conflicts rather than gradual declines. All four had led inconspicuous lives throughout their childhoods and most of their teenage years, including regular schooling, decent grades, and relatively unproblematic relationships with their parents. They all had good-to-very-good social skills and did not stand out in any way from their peers in their age group, although all four admitted to using drugs recreationally, most notably cannabis (as do up to 30 percent of their peers in Germany, a "narcotic society"; Ludwig and Neumeyer 1991). They all became homeless because of conflicts with their parents, with whom they lived, that resulted either in the parents' decision to throw them out (three cases) or the respondent's personal choice to leave, both of which resulted in immediate homelessness.

The key difference from the older homeless was that the four younger respondents never really had to look out for themselves or take responsibility for their material well-being. Moreover, because none of them had regular employment in the past, they did not receive unemployment insurance or other types of welfare assistance at the beginning of their homelessness. Given their young age and the lack of previous economic integration as a reference point, unemployment and homelessness had less-severe psychological consequences. The respondents were, at the time I interviewed them, relatively optimistic and upbeat and fairly content with living in the Wohnheim Trachenbergring, with the private rooms and other resources it afforded. Bob said:

> I'm not worried about all that. Look, most of my buddies still live with their parents and have not begun working yet. I'm still young, you know? If I were older, however, this would be a different story. If I look at the older guys [shelter residents] here, I can somehow understand why they are worried shitless and drink all day. (Bob, age 24, shelter resident, younger regular life course, interview, February 25, 1998)

Homeless People with "Transient" Life Courses

One important variable that immediately differentiated people with more regular life courses from those with more irregular ones was their migratory status and residential history. The question of whether people were indigenous[14] to the place in which homelessness occurred had important ramifications for how people became homeless and experienced homelessness. Migrants typically lacked information about the city and its infrastructure, had no or few local social networks, and consequently were more socially isolated than indigenous people. This fundamental difference prompted me to create a separate category for eight men described as homeless migrants with "transient" life courses (Dan, Harri, Jens, Leo, Martin, Matze, Schlöter, and Tobias). The reason for describing such life-course experiences as "transient" is that most of them had had fairly unsettled lives, frequently moving from one place to another. All of them moved often and, by their own account, never developed roots in any of the places they used to live. Also among the group were two people with international pathways, encompassing the United States and Korea (Dan, a college-educated U.S. citizen) and South Africa (Tobias, a German citizen who applied for a visa to return to South Africa, where he had lived for ten years). Although migration per se is not an irregular activity in contemporary German society, and some of the older migrants had been economically integrated in the sense that they had had relatively steady income in the past (Dan, Harri, Leo, and Schlöter), the nature of their previous employment (traveling day labor, contract work), the greater extent of prior social isolation, and a high prevalence of alcohol problems throughout life as well as previous experiences with homelessness (Harri, Matze) led me to address their life experiences in a separate category.

Another reason to address their experiences separately is that these respondents were more likely to experience delays in the receipt of welfare, because they had to figure out which agency was responsible. In three cases, it took up to four weeks until eligibility was finally determined. Some respondents even suspected that they might be victim to some intentional harassment. Leo explained:

> I'm telling you, they are doing this intentionally. When I first went there [social-welfare office], she [caseworker] gave me a list of things I needed to get. So I did that, and it took me a while, because I had to first contact my brother in Rostock to send me the stuff [to a friend's place]. So I went there again. Now this stupid cow [caseworker] told me that something else was missing. So I left and took care of it. And then the third time, the same shit. I was close to losing my temper. (Leo, age 32, shelter resident, transient life course, interview, February 23, 1998)

Such hassles notwithstanding, they were not left without assistance. While waiting to have their eligibility determined, they were temporarily issued a daily cash allowance (DM 18/$10 per day in 1998) and referred to an emergency shelter until they were able to produce all the required documentation to satisfy the eligibility requirements. Despite all the bureaucratic hurdles, all eight migrants, including U.S. citizen Dan, became eligible to receive welfare benefits and started claiming them immediately.

Homeless People with "Deviant" Life Courses

The remaining two groups among homeless people with irregular life courses were differentiated by the extent to which a variety of social problems (such as alcohol and substance abuse or mental and physical health problems) played a role in their lives and in the ways in which they became homeless.[15] Although younger homeless, for the most part, tended to be less affected by social problems, being in better physical health and significantly less affected by debilitating alcohol problems at the time,[16] four exceptions caused me to devise a separate category of irregular life courses—namely, homeless people with "deviant" life courses. This group included three younger men (FTW, Oliver, and Sioux) and one young woman (Marita) who had had turbulent lives that were all characterized by childhood abuse and neglect, violence, drug addiction (polytoxicomania), crime, and incarceration as well as chronic marginality and previous homeless episodes. Considering the combination of social problems, I deliberately use the term "deviant" to describe their life experiences, because they themselves felt alienated and ostracized by mainstream society and regarded themselves as being at the absolute margins of society, margins that, at some point in their young lives, involved the drug scene, the punk scene, or the milieu of street prostitution. These circumstances also affected the ways they perceived any type of "public" intervention. Oliver explained:

> If you look at my life, no parents, no love, no qualifications, my heroin addiction, you see it's all shit. You ask how the welfare state impacted my life? Foster care, jail, social workers who always tell you what to do and never listen to what you need, the assholes at the labor office who don't even try to find you a job. . . . Hey, what do you expect? I set my expectations low. I have no reason to trust them. In the end, it's up to me, me alone. (Oliver, age 26, shelter resident, deviant life course, interview, March 10, 1998)

It is not difficult to imagine that this group's members with their perhaps understandable suspicion constituted a small subpopulation among the homeless that remained hard to reach.

Homeless People with "Disabilities"

A fifth life-course category based on existing social problems included four homeless people with disabilities: two women who had been physically (Monika, legally blind) or mentally disabled (Andrea) their entire lives, and two men who had acquired either a mental (Paule) or physical illness (Biker) in their adult years after having led relatively "normal" lives in the past. I decided to put these four respondents into a separate category, simply because "disability"—in itself a contested label—poses a different challenge to social policy intervention, involving different administrative and legal entities. Moreover, unlike with most other respondents, the existence of such disabilities limited their ability to find work or be referred to viable job opportunities and thus affected their possibilities for economic integration. Although three of the four respondents desired to find work, their disabilities rendered them "unemployable." After many years outside the service system, they all needed some sort of independent or supportive housing. At the time of my interviews, only the two women had accomplished this goal and were, at the time, adequately housed in supportive facilities. In Monika's case, however, it took nine years to accomplish this basic reintegration. Like Marita in the deviant life-course category, her adult years were characterized by prostitution, precariousness, homelessness, and neglect after an inconspicuous but unloving childhood.

The example of homeless people with "disabilities" demonstrates that it is difficult to devise case-appropriate, let alone proactive, solutions to problems that involve so many different administrative entities. Biker completely avoided the homeless service sector and voluntarily lived in cars and minivans for nine years. During that time period, he underwent eight reconstructive leg surgeries following a motorcycle accident in 1989. In Monika's case, after years of public neglect, her step-by-step process toward finding appropriate housing in Berlin involved a former teacher (persuading her to seek help), the local social-welfare agency (providing basic cash assistance, shelter, and approval for additional measures), caseworkers at a domestic-violence shelter (offering psychological counseling and assistance with identifying housing options), the health department (verifying disability), and a youth welfare agency's final referral to a state-of-the-art assisted-living facility for visually impaired people in a nice neighborhood in Steglitz. In the end, it took about three months to achieve this stabilization, showing that Berlin's system can be successful. The question arises: Were welfare intervention and the various entities involved similarly successful in the case of homeless people in the other life-course groups? In the next section, I discuss the challenges involved in addressing the needs of the different groups with regard to the local welfare state.

Implications of the Life Course on Homeless Policy

The foregoing discussion of similarities and differences in homeless people's life courses reveals that different, often interrelated factors and problems may affect people's readiness for exit and, at the same time, the ability of welfare to intervene in proactive ways. The relationship between exit potential and policy is different for each group, because the different life-course trajectories and expectations suggest different normative objectives and challenges for the welfare state.

When Berlin's welfare, shelter, and service options are compared with homeless people's distinct service needs, most expectations and demands correspond to difficult but doable policy objectives. Policy instruments and services are available to address most of the problems homeless people face, including shelter and rehousing policies, job-qualification and reemployment policies, and health-care policies. Yet when asked their opinions of the welfare system and its impact on their poverty management up to the time of our interviews—which occurred on average twenty-three months into the subjects' homelessness—most respondents expressed grave dissatisfaction with the local welfare system. This dissatisfaction provides a starting point to examine in more detail how local welfare-state deficiencies contribute to homeless people's deteriorating life circumstances and their inability to reenter job and housing markets and normalize their social relations.

Homeless People's Service Needs: Doable Objectives?

From the analysis of people with distinct life-course trajectories and often-complex personal problems, we can isolate policy needs and challenges for each group in order of presumed difficulty, beginning with the least difficult.

Younger homeless people with regular life courses who are generally less affected by accompanying social problems are likely to pose the least-difficult challenge for policy intervention. Their most urgent policy need, besides immediate shelter and income support, is the acquisition of job training in preparation for independent lives in the societal mainstream. Older homeless respondents with regular life courses, most of whom have been integrated into the mainstream in the past, have shown their ability to live independent and economically secure lives. Considering their previous experiences with welfare intervention, such respondents clearly expect assistance from the welfare state in fulfilling their goal of reentering the mainstream, especially with regard to job and housing searches. Yet their age and the complex nature of social and economic problems (e.g., debts, health and alcohol problems) that accompany their gradual descent into homelessness pose challenges to the welfare state and may consequently complicate their chances for exit. Furthermore, some of them have expertise in rather obsolete professions and thus require retraining to be competitive in Berlin's tight labor market.

Migrants with transient life courses, a diverse and rather socially isolated group with little information about the city and its infrastructure, need assistance with initial entry rather than reintegration into the labor and housing markets. Some younger people in this group who lack qualifications and are thus at a competitive disadvantage may also need job training. Yet given the fact that many of the transient homeless have been out of the mainstream for quite some time, and considering the complexity of underlying social problems, their integration is likely a difficult challenge. Providing services to homeless people with disabilities and severe health problems may be similarly complicated, because a concerted effort between different administrative entities is needed. These people are likely to require some sort of assisted living arrangement or continuous long-term care to accommodate their specific needs. Finding suitable employment, as desired by three respondents in this group, also poses a challenge. Most problematic, however, appears to be the integration of people with deviant life courses because of the extent of adversity these people have faced in the past as well as the severity and complexity of their multiple social problems. Moreover, it may be difficult to overcome their reservations and doubts about trusting welfare intervention to help them overcome their problems.

Regarding access to services, most respondents accomplished it within their first two visits to the welfare agency, although the application process often involved an excruciating amount of paperwork and bureaucratic hassles. Six older homeless people with regular life courses and more recent employment were already in the system, because they received unemployment compensation; upon informing their caseworkers of the loss of their homes, they were immediately referred to a local welfare office to deal with shelter and other social needs. Most other homeless people with a previous address in Berlin were issued cash assistance and referral to a nearby shelter after their first or second visit to the local welfare office in the district of their last residence. Only homeless people with transient life courses and thus no prior residence in the city reported delays until their eligibility was determined. But even they were not left without help, being issued a daily welfare allowance (DM 18/$10 per day) and a place at one of Berlin's emergency shelters. Because of their legal obligation to do so, twenty-two respondents deemed able to work registered with the local labor office and started receiving referrals. People also reported no problems having their physical and mental health-care needs met since becoming homeless. Furthermore, people who knew about and sought specific social services, including domestic-violence counseling, debt consultation, or legal advice, reported few problems obtaining such services. This relatively unproblematic access to the local welfare system and the many services it offers is evidence for the comparatively higher social-welfare capital Berlin's homeless people possess vis-à-vis homeless people in Los Angeles, the majority of whom receive no direct public assistance whatsoever.

Homeless People's Service Experiences: Objectives Missed?

Yet when I asked the respondents for their opinions about the services they had received by the time I first interviewed them, I received primarily negative reviews: The vast majority of respondents were either dissatisfied or very dissatisfied with the nature and extent of local welfare provisions. A small minority felt the public response to be adequate or satisfactory, but none rated it as good or excellent. Among the chief complaints were substandard service and a lack of individualized assistance (twenty-four respondents), insufficient referrals to realistic job and housing opportunities (twenty-two), substandard shelter provision and warehousing (eighteen), and insufficient cash assistance (twenty-two; von Mahs 2005a, 941–946). Such complaints are frequently echoed in a range of evaluative and ethnographic studies from the United States (Burt et al. 2001; Desjarlais 1997; Hopper 2003; Snow and Anderson 1993; Wolch and Dear 1993; J. Wright, Rubin, and Devine 1998). This finding, in turn, raises the question: Why are the perceptions of the respondents so overwhelmingly negative, despite the fact that, in theory at least, services are available to deal with virtually all their individually specific needs?

To answer this overarching question, I examine the interrelationship between homeless people's exit strategies and homeless policy, paying particular attention to the likely differences among the five groups. Given that homelessness is a condition that unfolds over time and space and thus is a process, I first address homeless people's attempts to satisfy their immediate needs to generate income and thus stabilize their life courses (Chapter 3) and then to find shelter (Chapter 4). Then I focus on their long-term strategies to find employment and housing and, in succeeding, ideally to optimize their life courses (Chapter 5).

3

Not Allowed

Legal Exclusion, Human Rights, and Global Capital

Perhaps the most pressing need a homeless person has is to generate income to ensure his or her basic survival. Income, however derived, is an important component of stabilizing homeless people's lives en route to, ideally, overcoming homelessness. In this chapter, I demonstrate how in Los Angeles and, to a lesser extent, in Berlin, insufficient public cash assistance forces many, if not most, homeless people to resort to informal material survival strategies. Such strategies are frequently met with deliberate spatial exclusion by public and/or private security through legal means in the form of displacement, deportation, and prosecution of fare dodging. To support this argument, I first provide a brief discussion of U.S. research to set the stage for a more in-depth investigation of homeless people's material survival strategies in Berlin and how these strategies, along with homeless people's mere existence, are met with punitive responses, effectively limiting their use of urban space. In differentiating experiences by life course, I shed light on the consequences of punitive policy and subsequently synthesize the results by introducing a model of "legal exclusion" that demonstrates how public policy aggravates homeless people's personal circumstances and complicates their attempts to overcome homelessness.

Material Survival and Its Criminalization: Evidence from Los Angeles

Homeless people need income to procure food and clothing and often pay shelter fees. Given that few homeless people in Los Angeles, or in other U.S. cities for that matter, receive public-income assistance, they inevitably must rely on other material survival strategies to make ends meet. American homeless people employ an often astonishing extent of such strategies, which, using David Snow and Leon Anderson's (1993) typology, involve wage labor, institutional assistance, social networks, and shadow work, the last encompassing a variety of informal and often sanctioned survival methods commonly associated with homelessness (e.g., panhandling, scavenging, recycling, donating blood plasma, etc.).

Yet shadow work and, perhaps more generally, homeless people's mere existence have been met with punitive policies across the United States. Since the early 1980s, antihomeless ordinances have mushroomed in cities across the country, outlawing virtually every aspect of homeless people's lives and activities, including panhandling, scavenging, loitering, camping, sleeping, sitting, or violating public dress or behavioral codes.[1] The fact that even mobile feeding programs, which use vans to provide free meals to homeless people living on the street, have been outlawed has been discussed by Don Mitchell and Nik Heynen (2009). In many ways, the criminalization of homeless people is perhaps the most extensively studied geographic aspect of contemporary homelessness in U.S. cities and, more recently, in Europe (for overviews, see Amster 2008; Busch-Geertsema 2008; Mitchell 2003; Doherty et al. 2008; Toro et al. 2007; von Mahs 2011a). Borrowing insights from a variety of academic disciplines, these studies provide a persuasive basis for understanding the rationale behind punitive policy and serve to unmask those responsible.[2] The academic interest in homeless exclusion is unsurprising, as there is hardly a more blatant example of injustice across urban space than the deliberate spatial exclusion of people for the purpose of benefiting capitalist interests (Mitchell 1997, 2003; Mitchell and Heynen 2009; Amster 2008). The tenor of virtually all these critical studies is that cities, increasingly governed by public-private ventures, are reimagined as places of consumption in which homeless people, as potentially dangerous nonconsumers, have no place. Homeless people are deliberately portrayed as threatening and culpable deterrents to consumer activities who consequently must be removed, signaling Neil Smith's (1996) "revanchism."[3] Compelling evidence suggests that virtually every U.S. city has been enforcing specific "antihomeless" ordinances to facilitate homeless removal from prime urban spaces (Vitale 2010; Foscarinis 1996; NLCHP 2011).

Los Angeles has long been in the forefront of finding expedient ways to rid commercially important areas of homeless people, as aptly described in Mike Davis's seminal *City of Quartz* (1990). The city, its police, and local businesses resort to exclusionary measures that encompass myriad legal and architectural means, including the much-cited convex and divided "bum-proof benches," automatic sprinkler systems to wash people and cardboard homes away, and barbed-wire trash containers designed to dissuade scavengers. To facilitate actual displacement, police rely on a broad range of existing public order and safety laws (e.g., against public urination or public alcohol consumption) and, over time and with increasing intensity, local ordinances explicitly directed against homeless people and their behavior (Reese, DeVerteuil, and Thach 2010; Blasi and Stuart 2008; Wolch and Dear 1993; DeVerteuil 2006). Local jurisdictions enforce these laws despite the fact that most of these exclusionary practices are deemed illegal and often unconstitutional by the courts when challenged by homeless people or their advocates (Mitchell 1998a, 1998b). Yet, each time a local ordinance directly targeting homeless people is challenged by advocates litigating on behalf of the homeless and is removed upon a judge's orders (most judges side with the homeless), new ordinances are swiftly created, effectively replacing old ones at a faster pace than they can be removed.[4] In more recent years, under the leadership of Chief William Bratton, former New York City police commissioner under Mayor Rudolph W. Giuliani, the LAPD has stepped up its efforts to displace the homeless from the streets of downtown and even Skid Row itself in an effort to deconcentrate street homelessness and ensuing crime (Reese, DeVerteuil, and Thach 2010). Even if such "Safer City" initiatives really do lead to a decrease in crime and success in deconcentrating Skid Row, they remain questionable simply because they do not reduce homelessness or address its causes (Blasi and Stuart 2008).

In Europe, too, we find mounting evidence for the proliferation of homeless exclusion, albeit through existing public order and safety regulations, not explicit antihomeless laws (Doherty et al. 2008; von Mahs 2011a). Berlin, according to Volker Eick (1996, 1998), witnessed a clear proliferation of the use of public order and safety laws throughout the 1990s to exclude *Randgruppen* (marginalized groups) from commercially important urban areas, although it is unknown precisely how many displaced people were actually homeless (police statistics do not differentiate by housing status).

We also do not know the consequences of such punitive measures for homeless people and their life chances. In fact, the literature on homeless exclusion has come under scrutiny lately, as a number of critics have argued that existing studies are rather theoretical and are based on weak empirical footing. Specifically, the studies fail to consider the voices and experiences of the homeless themselves and consequently reveal little about the actual consequences of punitive action on homeless people's lives and life chances (DeVerteuil, May, and von Mahs 2009; May 2004). Critical studies from the United States (Amster 2008), the UK (May 2008), and Germany (von Mahs 2005a; Busch-Geertsema 2008) suggest that the extent and consequences of punitive action may vary and that homeless people are perhaps more adept in responding to social and spatial exclusion than the literature gives them credit for. After all, homeless street people continue to be present in most cities, despite rigorous efforts to remove them. To fill this void in our current understanding, I now focus on homeless people's experiences in Berlin, starting with an examination of homeless people's material survival strategies and why the public-income assistance that all respondents received was deemed insufficient, thus necessitating the use of these informal, often prosecuted strategies.

Making Ends Meet in Berlin: Homeless People's Material Survival Strategies

To differentiate the discussion of material survival strategies, I first elaborate on the role and impact of public-cash assistance on material survival and then, upon demonstrating that public-income support remains insufficient, describe homeless people's alternative, more-informal survival strategies, including wage labor, social networks, and shadow work.

Public-Income Support and Its Insufficiency

It certainly is a positive point that homeless people in Berlin and Germany have much easier access to cash assistance and reported few problems applying for and receiving it, as I discuss in the previous chapter. Twenty-two respondents, including seven with transient life courses who experienced some delays, began receiving social-assistance (*Sozialhilfe*) payments upon applying for them, which granted DM 540 ($300) per month in cash assistance in 1998. The remaining six respondents, all with comparably more-regular life courses and not-so-distant employment, initially received substantially higher unemployment insurance payments (53 percent of their previous income, averaging DM 1,800/$1,000); yet, over time, they saw their eligibility lapse, whereupon they joined the remaining welfare recipients in receiving, to their alarm, less than half the income they were accustomed to. Furthermore, five respondents who were living at the Wohnheim Trachenbergring applied for and were given the opportunity to earn some token income (DM 3/$1.70 per hour) through publicly funded community work (*Gemeinnützige zusätzliche Arbeit* [GZA]) in exchange for performing basic janitorial and cleaning duties at the facility. Although two of them (Kalle and Hanno) appreciated having something to do and an opportunity to "pay back," three (Bob, Markus, and Leo) thought that the income was ridiculously inadequate and pursued such opportunities rather haphazardly and with little effort. Respondents' public assistance is shown in Table 3.1.

It became apparent that an alarming three-quarters of the twenty-two welfare recipients felt that their cash assistance was insufficient to meet their needs. Except for the six older respondents who initially received substantially higher unemployment compensation and a handful of people who lived very spartan lives and did not consume alcohol or drugs, all respondents reported that they eventually ran out of money, typically toward the end of a benefit month. Leo explained:

> They calculated that amount quite narrowly. You know, I don't drink, with the exception of the occasional beer maybe, but even I can barely live off that money. Every month, I run out of money and then have no choice but to borrow some cash or get it somewhere else. (Leo, age 32, shelter resident, transient life course, interview, February 23, 1998)

Furthermore, not all eligible welfare recipients were granted additional benefits, such as subsidized transportation passes (a 50 percent discount) and the biannual clothing allowance (cash benefit of approximately DM 540/$300), in large part because they were unaware of them. Caseworkers in Berlin's welfare offices often failed to inform clients about such benefits.

TABLE 3.1 Homeless People's Use of Public Assistance in Berlin

Public assistance	Older homeless people with regular life courses (n = 8)	Younger homeless people with regular life courses (n = 4)	Homeless people with transient life courses (n = 8)	Homeless people with deviant life courses (n = 4)	Homeless people with disabilities (n = 4)	Total
Monetary assistance						
Social assistance (delay*)	3 (1)	3 (0)	7 (7)	4 (2)	4 (2)	21
Unemployment compensation†	5	0	1	0	0	6
Clothing allowance	2	3	6	2	4	17
Transportation allowance	1	1	1	0	2	5
Welfare supplement for communal work (GZA)‡	2	2	1	0	0	5
Additional services						
Soup kitchen (within 1st month)	3 (0)	2 (0)	7 (5)	2 (2)	1 (0)	15
Day center (within 1st month)	2 (0)	0	6 (3)	1 (0)	2 (1)	11
Respondents by name§	Helmut, Sachse, Kalle, Hanno, Det, Hans, Bernie, Maria	Mario, Bob, Markus, Radek	Tobias, Dan, Schlöter, Harri, Matze, Martin, Leo, Jens	Oliver, Sioux, FTW, Marita	Andrea, Monika, Paule, Biker	

* Delay of more than one week after application.

† All recipients of unemployment compensation unable to find social-insurance-based employment eventually saw their eligibility expire (typically after two years) and had to rely on substantially lower social assistance payments, at less than half their previous income.

‡ GZA (*Gemeinnützige zusätzliche Arbeit*) is a modest welfare supplement allowing selected welfare recipients to earn $2 (DM 3.60) per hour for community work such as cleaning or janitorial tasks at the facility.

§ Short biographies of the respondents are provided in Appendix 1. The respondents listed in the table are male, except for Maria, Marita, Andrea, and Monika.

But why were such welfare incomes perceived to be too low? In most cases, increasingly heavy alcohol or drug use over time consumed greater portions of a person's disposable income. Although I explain in the next chapter why people's alcohol and drug intake increased, suffice it to say that heavy alcohol use and resulting health problems are psychologically and financially expensive. More than half the sixteen respondents I identified as having "substantial" substance-abuse problems at the time of the interviews spent their entire welfare allowances, and sometimes more, on sustaining their addictions. The most extreme cases involved past, and in one case present, heroin use. Marita, a nineteen-year-old woman who had been homeless and addicted since the age of fourteen, had to generate approximately DM 300 ($170) per day to sustain her addiction. Moreover, all but one respondent smoked cigarettes, an expense that, assuming one pack a day (as was common), consumed almost one-third of the welfare income.

Once their welfare incomes eventually ran out, homeless people had no choice but to rely on a number of informal survival strategies to make ends meet. In so doing, they displayed quite a bit of ingenuity and improvisation skills, essentially employing the entire range of informal means that Snow and Anderson (1993) and a host of other researchers from the United States and elsewhere have identified as homeless people's primary material survival strategies.

Informal Survival Strategies: Necessity, Not Choice

When looking at homeless people's diverse set of material survival strategies in Berlin, we notice surprising similarities to the United States in terms of the breadth and ingenuity of attempts to generate income (compare with Duneier 1999; Snow and Anderson 1993; Rowe and Wolch 1990; Knowles 1999; Ruddick 1996). At the same time, it becomes obvious that many homeless respondents, especially those with more-regular life courses and comparatively higher human and social capital, tried to avoid shadow work, which most of them considered humiliating and degrading. Rather, they pursued other options for as long as they could. People with more-irregular life courses and those with substantial and increasing substance-abuse problems, on the other hand, often had no choice but to resort to informal survival strategies or had long shed their reservations about using them (Hans, Harri, and Matze). Table 3.2, borrowing Snow and Anderson's (1993) typology of homeless people's informal material survival strategies, provides an overview of the different types of informal material survival strategies the respondents had applied over the course of their homelessness. Prevalent factors (those used by more than half of the respondents) are highlighted in the table with boldface type.

Informal Wage Labor

Eight respondents with previous job experience, including four older homeless people with regular life courses and four of the older homeless with transient life courses or disabilities and thus higher extents of human capital, reported using temporary, informal employment, which Germans call "black work" (*Schwarzarbeit*), as an occasional income source, and two of them (Hans and Schlöter) more regularly. Relying on their old connections to employers and being comparatively more familiar with Berlin's labor market, they tried to obtain such part-time and temporary employment whenever possible, hoping it could translate

TABLE 3.2 Homeless People's Use of Informal Material Survival Strategies in Berlin

Informal material survival strategies*	Older homeless people with regular life courses (n = 8)	Younger homeless people with regular life courses (n = 4)	Homeless people with transient life courses (n = 8)	Homeless people with deviant life courses (n = 4)	Homeless people with disabilities (n = 4)	Total
Informal wage labor	**4**	0	3	0	1	8
Regular/monthly work	1	0	1	0	0	2
Paid apprenticeship	0	1	0	0	0	1
Social networks						
Nonhomeless	**5**	**4**	3	2	2	16
Diminished over time	4	1	2	1	2	10
Homeless	7	4	**6**	2	**3**	22
Shadow work						
Panhandling	3	2	**6**	**4**	0	15
Shoplifting	**5**	**3**	**5**	**4**	2	19
Selling street newspapers	0	0	**4**	1	0	5
Performances	0	1	1	0	0	2
Scavenging	1	0	3	**4**	1	9
Prostitution	0	0	0	1	2	3
Drug dealing	0	1	2	**4**	0	7
Miscellaneous crime	0	0	1	**4**	0	5
Respondents by name*	Helmut, Sachse, Kalle, Hanno, Det, Hans, Bernie, Maria	Mario, Bob, Markus, Radek	Tobias, Dan, Schlöter, Harri, Matze, Martin, Leo, Jens	Oliver, Sioux, FTW, Marita	Andrea, Monika, Paule, Biker	

Note: Numbers for prevalent factors (used by more than half of the respondents) are shown in **boldface** type.

* Short biographies of the respondents are provided in Appendix 1. The respondents listed in the table are male, except for Maria, Marita, Andrea, and Monika.

into long-term, regular employment opportunities. Schlöter, for instance, would supplement his income through undocumented wage labor using his existing connection with a former employer:

> Every now and then I would call Harold [name changed] to find out whether he had something for me. Harold was my former boss, you know. Unfortunately, his business isn't doing so well, especially in the winter, and so he doesn't have anything permanent. On occasions he would give me some tem-

> porary work if he had a shortage or deadline. At least a little money. Harold told me, however, that I'd be the first he would hire if the business is doing better. You know, I might be a drunk, but I am a damn good painter, and I never missed a day of work. (Schlöter, age 52, shelter resident, transient life course, interview, February 26, 1998)

Like Schlöter, Kalle expressed explicit hope that informal day labor could be parlayed into permanent employment:

> Somewhere one hopes that *Schwarzarbeit* leads to something permanent and that your boss recognizes that you have the skills and that you work hard. Unfortunately, however, it did not work out yet. But you've got to keep on trying. (Kalle, age 44, shelter resident, older regular life course, interview, February 28, 1998)

The biggest problem with this type of employment is that it is unreliable and sporadic; only two respondents could rely on such income on a predictable basis. Moreover, the competition for such jobs, most often in the construction sector, is fierce; the pay, although better than most other informal income options, is relatively low; working conditions are substandard; and employers are notorious for hiring undocumented workers (Krätke 2001; Mayer 1997). And it goes without saying that such informal work circumvents and undermines the social-insurance system and does not count toward people's social insurance or pensions. Still, those respondents who were able to find such informal work appreciated this option as the most dignified income strategy and retained the hope that it would lead to more stable, long-term job opportunities, something Germans call *Klebeffekt* (sticking effect), which is generally quite low in Germany, regardless of housing status (DGB 2010).

Social Networks

Another very important source of income as well as other material and emotional support is social networks. Sixteen people with existing social networks in Berlin, and thus higher social capital, relied heavily on kinship support and other nonhomeless connections. Unfortunately, ten of them stated that such support networks diminished over time, an occurrence that is, as I explain in Chapter 4, frequently associated with the deteriorating life circumstances in "homeless spaces." So although such important outside networks often dwindle, inside networks to other homeless people become increasingly important in providing material, logistical, and social support. Twenty-two of the twenty-eight respondents, including all respondents I interviewed in the shelter, reported that they relied on other homeless people for material support. Usually if someone ran out of money toward the end of the benefit month, someone else would lend him or her cash, which was generally promptly paid back once the borrower received his or her next welfare payment or earned some money doing informal work. According to Biker, an unwritten code of honor underlay this practice, as did sheer pragmatism. By participating in this reciprocal system, people ensured their trustworthiness and received support when it was needed. They realized that once they violated this unwritten agreement and abused the trust of others, they would be chastised, and nobody would help out anymore. Although this trust was not always honored and some people had lost money, this honor system of reciprocity seemed to work, as Mario explained:

> So, from my perspective, things here work well, because I get along with the people, and everybody helps everybody, and if somebody has no money, people help you out, and as soon as you get money again, you just pay back. Same with food and so on. People help each other out. I think it's a good sense of community here. (Mario, age 22, shelter resident, younger regular life course, interview, February 2, 1998)

I myself occasionally lent money, and I received it all back without having to ask for it. Conversely, Biker once helped me out, without questions or conditions, after my ATM card failed and I was stranded in Berlin without money. Given, however, that fellow homeless people had limited income to lend (the typical loan amount was DM 20/$11), even this option was finite, requiring people to resort to more unconventional informal survival strategies, the ones Snow and Anderson (1993) aptly describe as "shadow work."

Shadow Work

Although respondents with more-regular life courses were able to rely more heavily on wage labor and their social networks, people with more-irregular life courses and thus lower extents of human and social capital often had no choice but to rely more heavily on shadow work, encompassing a range of strategies.

The most frequent strategy—used by respondents across the life-course spectrum—was the shoplifting of alcohol, food, cigarettes, and occasionally clothing, in that order. Most respondents made it clear that they considered shoplifting a means of last resort and felt bad about doing it. Respondents, especially those with more-regular life courses, shoplifted infrequently and reluctantly and only if all other options were exhausted. In many cases, alcohol cravings caused people to steal. Five people were caught and received fines, adding to the already high debts many of them had accumulated over the years. One exception was Helmut, who, as a previous supermarket manager, negotiated a deal with the store owner. After working off his fine unloading trucks, he got occasional work at that particular store as well as regular help in the form of free leftovers at the end of the day.

The second-most-frequent strategy, employed at some point by more than half the respondents, was panhandling for donations. Here, too, most people, especially those with regular life courses, resorted to this strategy only in the direst circumstances and with great hesitation. Ultimately, only seven respondents, all with irregular life courses, regularly panhandled, in time becoming relatively proficient and generating modest amounts of income (on average DM 10 to DM 30/$5.50 to $17 per day).

Another strategy frequently associated with homelessness was scavenging for food, alcohol, or recyclables to be redeemed for cash. In this sample, nine respondents—all with severe addictions and thus financial problems—resorted to this practice, typically looking for recyclables, not food, to turn into modest amounts of cash. Given an increase in deposit amounts, fewer users were throwing bottles or cans away, making scavenging less lucrative than it used to be. Only one person, Andrea, a mentally disabled women who became homeless after her mother and guardian died, lived almost exclusively from scavenging and, at the time, resembled the stereotypical "bag lady." Making herself unattractive was also a defense mechanism she adopted to deter sexual predators after she was raped and abused by a man who had offered her a place to stay. She and another woman with a disability (Monika) had experienced such housing prostitution in the past.

Prostitution became the primary means of survival for Marita, who saw no other choice to sustain her up to DM 300 ($170) daily heroin addiction; in the process, she experienced violence on an almost weekly basis. Because of the dangers associated with this line of work, she had already endured multiple health and dental problems with little help to resolve them. She had also tried therapy and rehabilitation multiple times, but the urge of her addiction, and being released into more or less the same milieu upon completion of rehab, caused her to relapse repeatedly.

Strictly criminal activities, including drug dealing, grand theft, burglary, and robbery, were rather rare occurrences and were almost exclusively linked to people with more-irregular life courses. All those with more-deviant life courses had accumulated sizable criminal records and experienced multiyear incarcerations in juvenile or adult correctional facilities. All of them received monthly welfare, which allowed at least two of them (Sioux and Oliver) to cease engaging in criminal activities. FTW, on the other hand, continued to deal cannabis on occasion (he called it "sharing"), whereas Marita relied on daily prostitution to satisfy her craving for heroin. But another occasional criminal activity involved the destruction of private property and vandalism, specifically tampering with and raiding cigarette vending machines, a practice three younger respondents admitted to.

Finally, and certainly less common among homeless people overall, was the strategy of selling street newspapers, which, unlike all other informal survival strategies with the exception of giving performances, was voluntary and ultimately perceived as rewarding yet was met with fierce persecution, as I detail later in this chapter.

Performing any of these informal survival strategies requires quite a lot of effort and time as well as a substantial amount of mobility. Moreover, some of these activities—most notably panhandling, giving performances, or selling street newspapers—require locations with high pedestrian flows, simply because few people will actually make a donation, reward an act, or buy a paper. At the same time, it is precisely these types of activities in commercial or upscale spaces that have come under scrutiny and have resulted in the forceful displacement and criminalization of homeless people in Los Angeles and other U.S. cities. To what extent homeless people in Berlin become displaced for performing survival strategies and the consequences they experience are the focus of the next section.

Displacement and Criminalization in Berlin: Punitive Policy Experienced

That the displacement and removal of the homeless—observed in the United States and most postindustrial cities around the globe—have direct impacts on visible, easily recognizable homeless street people seems rather obvious. One of the startling discoveries of this research, therefore, is that well over half the respondents had been the target of some type of punitive approach, even though only six of them, subjectively speaking, even remotely resembled the stereotypical picture of a noticeable homeless street person. Specifically, nineteen people had been prosecuted for fare dodging, seventeen people had been asked to leave the premises of semipublic spaces (such as Berlin's public-transit system and the German railroad), and nine people had been displaced from public spaces. More alarmingly, five people reported having been deported to the urban fringe by the police force in violation of its own directives. It further became apparent that the vast majority of personal experiences with punitive policy occurred in the immediate city center, especially four predominant locations, in each of which more than three instances of bans had occurred: Breitscheidplatz–Bahnhof Zoo area, Kurfürstenstrasse, Alexanderplatz, and near the Reichstag building (see Fig. 3.1).

Given the respondents' frequent encounters with punitive urban policy, it is necessary to look into the reasons for, personal experiences with, and consequences of this policy. An understanding of these factors is, as I argue in Chapter 1, a main shortcoming of the contemporary literature on punitive policy in Germany and the United States.

Personal Experiences with and Consequences of Punitive Policy

Exploring homeless people's personal experiences reveals some variation in terms of the frequency and consequences of punitive policy and thus a more differentiated analysis. Most notably, I find substantial life-course differences, as Table 3.3 suggests.

Specifically, it becomes obvious that, accounting for duplications, homeless people with more-irregular life courses were much more likely to experience punitive policy, deal with it more frequently, and suffer more severe consequences than folks with more-regular life courses. The primary reason for this is that people with more-regular life courses were less distinguishable from the general public, familiar with the spaces they patronized, and, as suggested pre-

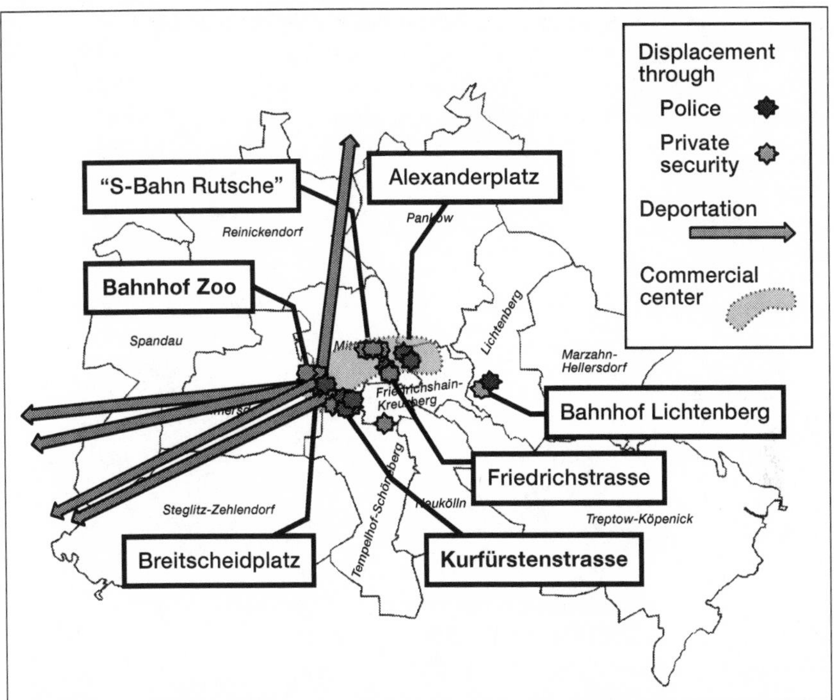

FIGURE 3.1 Locations of Displacement and Deportation of Homeless People in Berlin

viously, much less likely to perform shadow work or engage in behaviors commonly associated with homelessness. Most of their encounters with punitive policy involved loitering and public intoxication inside their *Kiez,* which can, frankly, happen to any Berliner standing at a kiosk too long for her or his own good while consuming more than one *Feierabendbier,* a practice that is quite common among Berliners on their way home. As a result, only one such person, Hans, incurred a permanent ban to leave the premises and, upon disobeying, was deported. Other than that, most respondents with more-regular life courses, older and younger alike, stated that they obeyed the first order to leave a place, moved on, and set up camp elsewhere relatively undeterred. Surprisingly, perhaps, almost half of them felt that the charge against them was justified, even if they did not necessarily agree with the consequence.

People with more-irregular life courses, on the other hand, were much more likely to experience punitive policy in the first place and then typically suffer more severe forms, such as bans against using particular spaces, trespassing violations in semiprivate spaces, and actual deportations to the urban fringe. Virtually all these increasingly severe forms of displacement and legal actions involved members of the deviant and transient life-course groups. First, members of these groups were generally a bit more noticeable as being "out of place,"

TABLE 3.3 Homeless People's Experiences with Punitive Policy in Berlin

Informal material survival strategies*	Older homeless people with regular life courses (n = 8)	Younger homeless people with regular life courses (n = 4)	Homeless people with transient life courses (n = 8)	Homeless people with deviant life courses (n = 4)	Homeless people with disabilities (n = 4)	Total
Displacement						
Temporary displacement						
From public spaces	2	1	5	4	1	13
From semipublic spaces	3	2	6	4	2	17
Permanent ban						
From public spaces	1	—	3	1	—	5
From semipublic spaces	—	—	2	3	—	5
Reasons for displacement						
Panhandling	1	1	3	2	1	8
Loitering	3	3	5	4	2	17
Intoxication	2	1	4	3	1	11
Prosecution of fare dodging						
Debts DM 0–900 ($0–500)	3	3	7	4	2	19
Debts >DM 900 (>$500)	—	1	3	2	1	7
Deportation to urban fringe	1	—	2	2	—	5
Total people (n = 28)	3	3	7	4	2	19

often congregating with other homeless people and fringe groups in the city's commercial center. Second, members of these two groups were much more likely to employ informal survival strategies. In fact, one-quarter of the respondents were asked to leave when performing such strategies. This behavior, again, makes it easier for public authorities and private security to spot, identify, and eventually displace such persons.

To make sense of the various types of punitive policies, the entities that enforced them, and their outcomes, I next differentiate my findings by type of space and the sets of escalating measures employed in them. Such classification is necessary, because different legal contexts resulted in different consequences, some of which were far reaching.

Public Spaces: Escalating Measures from Displacement to Deportation

In explicitly defined "public" spaces in Berlin (sidewalks, squares, parks, pedestrian zones), the police typically ensure adherence to general public order and safety laws and ordinances and not, as in the United States, to specific anti-homeless ordinances (Doherty et al. 2008; Busch-Geertsema 2008). The relatively broad scope of Berlin's ordinances gives individual police officers a great deal of discretion as to when, where, and under what circumstances to enforce them and, in so doing, to displace a person from a particular space. In this sample, almost all instances occurred in the context of loitering and public intoxication. Although it is legal in Germany to consume alcohol in public spaces, police officers are permitted to issue a temporary or permanent ban if an intoxicated person is perceived to be a nuisance or danger to other people. In most cases, respondents complied with the directives and moved on, preventing further escalation:

> The cops are not a problem. Listen, this is one of my lesser problems. You just say [stands in attention and salutes with a grin], "*Jawohl, Herr Wachtmeister*" [Yes, Officer!] and move on. They'll leave you alone as long as you do what they want. (Oliver, age 26, shelter resident, deviant life course, interview, March 10, 1998)

In a few cases, however, an immediate permanent ban was issued if the respondent dared to argue with an officer. In five cases, people received permanent bans and, upon further disagreements, were temporarily arrested and deported to the urban fringe. Five respondents, three of them citing repeated incidents, reported that they were handcuffed, loaded into police vans, often with others, driven to the outskirts of town, and released there. Although police officials admitted to this practice at a 1996 hearing of the Berlin parliament, they stated that police would not do so in cold temperatures, at night, or when the people were intoxicated. Yet all five respondents' experiences suggest that the police force violated its own directives. Hans's experience is exemplary, albeit with a twist:

> Yes, once they took me. I was loaded and argued with these guys [police]. They drove me out to that forest in Brandenburg, kicked me out, and said good night. Was in the middle of nowhere [*janz weit draussen*, JWD] and I got lost. Tried to orient myself by the city lights on the horizon. Froze my ass off, had no coat! A Brandenburg police patrol eventually picked me up on that country road and, upset about their idiot colleagues, drove me right back into town. With blue light! Dropped me off right at the same place where I was picked up and sober, too! Hey, but here is the kicker: I was back sooner than the other idiots [Berlin police officers], who must have gotten lost on their way back in [starts laughing]. They were utterly surprised to see me again—you should have seen their faces! [laughs]. (Hans, age 50, day-center visitor, older regular life course, interview, March 9, 1998)

For the others, such deportations were no laughing matter, as they literally endangered their physical well-being, clearly showing the harshness of police measures. Although none of them reported lasting effects, they found themselves exposed to hypothermia, disorientation, and stress. Fortunately, the Berlin parliament inquiry led to a discontinuation of this practice in 1997, although reports of occasional deportations have since surfaced, according to Sigi Deiß and Stefan Schneider, two of my key informants.

Semipublic Spaces: Fare Dodging, Displacement, and Trespassing

In "semipublic" spaces, such as previously public yet recently privatized public-transit facilities operated by the BVG or the German railroad, as well as in "private" spaces, such as malls or commercial establishments, specific "house rules" established by the legal owners spell out the terms and conditions of the facilities' use. Landlords or the management they hire have tremendous discretion, short of civil-liberties violations, regarding how, where, when, and for what reasons they can expel undesired patrons. As in U.S. cities, such house rules almost always include clauses that prohibit loitering with no intention to consume and ban any sort of commercial activity (panhandling, bartering) on the premises, sometimes explicitly singling out homeless people or other transient and marginalized groups. Yet many of these places are vital to homeless people, as they serve their transportation needs and, especially among people with more-irregular life courses, the need to generate income. The latter particularly pertains to any type of sales activity (e.g., street-newspaper sales) or activity involving soliciting donations (e.g., panhandling, playing music, giving public performances). Considering that most semipublic spaces have multiple public and private security entities patrolling the premises and are more highly secured (with omnipresent closed-circuit TVs) than public spaces, it is perhaps not surprising that most instances of displacement occurred in such semipublic spaces. More than two-thirds of all respondents—half of them at least twice—were asked to leave such places. Yet, as in public spaces, most respondents simply complied and thus avoided a further confrontation. Only five people, all homeless people with irregular life courses, experienced actual physical removal, being escorted out by security, usually after resisting orders to leave. The most severe consequence, on the other hand—actual legal prosecution for trespassing violations—exclusively involved street-newspaper vendors, whose experiences I discuss later in this chapter.

Perhaps the most damaging form of punitive measures applied in semipublic places is the targeting of fare dodgers in Berlin's public-transit system, which imparts substantial financial damage on the violators (debts between DM 200 and DM 2,000/$110 and $1,100) as a result. Although such prosecution is not explicitly aimed at homeless people and applies to anybody without a valid ticket, it was staggering that nineteen respondents had been caught dodging the fare at some point during their homelessness. Even more surprising, only five of them were in possession of subsidized public-transit tickets at the time of the interviews. Berlin's public-transit system, like many in Germany, operates on a trust basis, with the understanding that passengers must purchase tickets before departure. Considering that deliberate fare dodging constitutes substantial loss in revenue, the BVG has hired a private security company to conduct random checks to detect fare dodgers, with the incentive that the security company gets a share of the recovered revenue. In 1998, a conviction resulted in a DM 60 ($33) fine, payable within one week and subject to substantial interest thereafter. I witnessed how efficient the controls are, once counting seven random checks in one day by plainclothes security personnel who identified themselves with badges. Sachse's response was typical:

> Man, this happens all the time, you know? Can't afford the ticket, so I am already always on the lookout. I get out sometimes, but sometimes they come from both sides. Trapped! Another ticket. How many you ask? Oh, eight or nine. [pauses] With interest? Hmm, over DM 1,000 [$550] by now, I believe. (Sachse, age 35, shelter resident, older regular life course, interview, February 17, 1998)

The financial damage that Sachse incurred was not an isolated incident; seven respondents had been assessed more than DM 900 ($500) in fare-dodging debt, and because only four of them had made arrangements with the debt-collection agency (as welfare recipients, they could negotiate a temporary stop in interest payments), three continued to accumulate interest due (at an annual rate of approximately 20 percent). The BVG justified its approach not only on the basis of the substantial loss in revenue but also by maintaining that it was fulfilling its responsibility to poor passengers by providing discounted fares. Ingo Thederan, spokesperson for BVG's subway security, explained:

> You have to understand that a railroad station is not a service agency. And we do provide discounted fares for poor Berliners. It is not our fault that some people choose to spend the money on alcohol instead. The social ticket is affordable. (interview, September 12, 1998)

Although some of the blame most certainly has to be assigned to welfare caseworkers who neglected to tell their clients about subsidized tickets, the crackdown still posed huge problems and made respondents feel deliberately singled out. But although the prosecution of fare dodging and displacement from public-transit facilities affected individual respondents, resulting in substantial debts, its effects were particularly hard on homeless street-newspaper vendors—hence the ongoing standoff between the BVG and advocacy groups dedicated to ensuring homeless people's "right to the city."

Fighting Back: The Case of Street-Newspaper Vendors versus BVG

Street-newspaper vending, starting with the *Big Issue* in London, is a global phenomenon that can be witnessed in most European and North American cities (see Torck 2001). In all instances, the premise is that homeless vendors keep a portion of the proceeds plus tips. Depending on the size of the city and thus the market range, street-newspaper vending provides up to a few hundred homeless people with a flexible income opportunity. All those cities, however, share a prohibitive approach to the sales activities of homeless people and other fringe groups while they use public transit or are in other semipublic and public spaces.

It is perhaps not surprising that close to one-fourth of the previously discussed instances of displacement, and all instances of trespassing charges, were reported by the four respondents who were selling the *Strassenfeger*—one of two local street newspapers—to generate income at the time I interviewed them. They did so knowing that they ran the risk of running afoul of security officers and in deliberate defiance of such perceived persecution. Three of them (Harri, Martin, and Sioux) sold their merchandise exclusively in public-transit facilities or trains, as did most other vendors, and all of them reported being repeatedly caught and in danger of being charged with trespassing the next time.[5] They deliberately chose entry points to public transit or worked on the trains of Berlin's subway and commuter lines; entrances offered high pedestrian turnover, and the time afforded between train stops allowed for a quick sales pitch and up to two transactions (with tips, up to DM 3/$1.70). High turnover was important, because the majority of pedestrians and passengers did not buy papers or had already bought one earlier in the month. Additionally, all four vendors had been caught dodging the fare and thus had accumulated fines. Upon recommendation by social workers employed by the Mob e.V., three of them at the time of the interview carried a monthly subsidized ticket, thereby averting further charges of fare dodging and thus closing off that specific avenue of prosecution. Sioux mentioned that he knew most of the "blues" (colloquial for BVG private security officers) and that some of them did not even bother writing further citations, essentially letting him be. Still, despite some modus vivendi, the ongoing battle between the *Strassenfeger* and the BVG continues to the present day, and no compromise has been reached.

The BVG continues to disallow and prosecute the vending of street newspapers to avoid setting a precedent for other types of commercial activity that, in all likelihood, would not be appreciated by passengers, Thederan emphasized in an interview. He further pointed out that people have made complaints about overly aggressive or otherwise inappropriately behaving vendors posing a potential threat to passengers' safety. Although he expressed his sympathy with and appreciation for vendors' initiative, he explained plainly why a ban has to remain in effect:

> We know that most vendors are polite and do not bother anyone, but it is impossible for us to sort out the aggressive vendors. And since allowing their activities would set a precedent for all kinds of commercial activities, an all-encompassing ban of any sales activities has to remain in effect. (interview, September 12, 1998)

Although there is certainly some credence in this statement about the proliferation of business activity on trains, other assertions are less certain. Thederan suggested, for instance, that fully permitting the sale of street newspapers would likely meet the disapproval of passengers. In the survey I conducted among 176 BVG passengers in December 1998, I found primarily supportive attitudes toward vendors and their activities, and almost 40 percent stated that they regularly purchased and often read the paper. Ultimately, only four respondents approved of BVG's ban; others, although often disliking many vendors' approach of appealing to pity, acknowledged the vendors' effort and initiative and rejected a wholesale ban. Whether increased sales (and other commercial activity) would be appreciated is questionable, as passengers encountered vendors almost on a daily basis and expressed some concern about too frequent contact and the occasional nuisance. The Mob e.V. is mindful of a potential saturation of the market and how that would undermine vendors' profit margins and thus does not plan on expanding the number of vendors (Stefan Schneider, interview April 27, 1998).

The *Strassenfeger* and its vendors, in the meantime, remain insistent that the deliberate targeting of their activities infringes on their civil liberties, and the paper has taken numerous steps to address this injustice and create public awareness. During my investigation, the *Strassenfeger* joined with other advocacy groups to stage a large demonstration against displacement and the further privatization and securing of railroad stations, spurring a national movement titled "The City Belongs to All!" (*Die Stadt gehört allen!*). This demonstration created public awareness, as did others, as members of all segments of the homeless service industry, welfare administration, celebrities, and even politicians joined these activities in solidarity.

Vendors who are charged with trespassing can, in the case of repeated violations or an inability to pay fines, face jail time, sometimes in conjunction with other crimes (especially narcotics violations, as one-third of vendors are users or ex-users of heroin). To help their incarcerated comrades, Mob e.V. staff and vendors donate a portion of their proceeds to maintain a prison fund (*Knastkasse*) to help out with small cash allowances for daily needs. Eight of the eighty active street-newspaper vendors were in jail at the time of my investigation, and although vendors know that their prosecution is unconstitutional (Hecker 2002), they see few chances for change other than collective action. Martin explained:

> Of course I know that my constitutional rights are being stepped upon. I learned in school that the human dignity is untouchable. But, look, who is the judge going to believe? Me, the bum, or them, the police officers? You

> make the call. That's why we have to [starts singing the famous Bob Marley tune] "Get up, stand up, stand up for your rights . . ." [others start chiming in]. (Martin, age 33, transient life course, informal conversation, February 9, 1998, Berlin Breitscheidplatz)

Still, all four vendors I interviewed took pride in what they viewed as their role as advocates for other excluded groups and, with the paper and its contents, informing the public about the plight of the homeless and other social problems in Germany. Vendors further appreciate that this type of sales activity gives them a great deal of discretion regarding when, where, and with how much effort they engage in their sales. Moreover, depending on a vendor's skills, newspaper sales can be fairly lucrative, on average generating DM 50 to DM 90 ($28 to $50) over the course of five hours. Such income combined with regular welfare can be sufficient to pay for regular housing. In fact, two of the vendors, Sioux and Heinz, eventually succeeded in using such combined income to find and maintain agreeable housing solutions. The ongoing crackdown on vendors' activities, however, could have quickly brought this newfound stability to an end if either of them had been arrested for repeated trespassing violations. Fortunately, ten years later, both still lived in their respective homes and had optimized their life courses, due in large part to the empowering possibilities inherent in self-initiative and collective action. Heinz eventually retired, while Sioux started working for a cleaning company, where he quickly advanced to become a crew chief.

This productive grassroots activism, no matter how positive and enriching, only pertains to a relatively small number of homeless people. Street-newspaper sales, for instance, have a finite market range before saturation tests the goodwill of potential customers. Moreover, when I asked other homeless respondents about their interest in becoming involved in activism, most stated that they had neither the time, the energy, nor necessarily the desire to pursue such avenues:

> That's all I needed. . . . Spending all day dragging myself from one demonstration to the next, chanting? Listen, I have better things to do. For starters: I need a job. Then housing. And a healthy fuck wouldn't hurt either. Gotta set your priorities straight, see? (Helmut, age 37, shelter resident, older regular life course, interview, February 23, 1998)

Yet the others, too, showed remarkable resilience and improvisation skills and effort, thus demonstrating that they were quite capable of making strategic decisions about their poverty management. But it also became abundantly clear that they did not receive sufficient public assistance to make ends meet, and as a result they frequently encountered punitive policy and faced displacement and sometimes even worse consequences. In the next section, I discuss how the different factors are interrelated and how they, in turn, compare to circumstances and practices in Los Angeles.

Legal Exclusion: How Homelessness Is Rendered Invisible

One important finding of my research, confirming the tenor of a number of ethnographic studies from Germany and the United States, is that homeless people possess tremendous agency, all obstacles notwithstanding, yet in both Berlin and Los Angeles find themselves confronted with a range of policies and house rules that effectively displace them from commercially important urban areas in an alleged attempt to uphold public order and safety—in other words, legal exclusion with the purpose of upholding vital business interests, particularly in the commercial downtown areas (see also Eick 1996).

Explaining Legal Exclusion in Comparative Context

Figure 3.2 illustrates how this legal exclusion works and identifies the different constituents of such exclusion. This model starts with the premise that, to stabilize their life courses, homeless individuals must generate income to satisfy their most immediate personal and material needs. Because German welfare incomes are, across the board, insufficient and have not increased since the 2005 Hartz IV reforms, most homeless people must employ additional material survival strategies, the intensity of which depends on people's life courses and the extent of their personal problems and associated costs. This poses particular problems for homeless people with more-irregular life courses who lack human and social capital and thus have less-conspicuous income sources, such as informal wage labor or social networks. Consequently, they are more likely to use survival strategies associated with shadow work in public and semipublic spaces and, in so doing, become subject to exclusionary policies and practices. Although most respondents complied with authorities and faced few consequences for performing material survival strategies in such spaces, there were quite a few instances where homeless people's persecution had more severe financial and personal consequences, including actual endangerment, as in the case of repeated deportations.

Ultimately, however, the circumstances surrounding such exclusions are more dire in U.S. cities, simply because less public-income assistance is available in the first place, necessitating more frequent use of informal strategies that are consequently met with harsher, more direct punitive measures and concurrently more severe personal consequences. The German welfare state, in contrast, mitigates absolute income poverty, reducing homeless people's need to resort to informal means of support, yet still counters such means and homeless people's mere existence with less explicit yet similarly "successful" public order and safety ordinances and house rules, effectively removing homeless and other people from commercially important or gentrifying urban areas. As often visibly poor, low-end consumers, they are viewed as out of place and a potential threat to consumers, tourists, and visitors with means. Their deliberate removal through

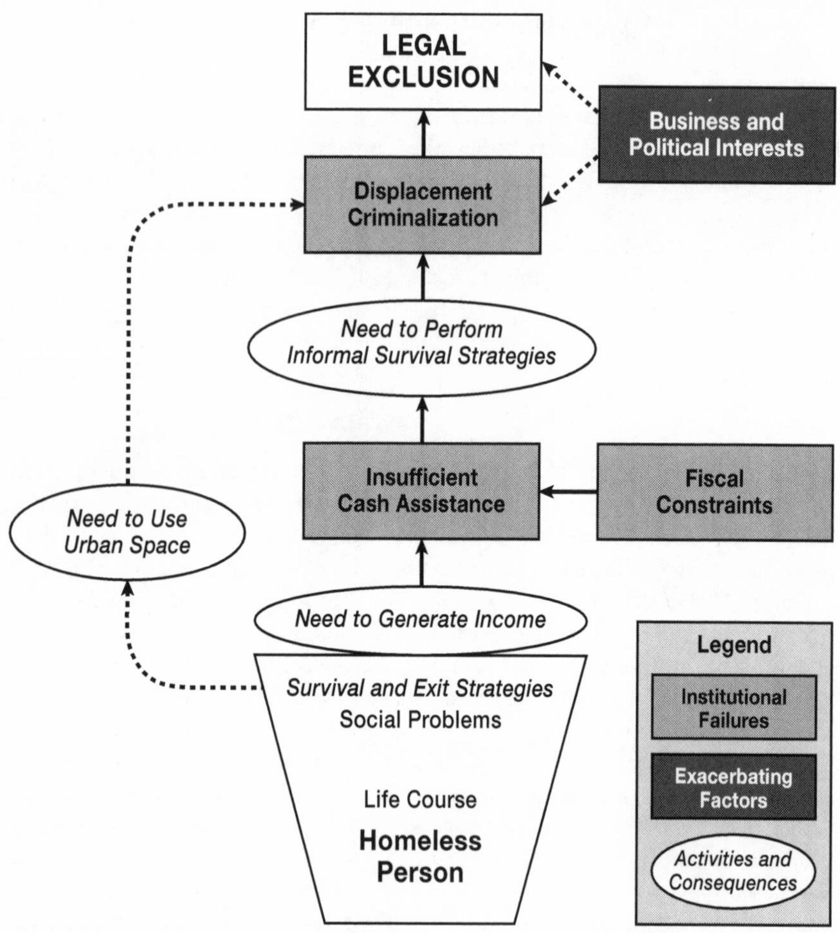

FIGURE 3.2 Model of Legal Exclusion

public law enforcement (police, border patrol) and, increasingly, private security is justified everywhere with similar protectionist probusiness rhetoric in the name of urban redevelopment (Belina 2003; Eick 1996, 1998; Mitchell 1997; Doherty et al. 2008). Eick (1998) in particular has shown how private and corporate business interests—from global to local—have applied considerable pressure on and found willing collaborators in Berlin's local government to advance security in the city. Although it is difficult to explicitly link capital and displacement, all my key informants, regardless of function, agreed that the deliberate displacement and criminalization of poor and homeless people in downtown Berlin served the interest of catering to and attracting global capital, be it in the form of investors, businesses, or tourists. Additionally, the deliberate removal of homeless people and other undesirable social groups in the commercial center is a quite profitable business opportunity in what has become a public-private growth industry dominated by a number of large national corporations (Eick 1998, 110).

The stigmatization of homeless people as "broken windows" that ought be removed to prevent further urban decay has become a global mantra as well as an opportunistic way to score cheap political points. It was telling that Interior Senator and Chief of Police Jörg Schönbohm invited former NYPD and current LAPD Chief Bratton in 1997 to share his experiences in urban crime fighting with colleagues in Berlin. In the name of safety and public health, homeless people and other social fringe groups have become easy targets for this new urban sanitation and, to borrow Smith's (1996) term, revanchism. It is further alarming that private security has extended its sphere of influence into previously public spaces, such as, for instance, commercial stands and seating arrangements on sidewalks and pedestrian zones (Eick 2008). All these developments clearly indicate a backlash against homeless people and confirm theoretical assumptions in U.S. research about power relations and the redefinition of "public space." This present research, then, adds to these discussions by providing important clarifications regarding who among the homeless are likely affected by punitive policies and what the personal consequences for homeless people are.

Conclusion: Public Welfare and Legal Exclusion

The ethnographic insights into legal exclusion in Berlin clearly show that the life course and thus extent of human and social capital has a great impact on whether and to what extent people must engage in shadow work and the extent to which their associations with other homeless people make them more noticeable, easier targets for displacement. This research also suggests that welfare-state deficiencies—most notably insufficient cash assistance and failure to disclose other service options—have created a precondition for why people ultimately face displacement and other punitive measures. In that way, the local welfare state actually becomes complicit in the deliberate exclusion of homeless people from public and semipublic spaces through the long arm of the law. One wonders whether it really was a mere administrative oversight that seventeen of the eligible twenty-two applicants were not informed about the existence of subsidized public-transportation tickets and that five people never heard about the biannual clothing allowance, a DM 550 ($306) benefit.

At the same time, it is important to point out that homeless people in Berlin receiving cash assistance in the first place have a huge advantage compared with Los Angeles's homeless. There, very few eligible homeless individuals receive public-income assistance at all, and if they do, benefit levels (at $211 per month) are much lower and, for able-bodied adults, limited to nine months. If we further consider that apartment rents and living expenses in Los Angeles are almost double those in Berlin, Los Angeles's homeless must rely on informal survival strategies more frequently or even exclusively, increasing the likelihood of encounters with law enforcement and the criminal justice system. One could consequently surmise that legal exclusion hits U.S. homeless people more explicitly, frequently, and with more severe consequences than in Berlin, where the right to welfare ensures that most homeless have at least DM 540 ($300) per month at their disposal.

One argument against the state's culpability in providing insufficient benefit levels is associated with the primary reason for why income was deemed insufficient: people's alcohol, drug, or even cigarette consumption. One could argue that it should not be the role of the state to actually sponsor and thus enable detrimental behaviors, or that alcohol and drug consumption is a personal choice, making the individual culpable and thus perhaps even less deserving of assistance. In response, I argue in support of a range of medical studies cautioning that addiction is a health problem that corresponds with concurrent mental-health problems (e.g., depression, bipolar disorder, post-traumatic stress disorder, etc.) and should be treated as such (Neale 2001; Winkelby and White 1992; Podschus and Dufeu 1995). In addition, the local welfare state has actually had some complicity in exacerbating homeless people's addiction problems by warehousing them in dilapidated shelters and service facilities in deprived urban quarters, right outside the spaces from which the homeless have become increasingly barred through legal exclusion. The spatial organization of the homeless service and shelter system and the life experiences in these shelters are the subject of the following chapter.

4

Not Wanted

Containment, Warehousing, and Service Exclusion

If, as demonstrated in the previous chapter, homeless people and some of their survival strategies are deliberately excluded from the commercial city center, what spaces remain for them? Do homeless people in Berlin, like their peers in Los Angeles, find themselves contained in deprived service ghettos? After providing evidence for the impact of the spatial organization of homeless service and shelter provision in Los Angeles on homeless people and their life chances, in this chapter I reveal the results of my analysis of the geographic organization of Berlin's homeless service infrastructure, which suggests that there are, indeed, similarities to the United States in that homeless service and shelter facilities are contained in the most deprived urban quarters. Yet rather than the containment of services per se, the warehousing into often-dilapidated multiple-occupancy shelters has the most devastating personal consequences, reinforcing the exact social problems, most notably alcohol consumption, that have contributed to insufficient income and thus displacement in the first place. Shelters therefore are places with positive and negative consequences. They provide homeless people with material and emotional support, yet they constitute a contagious environment of defeatism, alcohol and substance abuse, and (self-) isolation. Many respondents, especially people with more-regular life courses, self-isolate because of shame and cut ties with their nonhomeless social networks.

Based on these findings, I propose a model of "service exclusion" that explains how, in both Berlin and Los Angeles, warehousing into primarily low-quality shelters and the containment of shelters and service facilities adversely affects homeless people's chances to exit homelessness. I suggest that homeless people's life circumstances deteriorate in emergency and low-quality accommodations; mid-level shelters with in-house social workers are more effective at enhancing exit chances and saving money as well. Current practices in Berlin are ultimately counterproductive and expensive and needlessly prolong homelessness. They serve only the interests of commercial shelter providers, who ruthlessly exploit the fact that the local welfare state is legally mandated to provide shelter yet lacks the funds and infrastructure to provide better shelter options. The geography of homeless shelter and service provision provides a key to understanding how and where homeless people spend their lives, particularly if they are deliberately excluded from other urban spaces. This sets the stage for a more nuanced discussion of the consequences of such exclusion.

Los Angeles: Containment and the Shadow State

Considering that this question and the relevance of geographic processes remain seriously understudied in German research, it is useful to consider research from Los Angeles and other cities in the United States, where the geography of service provision in the context of homeless people's daily and periodic mobility has been studied in much more detail, as I discuss in Chapter 1 (for a summary, see Wolch and Dear 1993; for an update, see DeVerteuil 2003a, 2003b).

Such research suggests that the displacement of homeless people is reinforced by the spatial organization of homeless service and shelter facilities, which are contained in the most deprived urban communities, often in the vicinity of yet sufficiently far from important commercial and residential areas. Such service agglomerations—three of which, in Los Angeles County, contain more than twenty facilities within a square mile—can literally be described as "landscapes of despair" (Wolch and Dear 1987) that, although offering much needed services and support, truly reduce homeless people's long-term chances to pursue more promising labor and housing market opportunities. Thus homeless people, especially adult minority men, find themselves limited by the terms of the local "shadow state," experiencing a spatial mismatch between the location of shelters and more promising housing and labor market opportunities and therefore further intensifying the sense of entrapment that many homeless experience (Burns, Flaming, and Haydamack 2004; Tepper and Simpson 2003; Wolch and Dear 1993).

Such entrapment, it has been shown, also affects homeless people's tenuous ties to nonhomeless people, including their families, friends, and other social contacts. In place of them, homeless people, by necessity, must forge new social networks within the context of homelessness, with positive and negative ramifications. Although such networks are valuable sources of material and financial support, they also have negative consequences in that they increase exposure to people with similar problems (see Rowe and Wolch 1990).

Although relatively little information is available regarding how life inside homeless service and shelter facilities affects homeless people's exit chances in Los Angeles, we know from a number of ethnographic studies that life in such places exacerbates residents' problems and the "downward spiral" many of them experience (Desjarlais 1997; Wright and Donley 2008).

The reasons such containment exists are associated with the deliberate exclusion of services from more-upscale communities through NIMBY strategies at the expense of already impoverished, underrepresented, and politically disenfranchised communities (Dear 1992). Although almost twenty years have passed since the conclusion of the Los Angeles Homelessness Project's (LAHP's) research—and a number of service expansions and improvements have been noted since then—the basic geographic organization of the homeless service and shelter system remains largely unchanged despite public attempts to "deconcentrate" poverty, suggesting that the containment of homeless people continues to be a substantial problem in Los Angeles (DeVerteuil 2005; Tepper and Simpson 2003).

Whether such containment into "service-dependent ghettos" also exists in Berlin remained unknown, as did the effects of any such containment on homeless people's immediate life circumstances and their long-term chances to overcome homelessness. In the following section, I provide a geographic analysis of the spatial organization of Berlin's homeless service infrastructure by type, identify agglomerations, and elaborate on the characteristics of such locations to find out, more precisely, whether evidence shows containment in Berlin.

Containment: The Geography of Shelter and Service Distribution in Berlin

To examine the impact of homeless shelter and service provision on homeless people's immediate life circumstances and on their long-term life chances, it is first necessary to investigate the geographic organization of Berlin's homeless service and shelter infrastructure.[1] Where are service facilities located, and how are they distributed across the urban landscape and across administrative boundaries? What characterizes such locales? Are these facilities primarily contained in impoverished communities, as in the United States?

Fair Share? Service Distribution by District

One important aspect of the geography of homeless services is associated with the distribution of services across administrative boundaries. More precisely, how were the service locations related to the spatial-administrative structures and thus distributed among Berlin's twenty-three districts in 1998? Were there indications of inequitable service distribution, with impoverished central city districts carrying a disproportionate burden while more affluent communities often refused to provide their "fair" share of services?

To assess the distribution across districts, I divided Berlin's districts into four clusters: Center West, Center East, City West, and City East. I also created a separate category for the five most affluent districts across Berlin. For each cluster, I determined three variables: its share of the total population, its share of

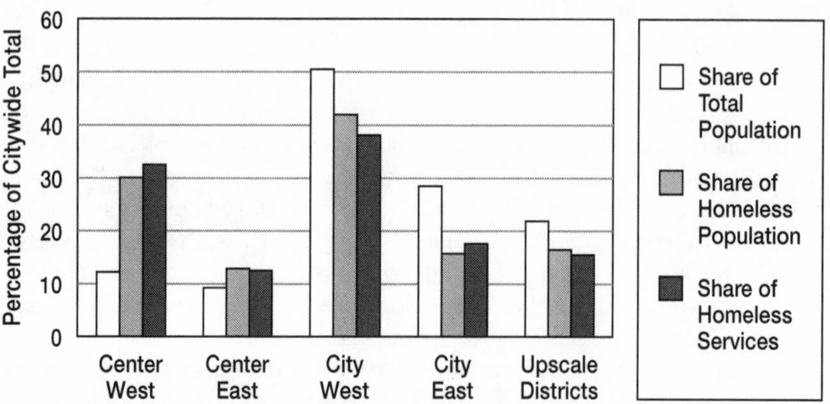

FIGURE 4.1 Distribution of Service Facilities in Berlin by District, 1998

homeless people, and its share of service facilities as a percentage of the citywide total (see Fig. 4.1). The analysis clearly shows that center city districts, particularly the three western "problem districts" of Kreuzberg, Wedding, and Tiergarten, provided a far greater share of homeless services relative to their share of the city's population. Almost half of all services (44.6 percent) were provided in center city districts, where roughly one-fifth of all Berliners (20.9 percent) resided. At the same time, such high service loads corresponded with the actual share of homeless people registered in these districts. Given that homeless people typically receive services in the districts in which they had their last residence, it is fair to say that most cases of homelessness originate in marginalized center city areas that have substantially higher poverty rates than the rest of the city.

This factor notwithstanding, it also becomes obvious that Berlin's more peripheral districts in the west and the east, including the most affluent districts, provided fewer services (55.4 percent) than their share of homeless residents (57.6 percent) and substantially less than their share of city residents (79.2 percent). This factor was particularly pronounced in the western part of the city, where the districts provided fewer services than their share of registered homeless people (–4.1 percent). Eastern districts, although not providing services according to their share of the general population, at least provided more services than their share of homeless people (+1.9 percent). The latter is remarkable insofar as the eastern districts did not have any homeless service infrastructure before unification, because homelessness did not—officially, at least—exist in the former East Germany.[2]

This analysis shows a clear concentration of both homeless services and homeless people in center city districts, as in U.S. cities. A more fine-grained analysis is needed to reveal how services are located within and across districts, how distributions vary by service type, and what the characteristics of service locations are.

Containment? Service Distribution by Facility Type

Looking at the geographic distribution of homeless service facilities differentiated by type provides a more nuanced picture. This analysis displays a very clear pattern that can be described as a "donut effect." Homeless service facilities were located primarily in a circle around the city's commercial center, in city districts that made up the so-called Wilhelminian Ring, consisting primarily of turn-of-the-century, low-rise apartment buildings of low to medium quality.[3] Figure 4.2 shows the distribution of facilities by service type in relation to the commercial center and the Wilhelminian Ring. Three important findings emerge that suggest similarities to and differences from the situation in Los Angeles.

First, almost all daytime facilities, such as day centers and soup kitchens, all large emergency shelters, and the vast majority of transitional shelters were located inside the Wilhelminian Ring yet outside the city's now-unified commercial center. This locational pattern—outside the central business district yet in close proximity to it—corresponds with a core finding from the previous chapter: Homeless people are deliberately displaced from the commercial center, and the facilities designed to help them are deliberately located outside it. At the same time, it must be remembered that most shelter and service operators rent their facilities and have to go where rents are affordable. The reconstructed and now-consolidated commercial center simply does not provide opportunities to rent facilities cheaply.[4]

A second important finding is that only a few emergency and smaller long-term shelters could be found outside the Wilhelminian Ring. These were often facilities that peripheral districts operated or funded themselves. Moreover, the four western districts (Charlottenburg, Wilmersdorf, Neukölln, and Schöneberg) that contained 90 percent of all City West service facilities all overlap the Wilhelminian Ring, and almost all these districts' homeless service facilities were located there, not in the districts' more-peripheral, affluent residential communities. This pattern reinforces the notion that peripheral and especially upscale districts do not provide their share of services.

Third, homeless service facilities were clustered in particular locations within the ring. Overlaying the maps for the different service types reveals a number of clusters—so-called service agglomerations—within a one-kilometer radius. As Figure 4.3 shows, four particularly dense service agglomerations exist in Berlin, with more than fifteen facilities within a one-kilometer radius: one in Wedding, one in Schöneberg North, and two in Kreuzberg. In addition, eleven other, less-dense service agglomerations contain between eight and fifteen facilities.

Characteristics of Shelter and Service Locations

To examine the locational characteristics of homeless service facilities, I used detailed maps to assess the socioeconomic and demographic characteristics of the neighborhood, the proximity to potentially negative land use, and the

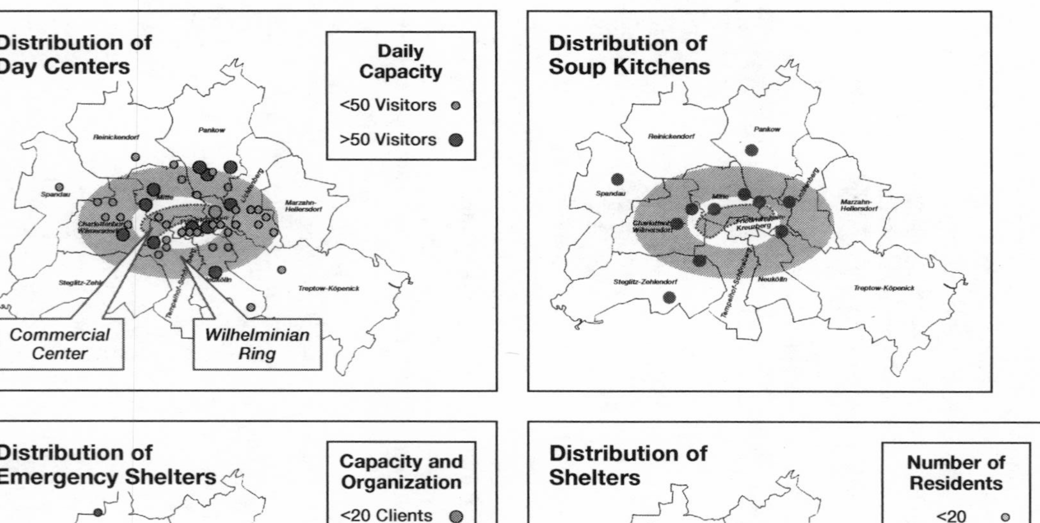

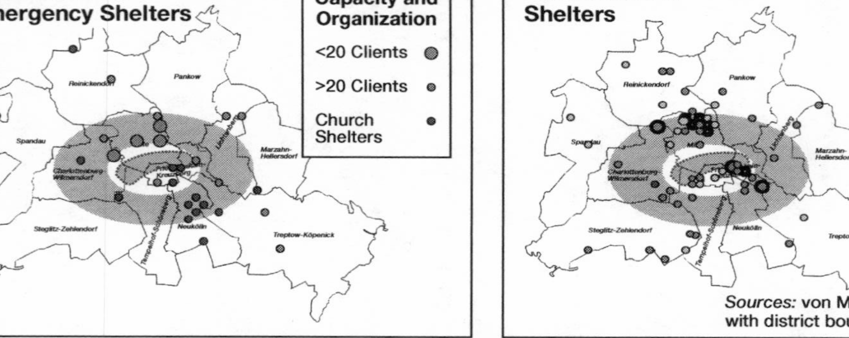

Sources: von Mahs 2012; base map with district boundaries: Dalet 2012.

FIGURE 4.2 Spatial Distribution of Homeless Services in Berlin by Type, 1998

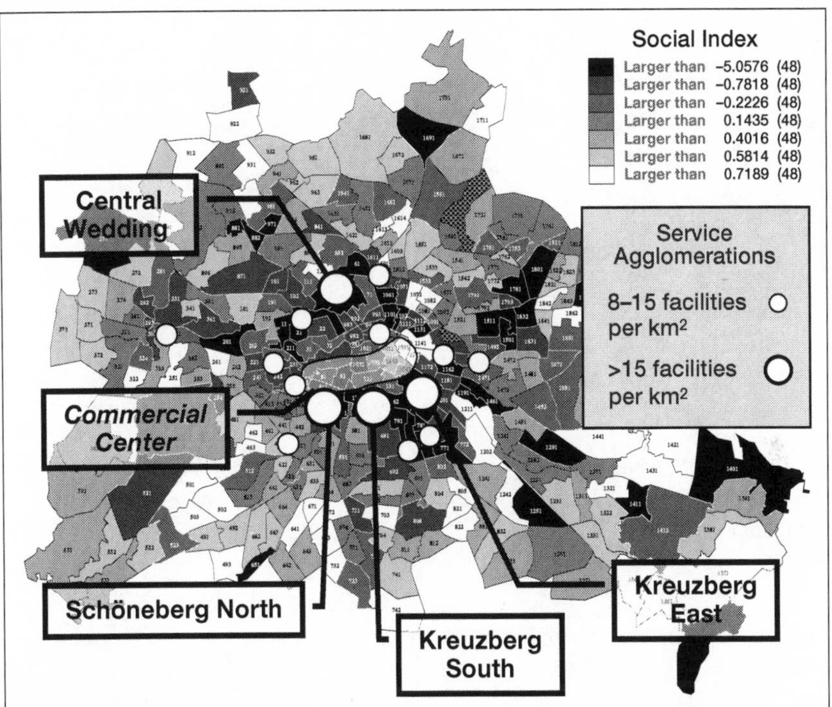

FIGURE 4.3 Service Agglomerations and Social Structure in Berlin, 1998

proximity to public transportation.[5] This analysis reveals that homeless service and shelter facilities were predominantly found in locales with negative attributes.

First, homeless service facilities in general were predominantly located in areas with low social indices and thus high poverty and unemployment, as Figure 4.4 indicates.[6] As judged by social index rank (on a seven-level scale), all four service agglomerations were located within the bottom 10 out of 338 spatial units (traffic cells) across Berlin. Moreover, 40 percent of all homeless service facilities were located in traffic cells with the lowest rank, and almost 80 percent were located in the three lowest-ranking cells. And the larger a facility, the more likely that it was associated with the lowest rank—almost two-thirds of facilities that served one hundred or more homeless clients were located in traffic cells with the lowest rank. The respondents in Berlin by and large confirmed the locational attributes and described most neighborhoods surrounding facilities as "bad places" (*üble Gegenden*). Oliver said about the Trachenbergring:

> A bit isolated, don't you think? Right in an industrial zone. First fifteen minutes walking, then waiting, and then twenty-five minutes to the center, and another twenty-five to the old neighborhood. (Oliver, age 26, shelter resident, deviant life course, interview, March 10, 1998)

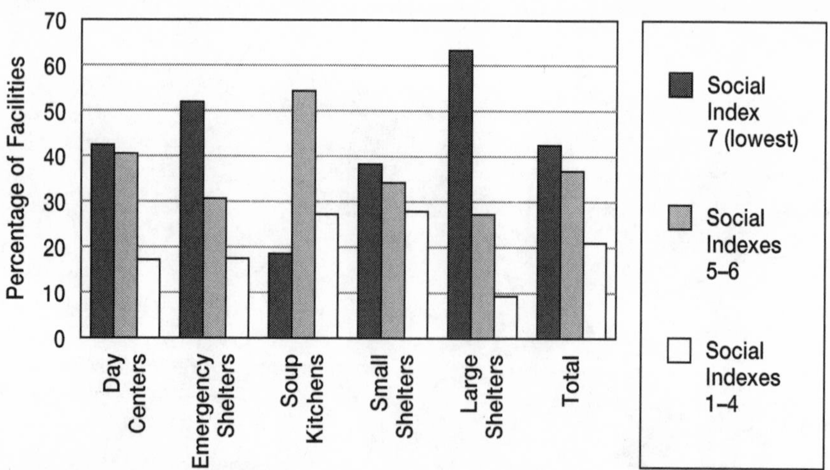

FIGURE 4.4 Homeless Service Facilities in Berlin in Relation to Social Index of Neighborhood, 1998

Second, homeless service facilities tended to be located in close vicinity to ecologically and socially negative land uses, including industrial sites, major motorways, railroad lines, or incinerators. More than half of all homeless service facilities in Berlin were located less than five hundred meters away from a negative land use, and more than half of these were in immediate vicinity of such land uses. Most affected by such close proximity were the more dispersed shelter facilities—especially large ones—whereas day centers and soup kitchens, closer to the city center, were typically located in mixed land use, residential areas, or commercial areas.

The only positive aspect of the locational characteristics of Berlin's homeless service facilities was their relatively good connection to the public-transportation system. Nine out of ten, including more peripheral ones, were within walking distance (less than five hundred meters) of a subway, tram, or bus station. This finding corresponds with the overall good evaluation of Berlin's extensive public-transportation system by the respondents and is certainly a great advantage vis-à-vis most North American cities, which often lack comprehensive and affordable public-transit systems and thus reinforce the spatial entrapment of homeless people (Jocoy and Del Casino 2010; Wolch and Dear 1993).

Yet if shelters and service locations are more readily accessible, why do homeless people experience a loss of their place-based social networks? Why can they not find jobs and housing from there? To find out, it is necessary to explore homeless people's experiences within homeless service and shelter facilities—which, as I indicate in Chapter 2, are primarily negative.

Warehousing? Life in Shelters and Homeless Service Facilities over Time

Shelter access is not a big problem in Berlin, compared with virtually any U.S. city (U.S. Conference of Mayors 2006). All twenty-eight respondents in my Berlin study had lived in a shelter before, and they could therefore compare different shelter and service types. In the following section, I describe the ways in which the homeless respondents in Berlin accessed and used the shelter and homeless service system and their experiences in different types of facilities. I provide evidence that homeless people developed a rather distrustful and ambivalent stance toward the homeless service system, often resisting some if not all services. Over time, however, many respondents began adapting to the system by necessity, an adaptation that came at a high price, prolonging their homelessness and deteriorating their life circumstances tremendously.

Service and Shelter Use over Time

My respondents certainly knew a lot about shelters. All twenty-eight respondents had lived in one or more shelters before, and twenty-four lived in a shelter at the time I interviewed them. Of the sixteen respondents with whom I cohabited in the Wohnheim Trachenbergring, twelve had lived in one or more other types of shelter before. They, along with three other respondents, could report in retrospective and comparative perspective about different shelter options in Berlin. I argue that the hierarchical structure of homeless shelter facilities—from emergency shelters up to high-level facilities—is clearly reflected in these homeless residents' opinions about such places, their experiences in them, and whether their use of such facilities assisted them in overcoming homelessness. I start by describing below how the respondents obtained entry into Berlin's shelter and homeless service system.

Accessing the Shelter System

To access Berlin's shelter system, homeless people have two principal options: going directly to a homeless shelter or service agency or, more commonly, going through the formal welfare system, specifically a referral by the local social-welfare office (*Sozialamt*) of the district where the applicant had his or her last formal residence. People without prior residence in Berlin are assigned to a welfare office by alphabetical code based on their last names and typically are just referred to emergency shelters and issued daily cash allowances (approximately DM 18/$10). After arrival, sign-in, and a long wait, applicants are each assigned to a caseworker and processed expediently within a few minutes. At the meeting, the caseworker finds a local shelter on a list giving only names, addresses, and telephone numbers—such lists contain no other information about the shelters, their service records, or their quality. Caseworkers, considerate of the resident's local affiliations, typically inquire about availabilities at a shelter nearby. If a place is available, the welfare recipient is sent there with a referral. The shelter operators then arrange payment directly with the local welfare office.

According to my respondents, the caseworkers' attitudes were often patronizing and uncooperative. Most meetings were conducted in impersonal, bureaucratic fashion.[7] The respondents were almost unanimously dissatisfied with the advice they received. The five respondents who contacted shelters or service providers directly, in contrast, had substantially better experiences and through such self-initiative found better shelter opportunities.

Once in the shelter and service system, the respondents generally had mixed, primarily negative experiences in different shelter types. To more accurately examine these experiences, I differentiate between different types of day and night service options and elaborate on the respondents' experiences in such places, their duration of stay, and their assessment of such facilities.

Emergency Shelters

Homeless people with transient life courses without prior residence in Berlin and those who have not contacted welfare agencies but need shelter immediately will typically encounter emergency shelters first. Most emergency shelters operate only in the winter and only between 6:00 P.M. and 7:00 A.M. They are usually hopelessly overcrowded, with up to fifty people sharing one room, frequently sleeping on the floor. Such accommodations are commonly used by people who are chronically homeless and living on the streets or those with severe alcohol and mental health problems who are often rejected by other shelter providers.

In this sample, five respondents with transient life courses had temporarily used such communal emergency shelters while waiting for confirmation of their eligibility for shelter and income provision. The volatile mix of people, the crowded conditions, and the lack of privacy, often exacerbated by noise and an unpleasant smell, make such places very unattractive, and every respondent who ever used such a facility tried to get out of there as quickly as possible, relying on them only on extremely cold nights. An exception was the emergency shelter operated by the Mob e.V. for up to eleven street-newspaper vendors, who may use the Mob e.V.'s editorial office for temporary accommodations. Although the office was relatively unsanitary, extremely crowded, and not void of conflict, three of the four vendors had used this option and were somewhat satisfied, because at least they cohabited with people they knew in a safe environment.

In addition to communal emergency shelters, seasonal emergency shelters are operated by voluntary organizations during the winter months. Such shelters, also called "night cafés," are operated by church congregations on a rotational basis, and they received much more favorable reviews than communal emergency shelters from my respondents, because they were less crowded and on occasion even offered a small meal.[8] Two people, Matze and Bernie, exclusively used such facilities and followed a regular routine, usually going to the same congregations every day of the week. They were generally very satisfied with this arrangement, appreciated the alcohol prohibition in such places, and certainly preferred them over conventional shelters.

Low-Level Shelters

People who consulted with the welfare office were typically referred to low-threshold, low-quality shelters, which constituted almost two-thirds of all shelter offerings in Berlin. They are operated either by the districts themselves (communal shelters, *Bezirkswohnheim*) or by commercial shelter providers (pensions and hostels).

The opinions of the eight respondents who had used communal shelters were unanimously negative. Usually up to four people had to share one tiny room, sleeping in bunk beds, which offered no privacy or space to securely store one's belongings. Hanno explained:

> Man, this was terrible! You have to share a tiny room with three guys you don't know. Their misery is contagious, and it's no wonder that you start drinking. And you have no privacy, your stuff gets stolen, and it stinks. (Hanno, age 36, shelter resident, older regular life course, interview, March 6, 1998)

People using such facilities reported appalling hygienic and social conditions and generally stated that their personal situations worsened in such accommodations, given that their alcohol consumption, through the proximity to chronic alcoholics, significantly increased. Four people reported incidents of theft or violence.

These conditions prompted virtually every respondent—regardless of life course—to leave eventually. Although three people moved to informal alternatives, such as sleeping outdoors, five people went back to the local welfare office and asked to be moved to different shelters. Although two of them were referred to a mid-level shelter (Wohnheim Trachenbergring), where they remained throughout my stay, the other three were referred to commercial shelters, where the situation was no better than in communal shelters, as I discuss next.

Commercial shelters are typically hotels or pensions that specialize in housing particular segments of Germany's marginalized welfare population, such as asylum seekers, refugees, and homeless people who, de jure, have a social right to accommodation, mandating municipalities to provide shelter, regardless of type. Such places, referred to as "lice pensions" (*Läusepensionen*) by the homeless, typically accommodate four people in bunk beds in one tiny room. The respondents confirmed written accounts about the dismal living situations in such pensions. The rooms are dilapidated, lack running water, and are only sporadically cleaned; there rarely is any supervision or security (see also Schneider 1998). Of the twelve respondents who used to live in such accommodations, none had anything positive to report. Biker explained:

> Sure. I would call these shelters "lice pensions" in the literal sense of the word. A car, even the street is more comfortable than that. I can understand that nobody wants to stay there. (Biker, age 39, shelter resident, homeless person with disability, interview, March 9, 1998)

Because of their negative experiences, ten respondents of all life-course types voluntarily left such places within three months, either going back to the welfare office or seeking informal sleeping arrangements. Although this resistance is evidence of homeless people's agency and initiative in not simply accepting unacceptable conditions, it often exacerbated people's health problems and made them more difficult to reach. Of the six respondents who slept rough rather than in shelters, four quickly realized that life on the street is difficult and dangerous, and therefore they reluctantly reconnected with the local welfare state, accepting the very arrangements they had previously rejected. They adapted to the system by necessity, not choice.

Mid-Level Shelters

Compared to communal and commercial shelters, specialized accommodations provided by voluntary organizations received more favorable reviews across the board. Most of these facilities, constituting 15 percent of all shelter offerings in 1998, are considered "mid-level shelters," because they provide better facilities and typically include social services. Particularly positive were the opinions about the Wohnheim Trachenbergring, where I lived for one month and conducted the bulk of my interviews. Mid-level shelters, which cost the same or less than commercial shelters, usually offer single rooms. All respondents, particularly those with experience in other shelters, were satisfied with the quality of the facility and the service they received. As Helmut (37, shelter resident, older regular life course) remarked, "I tell you, had they put me into this place here to begin with, I could have saved myself a lot of trouble" (interview, February 23, 1998). This positive assessment is also reflected in the fact that every respondent continuously stayed at such a facility until finding regular housing. It is notable that, although almost two-thirds of the Wohnheim's residents found housing, often relying on assistance by social workers on the premises, none of the respondents ever exited homelessness from a low-quality shelter (see Chapter 5). This suggests that mid-level shelters are more likely to facilitate exit from homelessness than low-quality accommodations.

High-Level Shelters

A final type of accommodation, mentioned by three of my female respondents, was the domestic-violence shelter. Such shelters, alongside specialized accommodations for people with severe social needs, such as disabilities or HIV/AIDS, are considered high-level shelters, because they offer more extensive counseling and other supportive services. In 1998, only 5 percent of all shelters in Berlin could be classified as such facilities. The German Social Welfare Act (§72) makes special legal provisions for such high-quality services, which are typically run by voluntary organizations. One woman, Monika, temporarily found shelter after having been brutally raped while working as a prostitute. Two other respondents escaped to such shelters from abusive relationships that they had pursued to avoid the dangers of sleeping rough.[9] These three women stayed in the shelters for approximately one month. Two of the women also had disabilities and received the necessary assistance to move into permanent institutionalized accommodations. Andrea now lives in a supervised group home with other mentally handicapped adult women, and Monika found a new home in a facility for visually impaired people in Steglitz. High-level shelters are by far the most expensive shelter option, costing up to DM 90 ($50) per client per night, but they generally claim faster turnover and more successful and faster referrals to case-appropriate housing, which was emphasized by most key informants I talked to.

Day Centers and Soup Kitchens

Given that many shelters, including all emergency shelters, close during the day, residents must leave in the early morning, with few affordable options to spend the daytime, especially in the cold winter months. In addition, material deprivation, a lack of food, or a need for advice prompt or, as I show, force homeless people to use Berlin's day centers and soup kitchens.

Respondents' experiences with such facilities clearly depended on life-course differences. Many homeless, especially those with regular life courses and some people with transient life courses, tried to avoid such facilities altogether. Schlöter explained why he avoided soup kitchens and day centers:

> I tell you honestly, I stay away [from soup kitchens]. I'd rather not eat, because I can't stand the misery. I once looked into one of these things, eh, that was the Warmer Otto in Moabit, and I saw those guys, and I said to myself, no way! So I left, though I didn't get anything to eat, not even coffee. Um, I simply can't put myself in that situation, because once you land there, it's a short step 'til you die in a dumpster. I've had enough. (Schlöter, age 56, shelter resident, transient life course, interview, February 26, 1998)

Quite similar was the attitude of many of the younger homeless. Mario, exemplary for most younger homeless, explained:

> Well, I always tried to avoid that. So, um, because I didn't want to have anything to do with these people. Although I'm somewhat one of them, I thought that if I have too much to do with them, I'd possibly slide down even further. I mean, I've already been pretty far down, drugs and stuff like that, but I said to myself, it could even get worse. Therefore, I had little contact with railroad stations, soup kitchens, and so on. And I simply did not want that. (Mario, age 22, shelter resident, younger regular life course, interview, February 22, 1998)

Thus, the avoidance of such facilities was due to fears of further social descent. Respondents' first impression of such places and their patrons was almost always negative, yet necessity drove people to use them. Although a mere five respondents used day facilities within a month of becoming homeless, almost half the respondents did so at least occasionally within a year, or by the time I interviewed them. Some of the older homeless people with regular life courses who saw their unemployment benefits expire and had to adjust to half the income (see Chapter 3) had no choice but to get food there at the end of the benefit month, when welfare incomes were depleted. Only a handful of respondents used such facilities regularly and appreciated their services. For Andrea, Bernie, Hans, and Maria, the Warmer Otto became part of their weekly routine and a place for socializing; they had long since shed their reservations. But as long as other people could, they avoided such places, which they perceived as harbingers of worse things to come.

The mixed experiences caused most respondents to pursue a "pick-and-choose" approach that ultimately created a great deal of ambivalence toward using homeless services as well as often deep-seated mistrust in the system. One key reason for such mistrust can be found in the detrimental life circumstances in these facilities, circumstances that, despite certain positive effects, often reinforce and magnify the diverse set of social problems homeless people have—most notably, their propensity to resort to collective alcohol consumption to numb the pain associated with their alarming and adverse social conditions.

The Consequences: Assistance, Alcohol, and Alienation

This analysis reveals the consequences of warehousing and containment on individual homeless people, which can be summarized in three words: assistance, alcohol, and alienation.

The field observations in the Wohnheim Trachenbergring in particular provided valuable insights regarding how the proximity to other homeless people in shelter and service facilities can have both positive and negative consequences. This rather ambivalent yet primarily negative assessment is also reflected in ethnographic studies from the United States (Desjarlais 1997; Rowe and Wolch 1990; J. Wright and Donley 2008) and Canada (Knowles 1999), although the respondents in those studies were more likely to have psychological problems.

Among the positive consequences is that shelter and service use—especially mid-level shelter facilities and day centers—enables homeless people to create peer networks that help them cope materially and emotionally. Homeless people learn from the experiences of others, help each other out, and provide consolation and friendship. Such inside social networks are important, but they also have potentially negative consequences. First, few fellow homeless residents can give advice regarding an exit strategy, because they have not figured it out themselves. Social networks in shelters therefore primarily provide immediate material and adaptive coping options. Second, the proximity to other people with alcohol or drug problems and the easy availability of alcohol in such places increase the likelihood of consumption. Third, life in shelters contributes to the gradual destruction of homeless people's social networks with the nonhomeless people they knew in Berlin. The extent to which people experience such negative effects depends on their life courses. Older homeless people with more-regular life courses and thus experience with regular accommodations and residential stability in their old neighborhoods are particularly affected.

Assistance: Inside Social Networks, Resources, and Information

Although shelters serve as a stark reminder of the crude realities of homelessness, they may also serve as places in which homeless people share resources and information as well as consolation and camaraderie. During my stay in the Wohnheim Trachenbergring and while living on the third floor, I witnessed an astonishing sense of solidarity and obligation. People shared material resources, such as food, cigarettes, and alcohol; cooked together; and, most important, lent money to each other, as explained in Chapter 3. Mutual assistance is also evident in the sharing of knowledge. Many of the younger homeless sought advice from older, more experienced homeless, such as Biker and Kalle. Kalle took pride in his role as advisor, which gave him a sense of purpose. Biker, the only elderly homeless who primarily socialized with younger homeless (he preferred cannabis over alcohol), proudly maintained his "outlaw" biker image (long hair, dark clothes, tattoos) and over time acquired a leadership function. Biker's room on the third floor frequently became a gathering point for the younger homeless residents (Bob, FTW, Jens, Mario, Markus, Radek), where Biker, with his authoritative, experienced, calm attitude, gave advice and told stories. Such advisory functions were also evident among street-newspaper vendors. Sioux, for instance, would voluntarily take new, inexperienced vendors and show them the tricks of successfully selling their merchandise. Sioux, who also worked as the vendor representative at the agency governing board and was engaged in a federal homeless initiative,[10] found a lot of value in the multiple roles he played:

> I am an activist, writer, advocate, advisor, social worker, partner, and friend, all in one person. Not bad for an ex-convict, huh? This is actually quite rewarding, as it allows me to have a positive impact on other people's lives. (Sioux, age 33, street-newspaper vendor, deviant life course, interview, March 8, 1998)

The contact with other homeless people not only was important in the pragmatic context of material survival but was also crucially important for my respondents' social and emotional well-being and their adaptive coping abilities. Consolation and companionship among people with shared experiences, thus relieving the pressure to constantly explain their circumstances, was important to most homeless people. Still, most respondents pointed out that these new relationships could not yet be considered true friendships:

> No, there is a difference between buddies and friends. I don't know whether I have friends here. They are more or less all buddies. Except for Mario, where I have the feeling that this could be more, although I don't know him that long. (Bob, age 24, shelter resident, younger regular life course, interview, February 26, 1998)

Developing true friendships takes time, and the frequent changes between shelter settings contributed to the short life of many of these newly formed relationships. Only a few people were able to maintain contact with people they met and became friendly with in other shelters.

Furthermore, I observed different patterns of social interaction among younger and older homeless people, particularly in group situations while living at the Wohnheim Trachenbergring. The mood among the younger homeless resembled more of a party atmosphere, whereas among the older homeless, I noticed a much more charged mood. During the evenings I spent with older homeless men drinking in groups, I noticed how storytelling and funny anecdotes suddenly ended in abrupt, painful silence until the next "cheers" signaled the start of a new story from the "good old days." This nostalgia was particularly apparent among my respondents from former East Germany or East Berlin. During an evening with Det, Hanno, and Barney, self-proclaimed "unification losers" (*Wendeverlierer*), I observed this "Eastalgia" (*Ostalgie*), as all three reported how their lives had turned for the worse since unification. They essentially wished the Wall back and longed for the social security and stability the communist system had offered.

The evenings I spent with younger homeless, on the other hand, reminded me of my own experiences living in an undergraduate dormitory. People regularly smoked cannabis, drank moderately compared to the older homeless, and listened to rock music or watched TV together. Due to the calming effect of cannabis, the mood was relaxed and peaceful. Radek would regularly play his guitar, and Bob, a former dancer, would give performances and do hilarious Eddie Murphy impersonations.

This contrast between the older and younger homeless was primarily the result of different attitudes toward life and the future. Although the younger homeless were generally much more optimistic, the older homeless faced tremendous anxiety from repeated rejections and legitimate worries about ever being able to find work again. The memories of their previous, rather "normal" middle-class lives made them perceive the current situation as a gradual, seemingly unstoppable social decline. Alcohol, and to a much-lesser extent other controlled substances (cannabis, prescription drugs), consequently became a means to cope with the anxiety and pain and a way to forget the present, indulge in the past, and temporarily block their worries about the future.

Alcohol and Drugs: Temporary Escape, Long-Term Effects

Common sense dictates that excessive alcohol and drug consumption has an adverse effect on people's life chances. In the previous chapter, I indicate that the inadequacy of public cash assistance, the need to generate additional income via informal survival strategies, and the persecution of such efforts and homeless people's activities are intrinsically related to alcohol and drug consumption. It is important to recognize, however, that my respondents' alcohol and drug consumption significantly increased over the course of homelessness, a factor highlighted in several medical studies on homelessness in Germany and in the United States.[11] Although approximately one-third of my respondents consumed "excessive" amounts of alcohol and drugs at the beginning of their homelessness, more than two-thirds of my respondents did so by the time of the interview.[12]

A major reason is the contagious nature of shelter settings. There is also a correlation with the quality of the shelter, as a number of studies have indicated.[13] Virtually every respondent who had experiences in communal and commercial shelters with shared rooms reported that he or she consumed more alcohol in such spaces, given that alcohol was always available. While living in mid-level shelters with single rooms, on the other hand, people reported less collective alcohol consumption, having the option to retreat into their personal rooms. Nonetheless, even in such places, alcohol and drug consumption was widespread and often excessive. Schlöter, a self-admitted alcoholic, explained:

> This is a compulsive group environment here, you simply need to get along with people, you understand? Out of necessity, you go over to one [fellow resident], because, as I said before, people drink. (Schlöter, age 56, shelter resident, transient life course, interview, February 26, 1998)

People clearly drink for a variety of reasons, most notably to cope with stress, anxieties, fears, and boredom. When people are not busy spending time in welfare offices, searching for work and housing, or performing informal survival strategies, all of which cost a considerable amount of time and energy, homeless people feel bored; in the case of shelter residents, their lives are often characterized by endless TV watching. Homeless people simply lack the resources to spend their "free time" in meaningful ways.[14] While we were watching TV together and after his seventh and my second beer, Helmut said:

> Oh boy . . . I am drunk again. Cheers! [takes a huge gulp] But what else do you want to do here? Well, okay, one could take a trip, and I do that occasionally. But where do you want to go in the winter? Ice skating? For that, you would need skates, and they cost money. This is how it starts. (Helmut, age 37, shelter resident, older regular life course, conversation, February 26, 1998)

Interestingly, only six of the sixteen people who consumed "excessive" amounts of alcohol or drugs considered their consumption a problem. Rather, most believed that the increased consumption was a temporary circumstance and that they would consume less when they found jobs and housing. Whether this was a feasible goal or simply a sign of denial is impossible to assess. Moreover, of the six people who admitted having a problem, only three took active steps toward recovery, and two of them failed once released into the same milieu that exacerbated their problems in the first place. The only respondent who successfully completed rehab and remained sober was Kalle, who withstood the temptation to resume drinking in the shelter. While drinking nonalcoholic beer, he did not mind that others were drinking the "real stuff," and none of them encouraged him to cease his sobriety. Rather, they all admired his willpower.[15]

As we know, alcoholism has a number of detrimental effects on the homeless. Homeless people depend on one another to keep up their increasingly excessive (and expensive) alcohol consumption, and shelters become places that enable homeless people to sustain and even to further their unhealthy habits with spiraling costs that, in turn, force people to rely on shadow work, thus increasing the likelihood of experiencing punitive policy (see Chapter 3). Excessive alcohol consumption also has negative health consequences; a number of my respondents began displaying the physical and psychological symptoms of alcoholism. Barney, one shelter resident whom I did not interview but was a close friend of my respondents Helmut, Det, and Hanno, died of liver cirrhosis during my investigation. Helmut, who was upbeat and relatively optimistic when I first met him, was a shadow of himself by the end of the study. He had lost a lot of weight, drank excessively on a daily basis, and had a hard time speaking coherent sentences. During my last visit to the shelter, he did not even recognize me anymore. Another consequence is that increasing alcohol dependence often alienates users from their nonhomeless social environment, a factor that partially contributed to changes in my respondents' social networks over time and to their increasing durations of homelessness.

Alienation: The Changing Nature of Social Networks

Social networks are, as virtually any study on homelessness emphasizes, important material, emotional, and informational resources for homeless people.[16] Stacy Rowe and Jennifer Wolch's (1990) publication on the inside and outside social networks of homeless women in Los Angeles offers a useful heuristic to assess changes in the nature and extent of homeless people's tenuous ties. The onset of homelessness creates a time-space discontinuity in that many previous outside (nonhomeless) networks disappear. Homeless people develop connections with other homeless people and with people affiliated with homelessness.

The discussion of homeless people's inside social networks in Berlin in the previous section confirms the positive and negative consequences. The Berlin research further reveals that maintaining outside networks is an important source of support and, in eight of my respondents' cases, a facilitator of exit.[17] Among the people who maintained preexisting social networks were three of the younger homeless with regular life courses who were less embarrassed by their situation. In all three cases, they waited until shared housing opportunities with old acquaintances presented themselves. Once such opportunities were found, they used welfare and housing subsidies to pay for their share of the rent.

Yet other people with preexisting social networks to nonhomeless people in Berlin were either unable or unwilling to use them to obtain housing or other meaningful material support. Among them were respondents who were *unable* to capitalize on outside networks because these networks were highly marginalized themselves and thus could not provide shelter or material support.[18] Rather *unwilling* to rely more heavily on external social networks were older homeless people with regular life courses, of whom six had very strong roots in their previous residential communities (their *Kieze*).[19] Most lost such connections within months of becoming homeless. Only two respondents maintained regular contacts with old friends. For both, maintaining their friendships was life-saving, as these valued contacts provided friendship, consolation, and hope. For the others, however, two major factors contributed to the gradual loss of such important place-based social networks: increasing spatial distance because of shelter assignments and self-isolation because of shame.

For one thing, the spatial distance between *Kieze* and shelters tended to grow with each new shelter assignment. Seven of the twelve residents of the Wohnheim Trachenbergring with previous addresses in Berlin had multiple shelter experiences and reported that the distance to their previous neighborhoods only increased, without their necessarily being admitted to better facilities until, at last, coming to the Trachenbergring shelter. Still, had people wanted to, they could have overcome such distances relatively easily because of Berlin's excellent public-transit system and the proximity of shelters to entry points.

Perhaps a better explanation for the loss of place-based social networks is the role that shame and deliberate self-isolation play. All older respondents with Berlin-based social ties felt ashamed of their situation. Most were too embarrassed to concede their situation, their drinking, and their failure in the marketplace to neighbors, work colleagues, acquaintances, or sometimes even family members. The stigma associated with homelessness, economic descent, alcoholism, and the eventual self-realization of being a "loser" wore heavily on them, despite their aforementioned attempts to resist the label. Helmut, whose entire extended family lived in Berlin and who had been a supermarket manager, explained why he did not have contacts:

> No, couldn't go to them. You know, that reflects on my entire family, my parents, siblings. Seventh-generation Berliners, you know? You've got to maintain a little bit of self-respect. (Helmut, age 37, shelter resident, older regular life course, conversation, February 26, 1998)

Others expressed with deep regret how they missed their social contacts. Schlöter, an outgoing and charismatic person, described how he occasionally ventured back into his *Kiez* yet maintained some distance to avoid being seen:

> Occasionally, I go back. I miss my *Kiez*. I then go to that park and sit there on an isolated bench. If I have something with me [alcohol], the better. I just don't want to run into anybody I know. So I stick to myself [long pause,

sighs]. (Schlöter, age 53, shelter resident, transient life course, interview, February 26, 1998)

The shame of being associated with homelessness and social descent was also reinforced by attitudes respondents perceived from people around them on the street, in stores, and in welfare offices; from social workers; or from the police. Most respondents, regardless of their life-course experiences, reported condescending attitudes from members of any of these groups once it became apparent that the respondents were homeless and in need of help. Some respondents reported that initial requests for help (money) to family members, former neighbors, or colleagues were frequently rejected, and contacts were severed. Paule explained in frustration:

> It hurts when you find out that many people you considered friends are not that friendly after all once you are in a shitty situation. The chaff separates from the wheat. You learn who your real friends are. In my case, nobody. . . . [long pause] Whatever. (Paule, age 35, shelter resident, homeless person with disability, interview, February 22, 1998)

Such rejections also affected people's willingness and ability to create new networks to nonhomeless people, let alone develop intimate relationships. Except for Sioux and Monika, who had a relationship with each other, and Sachse, who met his fiancée in a bar, none of the respondents had a boy- or girlfriend throughout their homelessness.[20] Even such an extroverted person as Bob conceded, when I asked him whether he had a girlfriend:

> What do you think? [laughs] Momentarily, I am not in the position to have a girlfriend. What would she think if I bring her here to the shelter? Besides, we are not allowed to have visitors past 10:00 P.M. I guess I have to wait a while. (Bob, age 24, shelter resident, younger regular life course, interview, February 26, 1998)

Bob's response also demonstrates the stigma that homeless people themselves attach to shelters—that they are places not worthy to be associated with. Still, he, along with all other younger homeless people with regular life courses and some of the other younger respondents, was less affected by life in a mid-level shelter, although his concerns began building.

In the end, it became abundantly clear that life in shelters, the bad social conditions, and the stigma associated with homeless service facilities had adverse consequences. Older respondents with regular and transient life courses in particular were ashamed of their situation and therefore self-isolated. Alarmed by the environment, they became increasingly anxious about their future. Many of the younger respondents, in contrast, perceived shelter provision and cash assistance as an opportune temporary solution and pragmatically adapted to the circumstances. In this context, it is important to point out that such deliberate and pragmatic adaptation and the eventual reward of exiting was only achieved from mid-level shelters, never low-quality shelters. In providing at least a bit of comfort, privacy, and service if needed, such facilities provided a more stable environment. Low-quality shelters—constituting 60 percent of all shelters in Berlin during the late 1990s—only exacerbated homeless people's problems. Why shelter provision is not better, why current practices are often counterproductive, and how all this compares to Los Angeles are discussed next.

Service Exclusion: Warehousing and Containment in Berlin and Los Angeles

I conclude this chapter with a summary of the main results by introducing a model of service exclusion and comparing my findings from Berlin with those from Los Angeles and other cities. I argue that service exclusion works in similar ways in these cities, is facilitated by similar processes, and ultimately has a highly detrimental effect on homeless people, their immediate life circumstances, and their long-term chances to overcome homelessness. The key difference between Berlin and Los Angeles is that containment per se is not as big a factor in Berlin, because none of the city's service agglomerations is as dense as those in Los Angeles, surrounding communities do not constitute ghettos, and the city's compact urban structure and excellent public transportation afford homeless people more mobility. The effects of warehousing, on the other hand, are comparably detrimental.

Service Exclusion: A Schematic Overview

To begin this discussion, I provide a schematic overview (Fig. 4.5) that illustrates the different components of service exclusion. The model starts with the premise that all homeless people, regardless of life course, need to satisfy their immediate need for shelter; all respondents had used the shelter and service system at some point. In using shelters, homeless people are immediately confronted with warehousing into primarily low-quality facilities and have no input into shelter-allocation decisions. The warehousing is then reinforced by the general geography of shelter and service facilities, which shows clear evidence of containment into the most impoverished parts of town, a factor that is more pronounced in Los Angeles than in Berlin. The consequences of such practices are negative for homeless people in that warehousing and containment reinforce shame, exacerbate alcohol and drug problems, and contribute to the demise of valuable external social networks linking to nonhomeless people, especially among older homeless people with regular life courses and strong local ties. Moreover, the negative experiences in shelters cause some homeless people to resist using homeless service facilities because of ubiquitous stigmatization and fear of further social decline. The social isolation is exacerbated by the location of shelters and the broader inequitable geographic distribution of services. This inequity is amplified by community resistance, which results in the refusal of wealthier districts to provide

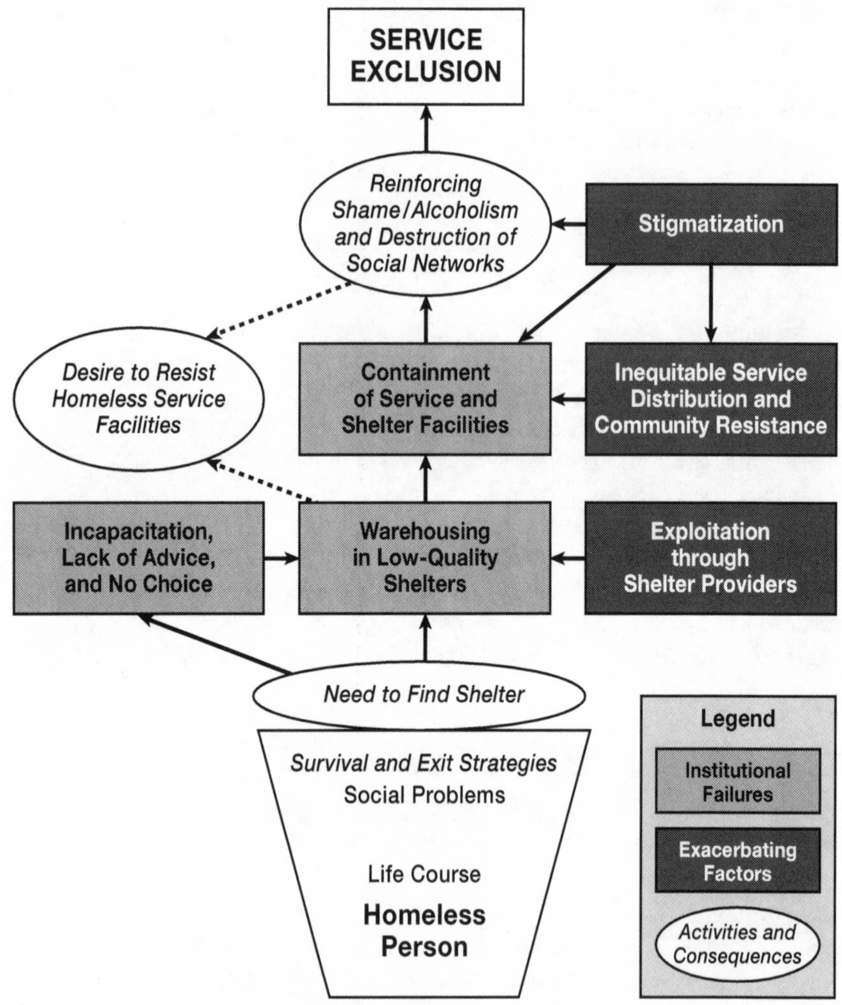

FIGURE 4.5 Model of Service Exclusion

their "fair" share of services, a factor that is more pronounced in Los Angeles and other U.S. cities than in Berlin and other German cities.

Containment and warehousing are the result of shortsighted shelter funding practices that ultimately serve only the interests of commercial shelter providers. These providers exploit the misfortune of homeless people and take advantage of the fact that the local welfare state in Germany is mandated by law (unlike the situation in the United States) to provide shelter yet does not have the means or infrastructure to provide better shelter facilities. Combined, these broader institutional and societal failures prolong homelessness, contribute to the decline of the quality of life of homeless people, and carry unnecessary costs, regardless of place or country. To demonstrate how service exclusion works and how social exclusion affects homeless people differently depending on life-course differences—and to highlight the similarities and differences between Los Angeles and Berlin—I address the institutional failures associated with service exclusion separately.

Containment: Service Ghettos in Berlin?

The Berlin study has demonstrated that inequitable service distributions have led to service agglomerations in Berlin. I have further shown that homeless shelter and service facilities are predominantly located in impoverished areas and near undesirable land-use forms, such as industrial and commercial land use, railroad lines, and busy highways. This description resembles accounts from a number of U.S. cities,[21] but, such similarities notwithstanding, containment in Berlin is nowhere near as pronounced as in Los Angeles. The term "ghetto" is certainly not applicable in Berlin, where even the most distressed neighborhoods do not exhibit the extreme segregation along class and racial lines as in Los Angeles.[22] Additionally, as shown in Figure 4.6, none of Berlin's fifteen service agglomerations is as dense as Los Angeles's three first-order service agglomerations, each of which contains more than twenty homeless service facilities in close proximity to one another. This includes the infamous Skid Row district right outside downtown, home to eleven thousand homeless people.[23] Finally, fierce community resistance, which has prevented homeless services from locating in better communities in the United States, is not a profound factor in Berlin.[24] The primary reason that service and shelter facilities in Berlin mostly exist in impoverished urban quarters has to do with costs and operational considerations, service providers told me. Facility operators typically rent their facilities and must do so where rents are affordable (and are likely to remain so). Proximity to the central city is important, because this is where most homeless people, by necessity, spend their days and early evenings before shelters open.

We can reasonably assume that the containment in Los Angeles more profoundly affects homeless people, who, in the absence of a reasonable transportation system, become entrapped in the service-dependent "ghetto." Why containment still contributed to a loss of place-based networks and caused a deterioration of life circumstances for the respondents in Berlin is more closely related to the consequences of warehousing for individual homeless people, especially those with more-regular life courses.

Warehousing, Incapacitation, and Exploitation

Although the containment of service and shelter facilities per se may have had a less-constraining effect on homeless people and their mobility in Berlin, the

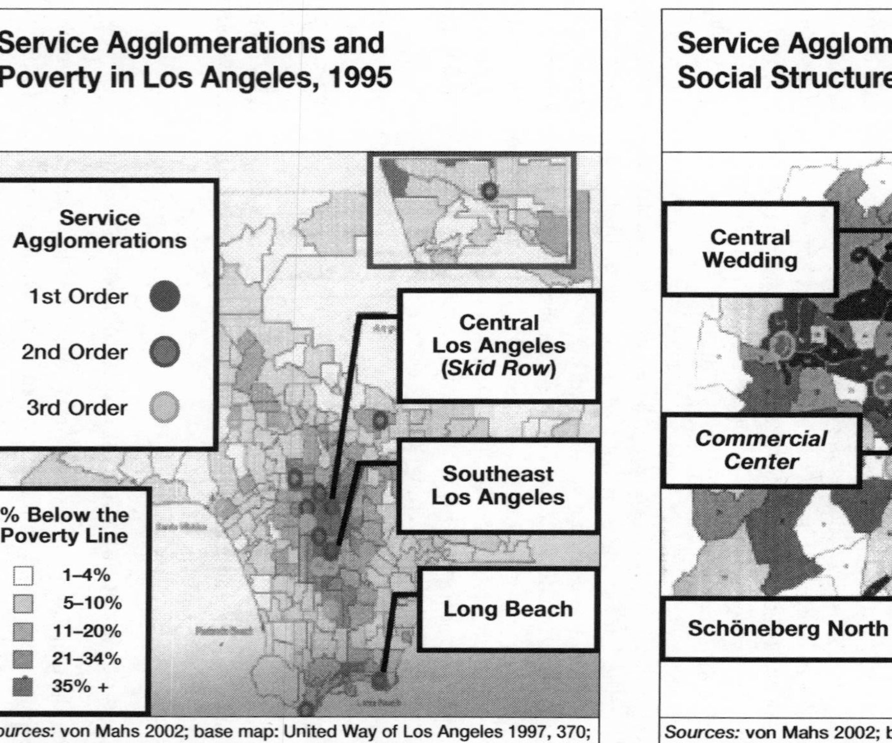

Sources: von Mahs 2002; base map: United Way of Los Angeles 1997, 370; agglomerations identified by Wolch and Dear 1993, 174.

Sources: von Mahs 2002; base map: Hermann, Imme, and Meinlschmidt 1998, 18.

FIGURE 4.6 Agglomerations of Homeless Gatekeeper Services in Los Angeles and Berlin

warehousing into shelters and the conditions within them most certainly had daunting and lasting effects. Perhaps the most important contribution of this chapter is to elucidate our understanding of the impact of shelter and homeless service facilities on homeless people over time and depending on their life courses. The discussion further reveals that personal experiences largely correspond with the *quality* of shelter provision—emergency shelters and low-quality communal and commercial shelters were perceived negatively by *all* respondents, whereas mid- and high-quality shelters received much more favorable reviews. Younger respondents and people with irregular life courses viewed these better accommodations as opportune temporary solutions. Older respondents, on the other hand, especially those with regular life courses, were wary of any shelter provision, regardless of quality, as they tended to compare this situation to the normalcy of their middle-class lives before their seemingly unstoppable social descent.

Personal experiences in shelters documented in U.S. research are similar in their assessment of their impact on homeless people's lives. Robert Desjarlais's (1997) ethnographic study in a homeless shelter in Boston in particular confirms many of the observations and findings from the Berlin study in terms of positive and negative consequences of shelter life (on the one hand, camaraderie and sharing of resources; one the other, defeatism and loss of hope). Also concurring with the Berlin investigation, U.S. studies have highlighted homeless people's agency and their deliberate attempts to change circumstances and the formidable institutional and structural forces arrayed against them (Desjarlais 1997; Rowe and Wolch 1990; Snow and Anderson 1993). Understandably, homeless people in both countries take an ambivalent stance toward the welfare and shelter systems, adapting to some aspects yet rejecting others. Whenever possible, homeless people avoid services intended specifically for the homeless, because they suggest further social descent. Ironically, in such places, they may find the help they seek, as opposed to public welfare and labor agencies, where respondents found little support for their efforts to overcome homelessness and unemployment.

Many respondents in Berlin emphasized that they became literally "incapacitated" (*entmündigt*) in shelters and by the local welfare system, a feeling also frequently reported in Stefan Schneider's (1998) investigations. They felt belittled and had no opportunity to state their problems and preferences. The big question: Why does the local welfare state allow this to happen? Why do administrators not make more use of mid-level shelters that are more likely to facilitate exit in less time, sometimes for less money?

The problem, ultimately, is associated with the local welfare administration's legal obligation to provide shelter while lacking the infrastructure to fund "better" facilities, leaving it no choice but to fund exploitative, expensive, and ultimately counterproductive "lice pensions" operated by commercial enterprises. Helga Burkert, head of the department for homeless affairs in the Berlin Senate Administration for Health and Social Services, explained:

TABLE 4.1 Shelter Allocation and Costs per Visitor in Berlin, 1998

	Shelter allocation		Daily costs (in DM/$)	Monthly costs (in DM/$)	Annual costs (in DM/$)	Exit chances
	1998	2001				
Rental apartment*			400 $222	4,800 $2,667		
Emergency shelter	15%	20%	30 $17	930 $517	10,920 $6,067	Low
Low-level shelter	65%	40%	25–40 $14–22	775–1,240 $431–689	9,100–14,560 $5,056–8,089	Low
Mid-level shelter	15%	35%	30 $17	930 $517	10,920 $6,067	Medium high
High-level shelter	5%	5%	90 $51	2,790 $1,550	32,760 $18,200	High
Shelter residents†	8,900	5,300				

* One-bedroom apartment with utilities at fair market rent.

† Figures based on shelter beds accounted for by the district offices (Senatsverwaltung für Gesundheit und Soziales 1997, 2004).

> You have to understand that our hands are tied. We are legally required to provide shelter, yet we have neither the resources nor the infrastructure to provide better shelter opportunities. We know that some shelter providers abuse this predicament and make profits on the backs of the homeless, but we momentarily have no other choice than to fund them since we must provide shelter. See, we would like to make better use of paragraph 72 [of the BSHG, allowing specialized shelters], yet we don't have the financial means. (interview, April 24, 1998)

This quotation makes it clear that administrators know about the problems and try to solve them, yet they often run into barriers imposed by overbureaucratization, lack of funds, or legal obligations and constraints.

Perhaps worse, according to Volker Eick (1998, 112), are instances in which the same corporations operate both lice pensions and the very security services that displace the homeless from the commercial center in the first place. He notes, "Penske and Garski [a large real estate corporation] not only derive tremendous extra profits—up to DM 1,000 [$550] per homeless person and month—the very same homeless people and illegalized immigrants are literally beaten out of the railroad stations conveniently into the company-owned shelters and kept under lock and key."

In the meantime, homeless people have continued to be warehoused in places that not only offer no chances for improvement but clearly exacerbate their personal problems. This practice comes at a high social cost and indicates fiscal mismanagement. Commercial enterprises that specialize in providing substandard shelter are able to make tremendous profits, a factor that numerous homeless respondents knew about:

> And do you know how much it costs to keep us locked up here? [raises his voice] Thirty marks [$17] a night! They are making all this money off this misery, nobody knows about this, and nobody gives a shit. And this is the real scandal here, Jürgen! (Leo, age 34, day-center visitor, transient life course, interview, February 28, 1998)

Leo was right about this, as the profit margins for commercial service providers at the time were enormous. By charging up to DM 40 (approximately $22) per resident per day to the local welfare agency and putting four people into one tiny room, commercial landlords could earn up to DM 4,960 ($2,756) per room per month, twelve times the cost of a regular one-bedroom apartment. Table 4.1 shows the shelter allocation and costs associated with different shelter options.

Fortunately, some recent positive developments have emerged since the conclusion of this research, as some of the reform initiatives in Berlin began to materialize and the rental market relaxed. As the numbers of officially registered homeless people and shelter residents declined (see Table 4.1), the extent of shelter offerings by voluntary organizations increased. In only three years, the proportion of mid-quality shelters doubled, and now almost 40 percent of all shelters constitute mid- or high-level shelters. Still, a number of key informants I talked to in 2007 indicated that they expected another surge of homelessness once housing prices, cyclical in nature, start rising again.[25] If that happens, the local welfare system will again have to rely on commercial providers to meet the increasing demand, a development that is, clearly, counterproductive.

Conclusion: Public Welfare and Service Exclusion

The results of the Berlin research and the comparisons to Los Angeles and other U.S. cities make clear that warehousing homeless people into dilapidated shelter facilities exacerbates homeless people's problems, regardless of place or country. The local welfare state in Berlin does provide more shelter than Los Angeles, in line with welfare regime theory, but serious problems are associated with the quality of shelter provision. Publicly sponsored emergency and low-quality shelters and commercial "lice pensions" are places that worsen homeless people's life circumstances. The local welfare state is squandering valuable public resources by sustaining such shelters and generously compensating commercial landlords without demanding any accountability.

Service exclusion, therefore, is first and foremost an administrative problem due to a number of deficiencies in the actual provision of shelter and services at the local level. Inadequately assisted, homeless people become preoccupied with the time-consuming and exhausting necessities of daily survival, unable to work toward exiting homelessness. Many homeless experience a downward spiral of defeatism, alcoholism, and despair that is ultimately reinforced by the lack of success in the marketplace. How homeless people try to find housing and jobs, and why some people succeed while others do not, is discussed in the next chapter.

5

Not Needed

Market Exclusion, Exit Strategies, and the Specter of Neoliberalism

It is not difficult to appreciate that the previously discussed forms of legal and service exclusion had an adverse impact on the respondents' immediate life circumstances and thus inevitable consequences for their ability to accomplish their long-term goals of securing housing and employment. In this chapter, I detail respondents' experiences with trying to find shelter and jobs, revealing primarily negative results with regard to employment but slightly better outcomes in terms of housing. Through a mix of assisted and unassisted search efforts, more than half of the respondents—most of them with regular life courses—found housing within one year, effectively stabilizing their poverty management; in four cases, they were able to optimize their situations by finding employment as well. Disappointingly, however, twelve respondents—most of them with irregular life courses—remained unsuccessful and thus became entrenched and dependent on public assistance. The widespread lack of success ultimately took a heavy toll on most respondents, especially older ones with previous economic integration.

To explain these outcomes, I provide an account of the types of exit strategies homeless respondents in Berlin employed and how their efforts unfolded over time, while highlighting the role that public intervention played. I show evidence that the referral services provided directly by public welfare and labor offices universally failed to facilitate successful housing or labor market access, whereas case-based interventions by social workers affiliated with nonprofits accounted for half of all successful housing placements and three of the successful job placements. Ongoing welfare intervention—most notably cash assistance and housing subsidies—ensured that most respondents who exited remained stably housed. In that sense, the local German welfare state remains superior, but it contains substantial flaws that contribute to rather than solve homeless people's problems with accessing local job and housing markets, flaws that could intensify as a result of Germany's 2005 neoliberal welfare overhaul and impending economic crisis.

To set the stage for a discussion of the potential policy implications of these neoliberal reforms on homeless people's exit chances in Berlin, I first provide a synoptic view of homeless people's attempts to gain market access in Los Angeles and other U.S. cities and how workfare and other neoliberal policy instruments have failed to ensure their quest to overcome homelessness and poverty for good. In this light, more recent experimentations with U.S.-style workfare in Germany should be viewed with utmost skepticism.

Homelessness, Market Access, and Workfare in Los Angeles

The following cursory analysis of homeless people's attempts to access housing and labor markets in Los Angeles demonstrates that, although the comparatively unregulated local labor market is easier for homeless people to penetrate than Berlin's, the largely substandard incomes generated thereby are barely sufficient to maintain rental apartments (Tepper and Simpson 2003). Most commentators agree that neoliberal policy and workfare, if anything, has contributed to the problem by facilitating an increasing pool of expendable working poor. These individuals constitute a growing class of "proto-homeless," who, largely excluded from mainstream welfare systems, remain constantly threatened by impending or recurring homelessness (Wolch and Dear 1993).

Homeless despite Work? Economic Prospects of the Working Poor

Over the past twenty years, a number of studies have examined facilitators and/ or barriers to exit from homelessness. The common tenor of these mainly quantitative, longitudinal panels is that homeless people in Los Angeles—and, for that matter, other U.S. cities in which homeless exit has been studied—may be able to find jobs, and subsequently housing, relatively rapidly due to less-regulated low-wage labor markets, but that such exit may be short-term, as many cycle back into homelessness after losing their jobs (for an overview, see Koegel 2004). Similar consensus exists regarding the importance of human capital as a facilitator of exit and, conversely, the lack thereof as a barrier.

The Course of Homelessness Study, in particular, provides evidence that access to regular work is a main facilitator of exit from homelessness in Los Angeles. Evidence from longitudinal studies shows that three-quarters of people who exited homelessness did so primarily by generating income through regular work (Schoeni and Koegel 1998, 299–300; B. Wright 1996, 97). According to a survey among homeless job seekers, 40 percent had managed to find jobs within one year and used such income to pay for housing (Burns, Flaming, and Haydamack 2004, 37–39; Einbinder et al. 1995, 2). Access to low-income work is, compared with Berlin's more rigid labor market, more readily available in Los Angeles (Burns, Flaming, and Haydamack 2004, 50; Schoeni and Koegel 1998; Tepper and Simpson 2003), yet advocates and research studies alike point out that low-income work does not result in economic security and self-sufficiency. As Bob Erlenbusch, director of the Los Angeles Coalition to End Hunger and Homelessness, told me:

> Sure, homeless people may find jobs rather easily, but they don't find long-term economic stability. You have to keep in mind that L.A.'s economy is ruthlessly exploitative, particularly with regards to the low-income service sector. (interview, September 23, 1997)

Erlenbusch's assessment holds up against longitudinal labor market data revealing that few homeless achieve economic self-sufficiency and move out of poverty, chiefly because they become entrapped in either the low-income, low-security, and low-gratifying formal labor market or the informal economy (Burns, Flaming, and Haydamack 2004, 49–52; Einbinder et al. 1995; Flaming 1995; LACEHH 2004; Schoeni and Koegel 1998; Tepper and Simpson 2003; Wolch and Sommer 1997). According to Burns, Flaming, and Haydamack's (2004) study on the long-term progress of 1,250 homeless participants in a Los Angeles job-training program, only one-sixth managed to overcome homelessness and poverty for good over a nine-year examination period. Thus, by placing a primary emphasis on the market, the liberal U.S. welfare regime may provide more flexible job access, but many working poor remain highly vulnerable to broader economic fluctuations, such as the current economic crisis (2008–?), as increasing numbers of foreclosures, rental distress, and ultimately homelessness demonstrate (Sard 2009).

Entrapped in the unstable low-wage labor market, formerly homeless people become or remain segregated into the impoverished communities in which they can afford rent, thereby staying poor and threatened by recurring homelessness. Such entrapment is reinforced by a spatial mismatch between the location of shelters and affordable housing opportunities and the location of more-promising job opportunities, which are often in suburban or exurban areas that are literally inaccessible to urban homeless people (Wolch and Dear 1993).

The Poverty of Public Policy: Why Workfare Will Not Work

To make matters worse, the public sector has been steadily reducing its involvement in providing homeless people with direct services and in providing nonprofits with sufficient funding. Such public disinvestment belies the fact that public policy and social-work intervention are, more often than not, positively correlated with successful exit from homelessness (Schoeni and Koegel 1998; Zlotnick, Robertson, and Lhiff 1999; Shinn 2009). Public programs that provide assistance with rental payments (e.g., Section 8, supportive housing) are similarly linked to successful and lasting exit from homelessness (Shinn et al. 1998). The importance of such interventions, especially client-centered, collaborative approaches, has also been documented in a range of ethnographic studies and in a broad array of evaluative research. However, the success of such programs and approaches remains limited, simply because few homeless people actually manage to gain access to such public benefits, and most homeless people, families included, remain outside the conventional welfare system (Burt et al. 2001).

If anything, the case of Los Angeles, and for that matter practically any U.S. city, shows that the public policy response in the United States toward facilitating exit from homelessness and poverty, and therefore ensuring upward social mobility, is abysmally low. Although the supply of services—including in some places excellent nonprofit service providers—has increased dramatically over the past twenty years, it still does not meet the demand (DeVerteuil, Lee, and Wolch 2002; Simpson and Tepper 2004; Wolch and Dinh 2001).

The fact that even homeless people who have completed job-training programs remain overwhelmingly unsuccessful is evidence of the limited possibilities of intervention in helping people surmount market barriers (Burns, Flaming, and Haydamack 2004). Similarly discouraging results can be noted in local evaluations of workfare policies inherent in the 1996 federal welfare reform that replaced Aid to Families with Dependent Children (AFDC) with Temporary Aid to Needy Families (TANF; the Personal Responsibility and Work Opportunity Reconciliation Act [PRWORA]). Most studies point out that forcing poor women with already-low human capital into the workforce does little to (1) advance them out of poverty, (2) account for their family and childcare needs, or (3) account for any aggravating personal problems (Wolch and Sommer 1997; DeVerteuil 2003b; Wolch and Dinh 2001).

Thus, the increasing supply of services has done little to enhance economic options; rather, it has furthered the spatial sequestering of homeless people into contained, service-dependent ghettos, where a broad range of largely uncoordinated service providers compete for inadequate public funding and, increasingly, funding from other sources (e.g., philanthropy, membership, fund-raising drives). The main problem—and a clear difference from Germany—is that the local welfare state does not have the legal, administrative, and funding support to link to and sustain the homeless support system, which therefore largely operates outside the mainstream social-welfare systems. The fact that homeless service provision remains inscribed in Germany's statutory federal welfare system should, in theory at least, give homeless people in Berlin a distinct advantage.

Advantage Berlin?

Information from Los Angeles and other U.S. cities suggests that the combination of the comparatively unregulated labor market, exclusive and prohibitively expensive rental markets, and minimalist welfare intervention and workfare has adverse effects on homeless people's exit chances and their long-term efforts to achieve upward mobility. Germany's homeless population should have better chances, in large part because a coherent social safety net exists on solid legal footing and covers the great majority of residents. Yet although approximately half the respondents of my 1998–1999 study eventually found housing, the success rate at finding jobs—four out of twenty-two active job seekers—was discouragingly low. This number seems to suggest that local welfare and labor office intervention have largely failed in facilitating homeless people's access to jobs. To understand why, we must examine first how homeless people in Berlin sought to achieve market entry or reentry and how such efforts unfolded over time.

Homeless People's Exit Strategies in Berlin

As I state in Chapter 2, all respondents included in the 1998–1999 Berlin study shared the desire to find appropriate housing and employment that would allow them to achieve or to regain economic self-sufficiency, although six had medical reasons for not pursuing work at the time. The other twenty-two respondents actively seeking employment had rather modest expectations, which, depending on their human capital, might have been specific to an occupational field (primarily in the construction sector) or might have encompassed any kind of unskilled paid labor. Whatever the expectations about type of job and extent of compensation, they were, if anything, lowered by the humbling experience of being repeatedly unsuccessful. Likewise, people were also willing to make concessions about housing in terms of location and quality. Although most indigenous Berliners would have preferred housing in their old *Kieze,* they eventually accepted the fact that any housing anywhere is better than no private housing at all. Biker explained:

> Expectations? Oh, sure! I wanna be a corporate executive with a villa in Zehlendorf! Now, don't we all? No, I don't think you fully appreciate my situation here: I am in a shelter. [pause] You understand? I am not in the position to make demands here! I'd be lucky if I get anything. (Biker, age 38, homeless person with disability, interview, March 9, 1998)

By the time I interviewed the respondents—on average three years into their unemployment and a year and a half into their homeless experience—most were more or less willing to accept any type of job and any type of independent living just to escape the degrading and humiliating milieu of homelessness. Only three older respondents with regular life courses said that they would continue to refuse low-paid or degrading jobs.

The reason homeless people lower their expectations is simple: Every respondent spent countless hours searching with the same discouraging result. This lack of success warrants scrutinizing the strategies homeless people use to find housing and employment. Considering that the respondents relied on the same set of search strategies for labor and housing markets, I differentiate the discussion of exit strategies between assisted (assistance provided by local welfare or labor offices or nonprofits) and individual, primarily unassisted efforts (searching newspaper ads, using social networks, making phone calls, and personally initiating contact). In this discussion, I further reflect on changes in the extent and intensity with which homeless respondents employed exit strategies over time and their often-continuous lack of success.

Unassisted Efforts and Self-Initiative

It is important to preface any discussion of homeless people's self-initiative with a reminder about the diminishing life circumstances that come with the containment and warehousing inherent in service exclusion. The immediately negative experiences that many homeless people face in such places likely increase their initial desires to find a way out of their predicaments as quickly as possible while simultaneously adversely affecting their chances to do so.

To find job and housing opportunities, most respondents employed a double strategy by studying the job postings and rental listings in one or more of Berlin's daily newspapers early in the morning. At the shelter and in many of the "better," more specialized facilities, staff members would post openings they had found in newspapers or on the Internet in a public display or provide them as handouts. Using pay phones (few respondents had cell phones at the time), respondents would try to call landlords or employers and, if they reached somebody and the position or place was still available, make arrangements to meet. Location played no important role; the respondents, desperate to find housing and employment, expressed almost universally that they would live and work anywhere within the city. Moreover, most respondents reported that they had little difficulty in finding or reaching places, given Berlin's excellent public-transit system. In following up on such leads, respondents would often spend considerable time and effort (up to 1.5 hours) to reach a potential housing or job location, only to hear the same bad news: The job was taken, or the apartment was already under contract. Sachse exemplified many when I met him, visibly frustrated and disappointed, in the stairwell of the Wohnheim Trachenbergring. When I asked him what was wrong, he replied:

> Oh well, just another one of these shitty days. This morning, I first went to the labor office. Like always, nothing. Then I saw this ad in the paper and talked to that landlord in Steglitz over the phone, and it all sounded very promising, and we arranged to meet at three o'clock. So I walked all the way over there [four kilometers]. And again, blah, blah, I'm so sorry, blah, blah. I guess he found out that I'm on welfare and in a shelter. Do you have any idea how often I hear that shit? I need a beer. Wanna come? (Sachse, age 35, older regular life course, informal conversation, February 25, 1998)

Sachse's response shows how the rejection he experienced translated into defeatism, depression, and consequently the desire to drown his frustration in alcohol. After two beers, he felt better, but the depression and discouragement lingered and added to his increasing fears and sense of hopelessness.

Another strategy that many respondents, especially with regular life courses, applied was to rely on social networks to find housing opportunities and perhaps even work. This strategy was particularly prevalent among younger respondents, who, less alarmed and ashamed by their situations, often maintained nonhomeless connections to other young people throughout Berlin (see Chapter 4). As a result, five of them took advantage of invitations to join shared housing arrangements. Two respondents, Schlöter and Hans, would also rely regularly on former employers to give them part-time work if available. Although this sporadic employment did not generate a sustainable flow of income, it provided an opportunity to stay involved, active, and connected and thus to break the boring routines of homeless life every now and then. Still, for them and most other older respondents, the shame that surrounds shelter life and the stigma of homelessness I describe in Chapter 4 foreclosed the possibility of relying more heavily on social support. This was particularly true for people with more-irregular life courses and thus lesser extents of local social capital.

Ultimately, self-initiative without direct welfare intervention enabled eight respondents to find housing and to enter into rental agreements. It is important to point out that all eight respondents relied on continuous welfare payments and housing allowance payments to maintain such independent or (in four cases) shared housing. Still, given that most unassisted efforts remain fruitless, it is not surprising that homeless people rely on institutional assistance to find housing and employment.

Institutional Assistance: Differentiated Outcomes

Like all welfare recipients in Germany, homeless people receive services directly from their district welfare offices (*Sozialämter*) and must, if deemed employable, also register with the local labor offices (*Arbeitsämter*) to receive job referrals or other services to facilitate labor market entry. All needs identified in social-welfare legislation as basic necessities—housing, shelter, and social services—are to be provided directly through the welfare offices or delegated to nonprofit service providers. In such fashion, the local welfare offices ought to function as the primary source for housing referrals. Many welfare offices also employ social workers for outreach and street work. Local welfare offices are, in theory, supposed to coordinate the welfare needs of eligible clients.

Social Welfare Offices

As discussed in the previous chapters, all respondents received services provided by their respective social-welfare offices, which respondents visited on a weekly basis to confirm their eligibility, show evidence for compliance with job and housing search requirements, receive referrals to shelters and other necessary services, obtain authorization for their monthly welfare payments, and, most important perhaps, receive referrals to housing opportunities. As I mention throughout the previous chapters, most respondents were gravely dissatisfied with their caseworkers, who, on average, spent ten minutes with each respondent, barely enough time even to state his or her needs. Caseworkers, at their discretion, could look up housing leads, as they had access to databases with rental market availabilities. Upon receiving leads, the respondents would typically try to reach the landlords by pay phone or would simply walk or take public transit to the location. In this context, I noticed a great deal of variation in the ways in which respondents viewed their caseworkers and their efforts, ranging from appreciation and understanding of the work conditions caseworkers face to very negative perceptions of them as unfriendly, unhelpful, or patronizing.

Frustratingly, however, not one of the leads provided by welfare caseworkers ever led to successful housing placement. By the time respondents received housing leads—hardly ever before 11:00 A.M.—most housing opportunities were long gone, especially in the tight urban rental market conditions that still existed in 1998–1999. Clearly, the local welfare offices did help stabilize people's life courses by providing basic cash assistance and sometimes additional services, but they failed in facilitating long-term exits from homelessness through direct referrals.

Local Labor Offices

A similarly poor performance can be attested for the efforts of Berlin's four metropolitan labor offices, where able-bodied and therefore employable welfare recipients must register to be eligible for social assistance or unemployment compensation.[1] Alarmingly, not one single job lead provided by a caseworker at a labor office resulted in a respondent's finding a job or job-training opportunity—not *one*. In virtually all cases, long waits and rather short and unproductive meetings at the labor office resulted in a few job leads that, upon contact with the potential employer, always turned out to be futile. Not surprisingly, many respondents began to wonder why they should even bother following such repeatedly fruitless leads. Schlöter, who had experienced unemployment many times throughout his life and had received unemployment insurance and compensation before, explained:

> If you ask me, an utter waste of time going there [*Arbeitsamt*]. Way too many people looking for work. I don't even think that they [caseworkers] are trying to find you a job. I would think that they would concentrate their efforts on more probable cases, not an old ass like me [shrugs and sighs]. (Schlöter, age 52, transient life course, interview, February 22, 1998)

Most respondents felt that they received insufficient time and opportunity to state their needs and, as in welfare offices, complained of being treated in bureaucratic, discriminatory, and condescending ways. As Oliver remarked:

> They have their laws that make sure you don't starve or freeze to death. You, on the other side of the desk, are just a number, a statistic. . . . It's this administrative mentality that I hate about this country. (Oliver, age 26, deviant life course, interview, March 10, 1998)

Virtually all respondents were gravely aware of the negative economic climate that perpetuated long and persistent urban unemployment (hovering around 18 percent in 1998–1999) and thus limited job opportunities (Statistisches Landesamt Berlin 2000). Older respondents understood their competitive disadvantage and were aware that they might not even be considered employable because of absences of a year or more from the formal economy. Biker reminded me rather sternly about his economic chances in light of his physical problems and limited opportunities:

> Just look at the news, man! [raises his voice] There are 4 million unemployed people in Germany. I am thirty-eight years old, crippled, and have not held a job in ten years. Do I need to say more? I have no illusion that I will ever find a regular job again. (Biker, age 38, homeless person with disability, interview, March 7, 1998)

Another problem, not as frequent yet noticeable among many younger respondents, involved difficulties following rules and directives and thus with navigating the complicated welfare and labor bureaucracy with its endless paperwork. In February 1998, I had the opportunity to accompany a respondent, Mario, to his welfare office to, in his words, see for myself how he was being treated there. And, indeed, from the hallway I overheard a loud and unpleasant conversation that culminated in the caseworker's throwing my respondent out of her office. On an unrelated occasion, I had a chance to talk with that particular caseworker, who, although not very friendly, gave me a different perspective of Mario as lazy, uncooperative, and unprepared, qualities to which Mario later admitted. He and a number of others did show some understanding for their caseworkers, who, as they could see plainly, were overworked and frustrated by their own ineffectiveness. I can confirm that most caseworkers are genuinely interested in helping their clients but also that many eventually succumb to burnout, which, given the miserable atmosphere in welfare and labor offices, is quite understandable.

When assisted efforts by mainstream welfare and labor offices turned out to be futile, what options remained for the respondents? One choice was to resist the local welfare state and try out other options, which five respondents began doing for extended periods of time, only to remain homeless (see Chapter 3). The other option, pursued by most respondents eventually, was to turn to social workers they had met or who had contacted them at the facilities they patronized. Such social work interventions, it turned out, were much more likely to yield success.

Social Work Intervention by Nonprofit Organizations

A third type of intervention consisted of the broad range of services provided by social workers at agencies specifically serving the homeless. All three case-study locations in this examination employed either full- or part-time social workers. Although at first sight, this seems no different from Los Angeles and other U.S. cities, where the task of service provision has been mostly delegated to the third sector, such third-sector service provision in Berlin and Germany is almost exclusively funded through public means, following Germany's social welfare principle of "subsidiarity" and a constitutionally inscribed collaboration between government and the voluntary sector.

Among the half of all respondents who eventually managed to overcome homelessness, social workers on the premises played instrumental roles. Their interventions were more successful, because specifically trained caseworkers were able to capitalize on their overall knowledge of the system and their familiarity with the condition of homelessness to provide homeless people with case-appropriate service and advice. Like most other shelter residents, Kalle had only good things to say about the caseworkers employed at the shelter:

> They [three social workers in the Wohnheim Trachenbergring] are wonderful. They'll do anything for you. They are not patronizing, they listen and treat you like a human being. At the welfare office, I always feel like a number, not a person. (Kalle, age 44, older regular life course, interview, February 28, 1998)

Social workers at all three facilities had university degrees and often years of experience working with homeless and other marginalized people. All social workers approached their clients carefully, taking the time to build relationships and slowly establish a basis for communication and trust. The key ingredients in virtually all these cases involved a willingness to listen and the patience to let clients seek advice of their own accord and initiative. As I describe shortly, such social work interventions were much more likely to facilitate a homeless client's stabilization and, in three cases, even optimization. This finding, as I discuss in the conclusion of this book, has major implications for reforms to improve, streamline, and enhance the effectiveness of local homeless service systems. Still, with regard to facilitating labor market access, even these types of intervention are likely to remain largely futile.

Efforts over Time and across Life-Course Types

Before revealing the ultimate outcomes of the Berlin study and thus answering the questions of whether and how people managed to overcome homelessness, it is important to examine how homeless people's efforts to find housing and jobs change over time. Initially, at least, the extent of individual effort was rather strong; the respondents, upon becoming homeless, followed about two housing and three job leads a week on average. Over time and with a consistent lack of success, their efforts clearly and perhaps understandably diminished, as virtually every ethnographic study on homelessness demonstrates (e.g., Snow and Anderson 1993; Hopper 2003). Respondents understood that they had competitive disadvantages in Berlin's tight labor and rental housing markets during 1998–1999. Bernie, a particularly diligent job seeker (that was the main reason he came to Berlin) explained what most respondents, in some variation, thought about their chances of finding suitable employment:

> Think about it. By the time we get something from a caseworker, contact the employer or landlord, get over there, well, guess what? The place is taken, the job not available. And think further: If an employer or a landlord has enough choices, why in God's name would they hire somebody like me without a fixed address who has not had a job in over two years? And as an automobile mechanic, nonetheless? I think that it is easy to see that we have few chances. And it gets worse over the years [shakes his head]. (Bernie, age 40, older regular life course, interview, March 9, 1998)

This realistic assessment summarizes the key factors in homeless people's diminishing human capital and competitiveness in the labor market. It is certainly understandable that their lack of success, relatively irrespective of their life courses, started wearing on the respondents. Hope and optimism gave way to a much more pessimistic, defeatist mind-set. Such deterioration even occurred in cases in which some degree of success was finally achieved, as Sachse's comment exemplifies:

> It really makes me sick, man! I'm trying, I really do, yet it's all in vain. I go there [labor office] almost every day, I study the newspapers. I call them up, and nothing. I've been doing this now for almost three years, and nothing. You have no idea how this feels. Sometimes I say to myself, fuck it. Why even bother? (Sachse, age 35, older regular life course, interview, February 17, 1998)

Particularly alarming was the noticeable decline in effort among older respondents. Although they were alarmed by the circumstances surrounding their unaccustomed new lives and thus initially particularly eager and diligent about looking for ways to change them, they experienced a correspondingly steep decline in effort. Schlöter aptly expressed the fear of getting old and remaining unsuccessful:

> Getting old is taking a toll on me. I am afraid of the future. I'm a fifty-two-year-old transient day laborer [*Wanderarbeiter*] with no meaningful social insurance contributions and therefore likely a low pension. My body is not working so well anymore, and the alcohol is a drain. I can't sleep at night unless I'm loaded [with alcohol]. I have problems in the morning, my concentration span is small, and I'm irritable. I'm telling you, this is not good. Not good at all. (Schlöter, age 52, transient life course, interview, February 26, 1998)

He continued drinking heavily, subsidizing his welfare income with occasional undocumented work as a painter and thus maintaining at least some hope that such work would parlay into more a permanent form of employment.

Because of the general lack of success, most respondents began perceiving job and housing searches prescribed by caseworkers at welfare and labor agencies as a deliberate hassle imposed on them just to keep them busy. The respondents called this practice "going stamping" (*stempeln gehen*), no longer believing that they had a chance to find either jobs or housing this way. Some respondents who used to be economically integrated were rather outraged at being mandated to accept any job to remain eligible for full benefits, a practice that already predated the much-heralded 2005 Hartz IV reforms. This is what Helmut, visibly angry, said when he was mandated to take a job as a communal street sweeper:

> Listen, I am not going to have those assholes give me a [DM] 5.50 [$3.06] an hour job as a street sweeper just to get me off the books. I have worked hard all my life, and I have some dignity left, and I do deserve some respect, you know? They give me a decent job, and I'll prove that I'm worth it. But sweeping streets for a hunger salary? Never! And then they treat you as work-shy because you are reluctant to take that kind of job. Should I be thankful? Kiss my ass! So I went to my doctor and had him write me a note that I can't take that job because of health reasons. That was the end of it. But I continue to look on my own terms. (Helmut, age 37, older regular life course, interview, February 23, 1998)

The disillusionment that came with the lack of success ultimately affected all respondents, including those within the categories of deviant and transient life courses who did not even show substantial effort in the first place. Already discouraged by their lack of success in their previous places of residence, many set their expectations low and, as evidenced in Chapter 3, often became preoccupied with comparatively time-consuming shadow work just to make ends meet and sustain their addictions.

It is precisely in light of diminishing life circumstances, decreasing effort, and largely inefficient public policy intervention that we now turn to the outcome of homeless people's efforts within one year of the initial interviews. The results, although offering some reasons for optimism, were largely negative, as almost half—twelve respondents—became increasingly entrapped in the condition of homelessness, with diminishing chances to escape their predicament.

Outcomes after One Year: Between Optimization, Stabilization, and Entrenchment in Berlin

The overall outcomes of homeless people's assisted and unassisted efforts to find housing provide some grounds for optimism but ultimately a rather discouraging picture, as the following overview in Table 5.1 suggests. The table differentiates, borrowing from Lutz Leisering and Stephan Leibfried's (1999) typology, among three types of outcomes: optimization, stabilization, and entrenchment. On the positive side, four respondents "optimized" their poverty management by finding jobs and housing, while twelve respondents managed to at least "stabilize" their life courses by finding agreeable housing solutions, but without obtaining jobs they remained on welfare. Discouragingly, twelve respondents—

TABLE 5.1 Job and Housing Search Outcomes after One Year for Homeless Respondents in Berlin

Housing / employment outcomes	Older homeless people with regular life courses (n = 8)	Younger homeless people with regular life courses (n = 4)	Homeless people with transient life courses (n = 8)	Homeless people with deviant life courses (n = 4)	Homeless people with disabilities (n = 4)	Total
			OPTIMIZATION			4
Housing / Employment	Kalle* Hanno*		Harri*‡			3
Military housing / Noncommissioned officer training		Mario				1
			STABILIZATION			12
Rental housing / Welfare	Hans	Radek†		Oliver*	Biker*§	4
Supportive housing / Welfare	Maria*||				Andrea*|| Monika*||	3
Shared housing / Welfare	Sachse*	Bob Markus	Leo	Sioux‡		5
			ENTRENCHMENT			12
Wohnheim Trachenberg-ring (same shelter) / Welfare	Det*§|| Helmut*§||		Tobias*||	FTW*†§		4
Welfare / Emergency shelters	Bernie		Martin‡ Matze‡			3
Low-level shelter (worse shelter) / Welfare			Jens§ Schlöter§ Dan§		Paule§	4
Street / Welfare				Marita§		1

Note: The categorization of outcomes as optimization, stabilization, and entrenchment is based on the typology of Leisering and Leibfried (1999). Short biographies of the respondents are provided in Appendix 1. The respondents listed in the table are male, except for Maria, Marita, Andrea, and Monika.

* Individual received substantial assistance from social workers.

† Individual was pursuing job training.

‡ Individual was pursuing alternative paths or activism.

§ Individual was experiencing serious defeatism and substance-abuse problems.

|| Individual was not looking for employment or was exempt from search requirements.

most with irregular life courses—found neither jobs nor housing and thus found themselves entrenched in the welfare system, living off welfare and in shelters or, in Marita's case, still on the streets of Berlin.

With an asterisk, the table also indicates which of the nine successful respondents owed their achievement to substantial social work intervention; notably, three of them were women. The fact that three of the four women in this investigation succeeded may be an indication of slightly better service options for groups presumably seen as more "deserving," such as women with mental or physical health problems.

Ultimately, however, it became painfully clear that many respondents failed to accomplish their goals and thus remained entrenched in the welfare system, more or less dependent on welfare payments and shelter provision. Although half of them still made some effort to stop their gradual personal decline and remained somewhat optimistic, the other half (indicated by a § symbol in the table) essentially resigned themselves to their fate—living dependent, disillusioned, and bored in shelters, places that ultimately only fueled their decline and increasing alcohol dependence (see Chapter 4). Despite living in a favorable shelter setting, two respondents (Helmut and Det) deteriorated to the point that even proactive interventions, such as case management, did not come to fruition. Even the most dedicated social workers can do little if people are so disillusioned and depressed that they are incapable of taking any action, let alone participating in day-to-day routines. Considering that each category has variations, I address the outcomes in turn, starting with a synopsis of the ways in which four respondents, at least temporarily, managed to optimize their life courses.

Optimized Poverty Management: Homelessness Averted?

Three of the four ultimately successful respondents owed their exits to both self-determination and substantial help they received from social workers at the facilities at which they stayed or worked. In all three cases, such social workers took advantage of their knowledge of local active labor market policies (ALMPs), including publicly subsidized employment, a practice that has been successfully implemented in social democratic welfare regimes. In Kalle's and Hanno's cases, social workers at the Wohnheim Trachenbergring were instrumental in finding, negotiating, and facilitating the respondents' access to regular rental housing and their reentry into the formal labor market. Harri received help at the Mob e.V. to parlay his volunteer activities as head of logistics and distribution there into a paid "social work" opportunity. All three recipients of ALMPs received the contractual minimum wage of approximately DM 1,800 ($1,000) per month. Such time-limited employment came with no guarantee of reemployment, but it did offer a chance to requalify for nominally higher unemployment compensation of approximately DM 954 ($530) per month, almost double the amount of social assistance benefit they received at the time. I know that Hanno and Kalle eventually lost their employment again and that Kalle, after five years of independent living, sought readmission to the Wohnheim Trachenbergring, where he still lives today, essentially entrenched in the welfare system (but sober again). Ultimately, only Harri achieved an annual renewal of his contract until his formal retirement from the organization a few years later. Given his social insurance contributions over the years, he now receives a modest pension and still lives in his converted trailer in Berlin-Karow, one of the few respondents who truly optimized his life-course management.

The fourth respondent, Mario, took advantage of his draft status and enlisted for four years in the German Army, embarking on an entry-level noncommissioned officer's (NCO's) career with the option to reenlist. NCO training comes with full compensation (approximately DM 2,300/$1,278 per month starting salary), training, and NCO housing, which in most German military installations includes shared apartments in the NCO barracks. Barring a dishonorable discharge, he was ensured stable housing and income for the next four years. He acknowledged that this step might help him acquire the self-discipline and time-management skills he had been lacking (something he was critically aware of). The last time we spoke, he was not really happy with military life but felt that it was certainly a step up from a shelter and the accompanying degradations, and he was hoping to pursue a career in private security upon discharge.

Stabilization: Temporary Fix or Permanent Solution?

As with optimized cases, stabilization often involved respondents' parallel use of assisted and unassisted efforts to ultimately succeed in finding housing; labor market access, however, was not achieved within one year. Five respondents could attribute their partial success to social workers on the premises. Nonprofit service providers, local welfare offices, and supportive housing providers worked relatively quickly to ensure solutions for three of the four female respondents, who had particularly pressing housing and service needs. In all three cases, less than a month passed between first contact and actual housing placement. Monika now lives in a state-of-the-art assisted-living facility for visually impaired people; Andrea moved into a socially supported group home with other older women with mild mental disabilities; and Maria lives in an apartment, where she regularly receives visits from social workers who help her with paperwork and household finances. All three women are very satisfied with these solutions. This positive assessment, however, should not mask the fact that at least two of the women (Monika and Andrea) remained homeless and excluded from the social safety net for many years before agreeable solutions were found.

Efforts to find shared housing solutions were almost exclusively based on self-initiative and sometimes a bit of luck; housing was typically obtained through social networks. Bob and Markus, two younger homeless people with regular life courses, found shared opportunities with nonhomeless friends and acquaintances and moved as soon as they were invited to join apartments. Sioux and

Sachse found romantic relationships that provided, temporarily at least, access to regular rental housing. Leo moved to Hamburg to live with a relative and try his luck at finding employment there. The last I heard of him, he had remained unsuccessful at finding a job but was stably housed at his aunt's place, appreciating her cooking.

The common denominator among all twelve respondents in this category after one year was that none of them had found regular employment, and most remained, despite the much-needed housing stability, at the crossroads of achieving optimization or experiencing further decline, especially in light of repeated rejections. I witnessed upward mobility and eventual optimization among two respondents. Radek was the only respondent to complete job training, as an apprentice for a mechanical-engineering firm; he moved into an apartment financed through welfare and housing allowances and eventually found a job with good income and full benefits in 2001. Likewise, Sioux, after six years of selling street newspapers and after moving in with Monika, managed to find a regular job in a cleaning company in 2002, where he quickly advanced to become a foreman. He maintained a nice apartment, amicably separated from Monika, established a new relationship, and reconciled with four of his five children from previous relationships. Although health problems forced him to stop working, requiring him to accept welfare again, he has remained stably housed since 2003. Whether such optimization has also occurred among the remaining respondents who experienced stabilization remains unknown, because I eventually lost contact with them.

I also cannot say whether any respondents who stabilized their housing situations eventually experienced a recurrence of homelessness. By the end of the investigation, the newly acquired and, by most accounts, satisfactory housing solutions had certainly provided welcome stability in people's lives. When I visited Biker in his apartment ten months after our first conversation, he said:

> Having a place of your own again is certainly an important step back to a normal life. You literally get your life back. It makes it so much easier. Sure, it is a bit empty in here [points to the empty walls and sparse furniture], and it will take time. But it is a step. (Biker, age 38, homeless person with disability, conversation, December 12, 1998)

A common denominator in making the newfound stability possible was the continuous receipt of welfare and additional assistance. Confirming a number of evaluative studies, such housing and income support allowed all those who stabilized their situations to remain stably housed for the duration of the study, and in three cases well beyond. In that way, we see a clear advantage of the German welfare system, which, if used properly and continuously, provides much better chances for formerly homeless people to stay in regular housing. This is, after all, the least-expensive solution and, from a fiscal perspective, clearly preferable over much-higher shelter expenditures, regardless of who receives those funds.

Entrenchment: Harbinger of Worse Things to Come?

The fact that twelve respondents remained unsuccessful despite the provision of welfare and shelter is rather discouraging. Perhaps even more alarming is the fact that more than half of them experienced a serious deterioration of their personal life circumstances, exacerbated by a substantial increase in defeatism and alcohol abuse, or remained, like Marita, in the same daunting predicament with diminishing hope of ever improving their lot.

Interestingly, however, not all respondents who continued living in shelters and on welfare were fully discouraged or discontent with their circumstances. FTW, who continued to live in the mid-level shelter and on welfare, actually improved his situation with the help of a social worker. Upon learning about FTW's fascination with motorcycles, the social worker managed to find him a one-year job-training opportunity at a local motorcycle repair shop that would earn him the title of assistant motorcycle mechanic. For the first time in his life, he had a realistic chance to pursue regular and paid employment (unfortunately, we lost touch after fifteen months). Three other respondents established agreeable routines alternating between dry emergency shelters in the winter and living rough in the summer and were content with this choice, which they either viewed as temporary (Bernie, who hoped to find stability for the family he left behind in Dortmund) or opportune for pursuing alternative strategies (Matze and Martin, street-newspaper vendors and activists). Also still optimistic was Tobias, who viewed his time in the mid-level shelter as temporary while he awaited the decision on his visa application, having accumulated enough savings for a one-way ticket to Cape Town, South Africa. He did not mind shelter life, as it provided him with an opportunity to save money, live spartanly, and deal with his health problems. (We lost touch before the visa decision was made.)

Whether their optimism and temporary sense of contentment would last was another matter—it was feasible that they, too, would become increasingly disillusioned, defeatist, and passive with ongoing lack of success and thus join the five respondents, primarily older, who had more or less given up on themselves. All five of these people—Helmut, Schlöter, Paule, Det, and Dan—experienced a substantial turn for the worse as their alcohol problems increased, adversely affecting their physical and mental health. All five respondents were clinically depressed and, by the end of the study, barely functioning in their day-to-day activities. Four of them also found themselves, sometimes through detours, in worse accommodations than the mid-level shelter where I first interviewed them. Schlöter, for instance, left to undergo alcohol rehabilitation but afterward was released into a low-level shelter, where he soon relapsed and deteriorated. Dan, on the other hand, took an international detour. He was deported in late 1998 for overstaying his visa and moved back to Pittsburgh, where he now lives in a homeless shelter, as he explained in a postcard to me. He also mentioned that Berlin's welfare and shelter system is much better in comparison:

> I am staying at a shelter, temporarily at least. Certainly worse than Trachenbergring and in worse company. Hope that I can find some use for my skills but it is pretty hopeless. I'll be alright but, who knows? (Dan, age 52, transient life course, postcard stamped January 13, 1999)

The defeatism these five truly entrenched respondents experienced comes at a very high price both from a fiscal perspective and in terms of social costs. Usually, ineffective long-term shelter stays are very expensive, costing between DM 25 and DM 40 (between $14 and $22) per day per resident. More important, perhaps, are the social and psychological costs of such entrenchment and the extinguishing of hope.

All respondents, including the ones who were ultimately successful, became increasingly disillusioned and discouraged with each rejection they experienced. Virtually all began to internalize feelings of being "losers" as their sense of self-worth and self-respect diminished. As their sense of shame increased, so did their desire to self-isolate, drown their frustration in alcohol, and abandon their social connections to nonhomeless people (see Chapter 4). It was painful to witness the rapid demise of previously outspoken and eloquent respondents, such as Helmut, who remained unsuccessful despite attempts by social workers to help him. During our last meeting in December 1999, he had lost a lot of weight, was constantly drunk, and was barely able to spin coherent sentences; he barely even recognized me. With these circumstances in mind, it is not surprising that three homeless acquaintances of my respondents committed suicide over the course of my investigation.

Development since 2000: Signs for Improvement?

One reason why some of the respondents with whom I stayed in touch beyond the one-year study eventually succeeded may very well be the economic recovery Berlin and most German cities experienced over the past decade. In that time, we have witnessed an overall decline or at least stabilization in homelessness in Berlin and nationwide. The number of homeless welfare recipients tracked by Berlin's Senate administration declined steadily from a high of more than 11,000 in 1997 to approximately 6,500 in 2004, the last year for which official numbers have been released; the number of homeless seems to have held steady since then (Abgeordnetenhaus von Berlin 2008; Senatsverwaltung für Gesundheit und Soziales 2004). The decline was accompanied by a decline in the percentage of unemployed people across the city, from a peak of 21 percent in 2004 to less than 14 percent in 2010 (Abgeordnetenhaus von Berlin 1999; Amt für Statistik Berlin-Brandenburg 2011, 16). The market recovery also affected the supply of affordable housing, which is perhaps greater in Berlin than in any other large German city, as I explain in more detail later in this chapter. We can consequently conclude that market fluctuations and especially the supply of affordable housing and regular social insurance–based employment are key factors in facilitating or hindering homeless people's chances to access local housing and labor markets, explaining why homelessness became so prevalent in the first decade following unification.

Such potentially positive developments notwithstanding, it is important to acknowledge that the number of homeless people is still very high. Moreover, even formerly homeless people who have managed to stabilize their situations are in danger of experiencing a recurrence of homelessness should economic and fiscal circumstances worsen again (which has not happened, as of 2012). In addition, the German government has made a significant step toward implementing U.S.-style social policy reforms, which, as I argue earlier, should be viewed very critically, as they remain largely incapable of meeting homeless people's complex needs.

To conclude this chapter, I first synthesize the results from the Berlin study, proposing a model of market exclusion that shows how and why many homeless people remain unsuccessful. Second, I discuss these findings from a comparative perspective, with particular emphasis on recent changes in Germany's welfare system and why, despite the country's economic recovery, the ultimate verdict on the success or failure of German-style workfare still remains to be seen.

Market Exclusion: Welfare State as Facilitator or Barrier to Exit?

Figure 5.1 illustrates the trajectory of market exclusion by depicting homeless people's long-term strategies to enter or reenter local housing and labor markets; welfare deficiencies of insufficient referrals and bureaucratic fragmentation; and, ultimately, substantial barriers to entering labor and housing markets.

The figure shows explicit welfare-state deficiencies to be of particular importance in explaining people's lack of success. Most alarming, perhaps, is the finding that neither local welfare nor labor offices provided viable job or housing leads, although they did provide much-needed income support and shelter and, where exit was achieved, long-term income and housing support. More promising were services provided by the third sector of nonprofit service providers, which in Berlin, unlike in Los Angeles, is still almost exclusively funded through public means.

In this context, we notice substantial differences between Berlin and Los Angeles, with different implications for people's experience of homelessness. As postulated by welfare regime theory, the U.S. liberal welfare regime is less regulated, making employment more accessible, while Germany's more rigid and conservative regime is more concerned with maintaining the status quo. So-called insiders, participants of Germany's social insurance system, enjoy excellent social protection, whereas so-called outsiders, including the homeless, find themselves increasingly and sometimes permanently excluded from the formal economy, entrenched in and dependent on welfare as their life circumstances

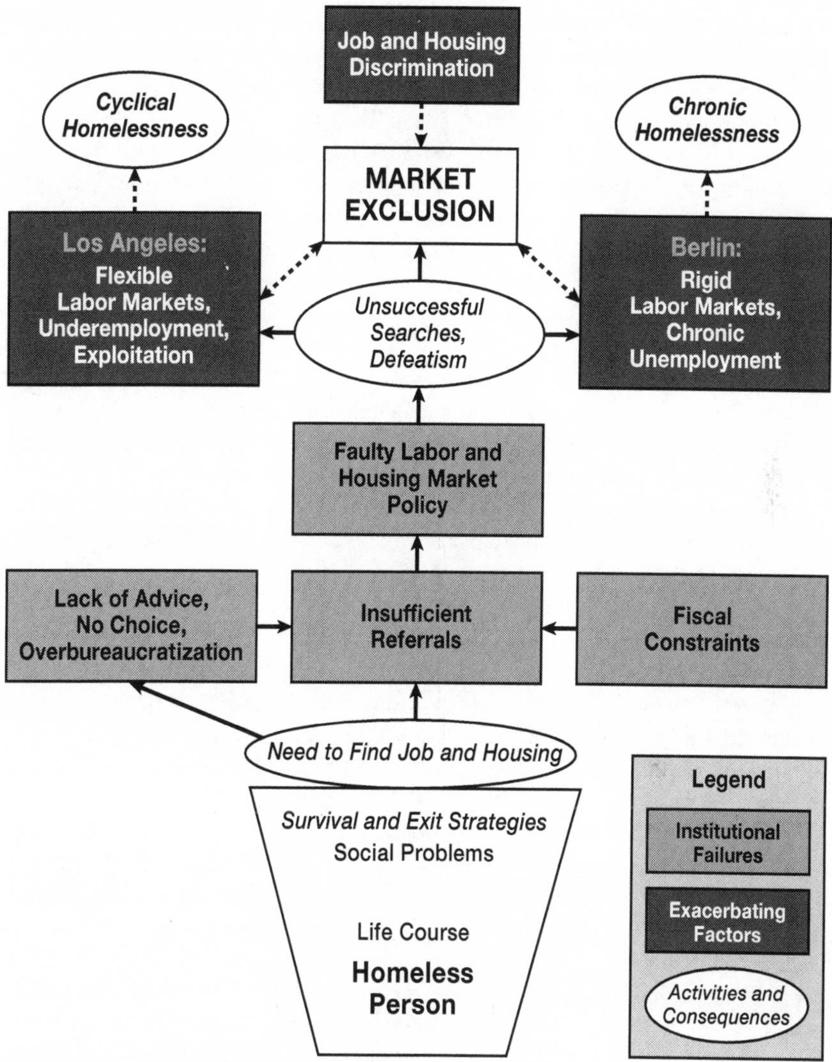

FIGURE 5.1 Model of Market Exclusion

deteriorate to the point of hopelessness. The often-inevitable result is long-term homelessness that comes with great personal and cumulative fiscal costs.

Compared with Berlin, Los Angeles and other U.S. cities have labor and housing markets that are much more vulnerable to market fluctuations, resulting, in many cases, in more cyclical forms of homelessness that mimic the ebb and flow of the local economy yet leave the homeless permanently at the margins of the local labor market, with few chances to truly improve their lot. The concern arises regarding whether recent neoliberal inroads inherent in Germany's

2005 Hartz IV reforms have similarly detrimental effects on homeless people. Although we still lack conclusive evidence on the impact of Hartz IV on homeless people and their life chances, we can surmise from U.S. insights that the workfare policies undercutting the social insurance system will do little to improve the lot of homeless people. Although they may now find jobs more easily, in large part because of the new low-wage sector that the German welfare legislation helped facilitate, such jobs rarely provide a living wage and economic self-sufficiency, as the example of Los Angeles has demonstrated.

Market Exclusion and Welfare Regime Theory: Path Dependence despite Neoliberalism

If neoliberal policies had such detrimental effects on so many homeless people in Los Angeles, why did the implementation of neoliberal workfare policies across Germany in 2005 not have the same adverse consequences in Berlin?

To answer this question, let us first review the nature and extent of Germany's 2005 Hartz IV welfare reforms. Charged by Chancellor Gerhard Schröder, a commission of representatives of employers and unions and others chaired by former Volkswagen executive Peter Hartz proposed policies to reform Germany's apparently ineffective welfare system and its inability to address persistent and increasingly long-term unemployment. Of the four reform proposals that were enacted by the federal coalition government of Social Democrats and Greens in 2000, Hartz IV—fully implemented in 2005—had the most far-reaching implications, involving fundamental changes to the second book of Germany's federal welfare law. Its fundamental philosophy was molded after Bill Clinton's welfare reform and Tony Blair's Third Way, putting a stronger emphasis on the principles of "demanding" and "facilitating" (*fordern* and *fördern*), which mandate labor market participation and impose stronger sanctions for noncompliance. Administratively, Hartz IV policy streamlines the previously separate entities of welfare offices and labor offices into one bureaucracy that maintains local "job centers" and employs a more customer-oriented approach, in which caseworker and client mutually develop a service plan. In terms of benefits, previously staggered income provisions of unemployment assistance (63 percent of previous income for one year), unemployment compensation (53 percent of previous income for two years), and social assistance (fixed amount, paid as long as need is documented) have been consolidated into two principal benefits. Unemployment Assistance I remains tied to previous employment income and is granted for one year. After that, unsuccessful job searchers and all those unable to work receive Unemployment Assistance II, which provides monthly cash benefits at roughly the same level as the previous social assistance. This measure, rather suddenly and without any differentiation among recipients, moved more than one million recipients of nominally higher unemployment compensation into the pool of *Hartz-empfänger*, the German nickname for the 4.9 million recipients of

Unemployment Assistance II in 2009, 438,000 of them in Berlin alone (Proksch 2011, 21).

The exact implications of these rather drastic changes remain to be studied in more detail. From some evaluative studies (Busch-Geertsema and Evers 2006), recent accounts by former respondents, and a critical analysis of the impact of workfare on homeless people in the United States (where it was instituted much earlier), we can surmise potentially positive and negative implications. The service consolidation and stated improvements in client-caseworker relationships are, clearly, positive departures that address some chief concerns my respondents expressed in 1998. The lack of transparency and the omnipresent problem of having to adhere to separate sets of guidelines had made homeless people's short- and long-term efforts to survive and overcome homelessness more difficult. Whether and to what extent more client-oriented approaches have really come to fruition are different questions. The experiences of those respondents with whom I have maintained contact suggest that, ultimately, relatively little has changed, as the atmosphere and helpfulness of overworked, underfunded, and understaffed job centers remain problematic. Moreover, the service consolidation, although undoubtedly needed, does not necessarily overcome coordination deficits with other public administrative entities, including health-care providers, substance-abuse counselors, the criminal justice system, or myriad nonprofit service providers. Therefore, the capacity of caseworkers at the job centers to assist people with multiple problems and to make cross-agency decisions still remains relatively limited.

More important, perhaps, is that some of the more stringent regulations and the now universally low benefit levels are likely to cause their own problems. First, many unemployed homeless people will now experience a more sudden (after one year) and drastic decrease in income, which already had been a major problem for the six respondents who were forced to make this transition after three years and who had difficulties adjusting to life with half their previous incomes. Benefit levels for single adults in 1998 were already perceived to be much too low, even by people without expensive addiction problems. Second, the more stringent work requirements will likely not suit homeless people, the often-complex personal problems they have, and the low or declining human capital they possess. As my research clearly shows, homeless people face particularly severe obstacles to entering the labor market, and more mandates to do so are unlikely to enhance their chances for success (see also Busch-Geertsema 2008).

In light of such reforms and the likely problems they may pose for homeless people, we have reason to assume that Berlin and Germany would experience negative outcomes similar to those witnessed in the United States, where the numbers of working poor and ultimately marginalized and homeless people have increased substantially, especially in the wake of the 2008–2009 global recession. That, however, has not happened. On the contrary, the number of homeless people in Berlin and elsewhere in Germany has been steadily declining from its peak in 1997 (Abgeordnetenhaus von Berlin 2008; BAG Wohnungslosenhilfe 2001; Senatsverwaltung für Gesundheit, Soziales und Verbraucherschutz 2002). Why the number has declined and why the recent implementation of workfare still needs to be viewed with caution are discussed next.

Declining Homeless Numbers despite Neoliberal Reforms?

Although we lack conclusive evidence for the ultimate impact of the Hartz reforms on homelessness, most experts concur that two fundamental reasons explains the declining numbers of homeless people in Germany and Berlin. For one, housing markets have slackened after initial waves of speculation and rental hikes following unification, especially in Berlin. Given that the projected population increase and rental market demands did not materialize—Berlin actually experienced a net loss in population—rental markets readjusted and eventually stabilized, providing a better supply of affordable housing, especially in the now-renovated apartment buildings of former East Berlin (Amt für Statistik Berlin-Brandenburg 2011). This trend started in the late 1990s and may, in fact, have abetted my respondents' efforts in finding regular rental apartments or shared housing opportunities at the time of the investigation and, presumably, since then.

A second reason is that workfare policies primarily pertain to income and reintegrative labor market policies and not to the entirety of Germany's social safety net. Specific legislation pertaining to homelessness inscribed in Germany's statutory federal Social Welfare Act—including, among many other provisions, eviction prevention, provisions for case-management, or high-quality service provisions—remains unaffected by the Hartz provisions. If anything, some provisions, especially those allowing preventive and proactive measures, have been improved, in large part due to lobbying by national and local homeless advocacy organizations (BAG Wohnungslosenhilfe 2010; AK Wohnungsnot 2007). In Berlin, considerable progress has been made in improving service and, by extension, market access for homeless and other marginalized groups. Recent revisions of Germany's Social Welfare Act have been attributed to improved usage of proactive and preventive public policy instruments, often in collaboration with the nonprofit sector of secular and religious service and shelter providers.

A particularly good example of a local homeless policy initiative originating in the mid-1990s in Berlin is the so-called protected market segment (*geschütztes Marktsegment*). After some experimentation and over time, the program singlehandedly was responsible for providing more than nine thousand people with affordable housing by mandating builders and developers to allocate 20 percent of newly available housing to participants of the *geschütztes Marktsegment* program. Half the beneficiaries were people who were already homeless, whereas the other half constituted cases of eviction prevention. In such fashion, a great number of potential cases of homelessness were prevented while simultaneously providing reintegrative chances for previously homeless people (Mühlich-Klinger 2010).

The declining numbers of officially homeless people have further allowed local administrators to make better use of mid- and high-level shelters and to circumvent exploitative commercial-shelter providers. This development alone will help immensely with facilitating people's exit from homelessness by effectively combating the literal warehousing of homeless people into the much-dreaded and unhelpful "lice pensions." Not only that, the experiences of my respondents suggest that the knowledgeable and helpful social workers on the premises of these "better" shelters and service providers may be more likely to provide the case-based interventions necessary to facilitate a lasting exit from homelessness.

All Clear in Berlin? Hartz, Homelessness, and the Life Course

Although there is some reason for optimism in light of declining homeless numbers and improved market conditions as of late, there are also compelling reasons to view the current developments in Berlin with caution, especially knowing that the favorable economic climate is not going to last. Germany may have weathered the 2008–2009 global recession and first banking crisis very well, but it remains to be seen what the implications of the current (2011–2012) European debt crisis will be on the national economy and on local labor markets.

Will the slimmed-down, workfarist local welfare state be able to absorb increasing demands in the next economic down cycle? This question is particularly pressing in light of the financial debt crisis in the southern European Union member states during 2010–2011. Given that Germany, once more, will likely have to foot a substantial portion of the bill associated with regional recovery, it is also likely that the German economy will experience a downturn with likely severe fiscal implications. Although the true economic implications of the European fiscal crisis are yet unknown, Berlin has to look no further than at its own recent economic history to find reasons to view the conditions with caution and concern.

If Berlin's own experiences during the chaotic post-unification years and insights from U.S. cities, such as Los Angeles, are any indication, we have reason to assume that market exclusion along with the previously discussed legal and service exclusions will proliferate again if, as in the post-unification years, the demand for service cannot be met with an adequate supply. During economic crisis and restructuring periods, the local welfare state will have neither the means nor the logistics to deal with a drastic increase in demand for services and most certainly will not possess the means to facilitate access in contested labor markets. As a result of declining public revenue and concurrent public debt (currently 50 billion euros/$60 billion for Berlin alone!), vital programs will likely face cuts, and commercial shelter providers will jump in to fill the void, again making substantial profits on the backs of the homeless. And considering that the urban fiscal crisis in Berlin at this time is even more substantial than during the post-unification years, we already have a precondition that might—out of necessity perhaps—open the doors for further U.S.-style neoliberal welfare-state restructuring and further implementation of roll-out neoliberalism, to use Neil Brenner and Nik Theodore's (2002) term. The "specter of neoliberalism" thus continues to loom over Germany and its new capital, Berlin.

It is further important to consider the various life-course trajectories, as they affect people's experiences with any form of exclusion differently. It is clear, for instance, that homeless people with more-regular life courses are likely to benefit from enhanced market access before other groups, simply because they often still possess higher extents of human and social capital. People with more-irregular life courses have been shown to be substantially less successful and to experience market exclusion more harshly, which leaves them largely outside the formal economy, more likely to engage in shadow work and subject to displacement and persecution in the process. Homeless people are well aware of their economic disadvantages in fiercely competitive urban labor markets. Many feel that they are, ultimately, not needed in the local economy. In an informal gathering with three previously East German shelter residents, Det, a former member of the Communist Party, provided me with a political explanation:

> I can finally use my Marxist training [laughs]. We are the "Industrial Reserve Army," that is what we are! You know what that is, right? Needed when the economy does well, redundant otherwise. Good old Karl was right! (Det, age 49, older regular life course, informal conversation, May 4, 1998)

The industrial reserve army may, indeed, be a fitting metaphor to conclude this chapter on market exclusion. The homeless are likely to be the ones who find themselves unneeded and unwanted in the formal economy and disposable in the low-wage service sector that workfare facilitates, again with adverse impacts on their immediate and long-term life situations. Such lack of success particularly affects those people with more-regular life courses and their painful memories of a better past.

It should be fairly clear by now that the three trajectories of exclusion—legal, service, and market—I describe in the previous three chapters interrelate and reinforce one another. How these factors work together, how public policy and geography play crucial roles in creating and reinforcing exclusion, and how to overcome such exclusions are discussed in the following chapter.

6

Sociospatial Exclusion of Homeless People

Comparative Perspective

The foregoing empirical chapters provide evidence for three distinct yet interrelated trajectories of exclusion that pertain to homeless people's immediate survival strategies to generate income (legal exclusion) and find shelter and housing (service exclusion) as well as their long-term exit strategies to find residential stability and economic self-sufficiency (market exclusion). In this concluding chapter, I use the evidence from the previous chapters to propose a model of sociospatial exclusion, explain how it works, apply it to important contemporary theoretical discussions, and suggest ways to surmount such exclusion.

Specifically, I show how sociospatial exclusion, despite some variation across and within countries and their underlying welfare regimes at different administrative levels, works surprisingly similarly in Berlin and Los Angeles. To showcase the usefulness of this model and account for such variations, I discuss sociospatial exclusion in the context of welfare regime theory, supporting the prevalent notion that Germany's system remains superior to that of the United States but cautioning that local welfare deficiencies often aggravate rather than solve homeless people's problems, just as in Los Angeles. I further demonstrate that such local problems are determined by the interplay of the economic and social geographies, the geographies of service and shelter provision, and the geographies of punitive exclusionary policies that underlie sociospatial exclusion. Yet whether and to what extent any of the trajectories of sociospatial exclusion affect homeless people is largely dependent on their life courses, which, given the wide variations in experiences, expectations, and skills, poses a tremendous challenge to proactive service provision. In the conclusion of this chapter, I propose possible solutions to overcome sociospatial exclusion, paying particular attention to national and local variations and, most important perhaps, to the issue of feasibility in times of economic crisis, fiscal constraints, and austerity measures.

Explaining Sociospatial Exclusion

To explain how and why homeless people in Berlin and Los Angeles, and arguably in other cities in Germany and the United States, face such tremendous difficulties overcoming homelessness, I combine the previously discussed trajectories of legal, service, and market exclusion into one coherent model of sociospatial exclusion (Fig. 6.1). This model indicates clearly that a number of welfare

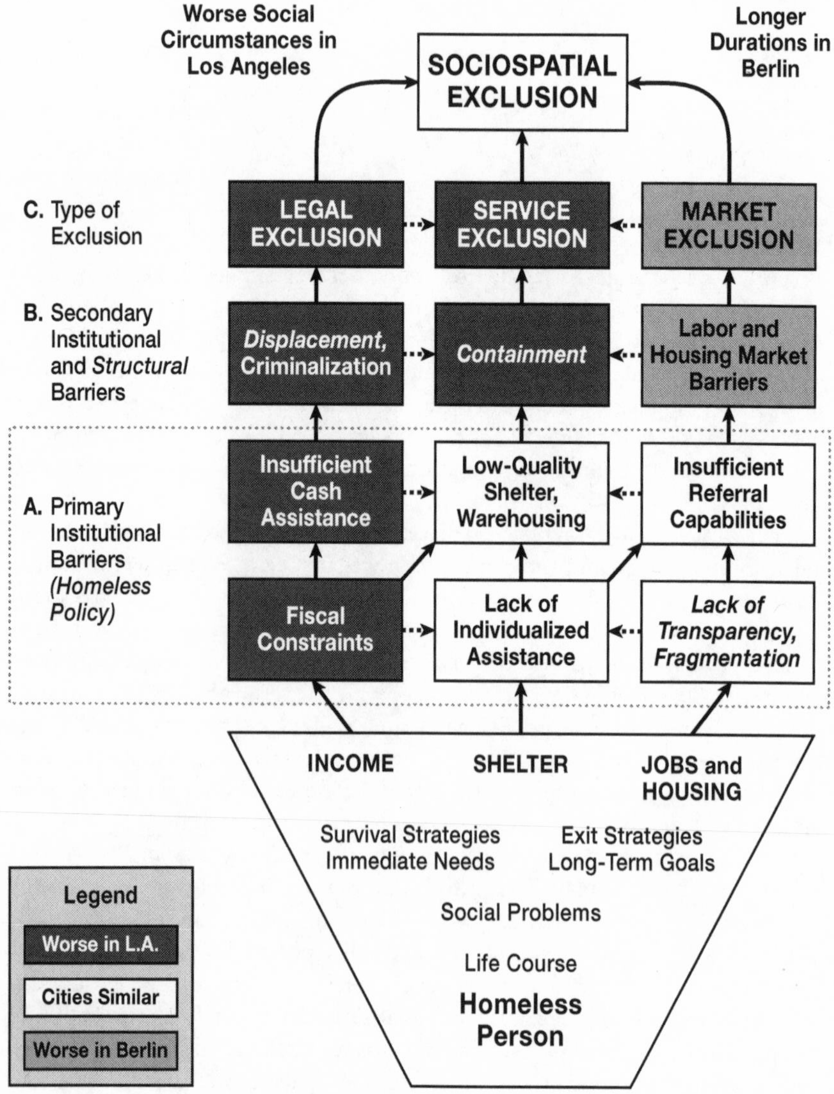

FIGURE 6.1 Model of Sociospatial Exclusion

state and service delivery problems at the local scale underlie and reinforce the social and, as I discuss in more detail later, spatial exclusion homeless people experience on their quest to stabilize and ideally to optimize their life circumstances and (using Leisering and Leibfried's [1999] terminology) their poverty management.

The model also indicates tentatively how these forms of exclusion compare internationally, suggesting that ultimately legal and service exclusion tend to be more pronounced in Los Angeles simply because of its comparatively much-weaker welfare infrastructure and the more-contested, polarized, and revanchist nature of urban space in U.S. cities. Market exclusion, on the other hand, tends to be more severe in Berlin for reasons associated with Germany's more-rigid and regulated economic system, despite recent neoliberal reforms. To provide more evidence for these findings, in the next section I situate this model of sociospatial exclusion in important theoretical debates, beginning by discussing the relevance of these findings in the context of comparative international social policy analyses and welfare regime theory.

Sociospatial Exclusion and Welfare Regime Theory

At face value, the experiences of the twenty-eight respondents seem to confirm a number of key findings of welfare regime theory when comparing the impact of public policy on homelessness in the liberal U.S. welfare regime with the conservative or corporatist German regime. Most notably, all respondents faced tremendous difficulties accessing markets, especially Germany's highly regulated labor market. True to welfare regime theory, the corporatist German system thereby fosters an increasingly persistent cleavage between insiders and outsiders, and homeless people, clearly, belong in the latter category. Welfare regime theory also proves useful by accounting for social disaffiliation in that many homeless either have low social capital and family ties to begin with or, over time and with service exclusion, tend to lose such valuable contacts. Figure 6.2 returns to the initial conceptual framework regarding the interplay between internal and external determinants of exit from which these deliberations began, but it adds the components of sociospatial exclusion—legal, service, and market exclusion—into the mix and identifies more explicitly the key institutional barriers to exit reported in this study and confirmed by a number of U.S. studies.

The Market: Market Exclusion, Regulation, and Diminishing Human Capital

Market barriers are clearly the main impediment for homeless job and housing seekers in Germany. The quest to (re)access highly regulated and persistently tight urban labor markets, fiercely protected by insiders, was one of the most-discouraging experiences the respondents in the Berlin study faced. In this context, it did not seem to matter how much human capital respondents possessed

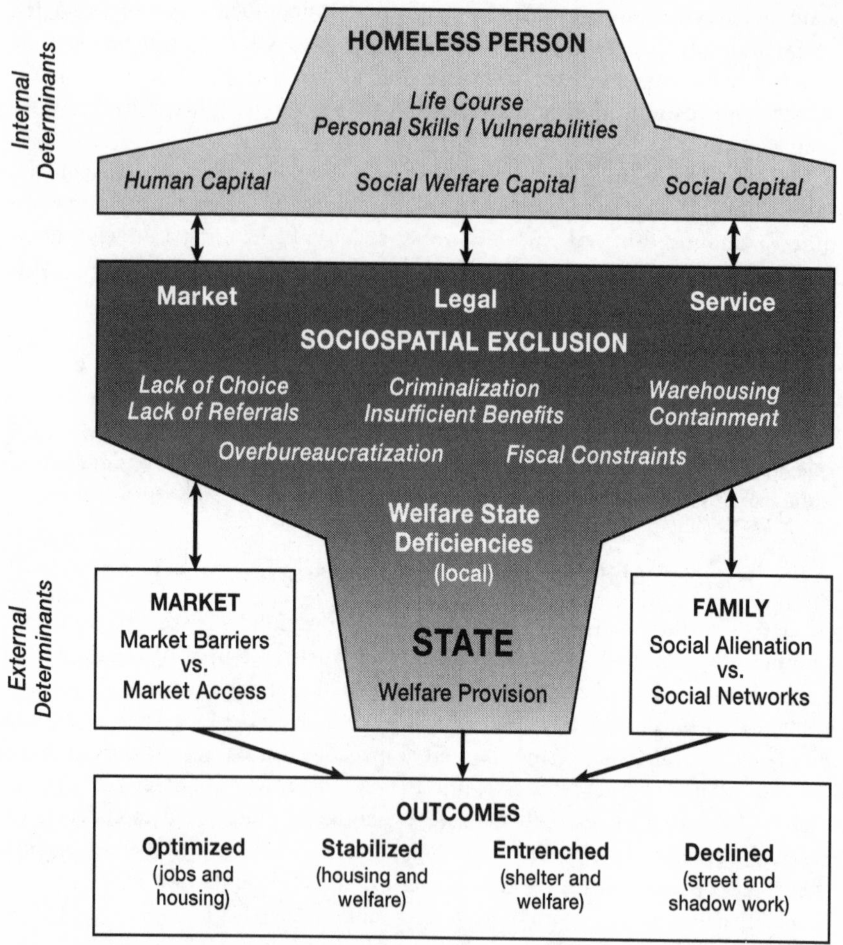

FIGURE 6.2 Exit from Homelessness in the Context of the Welfare Regime

or how strong their desire to find jobs was. The fact that only four respondents found jobs—all of them subsidized—speaks volumes. Considering the persistently high unemployment and the apparent ineffectiveness of existing labor-market policies, it is not surprising that German lawmakers—headed by Chancellor Gerhard Schröder's SPD/Green coalition government—began looking for alternative solutions molded after Bill Clinton's welfare reform and Tony Blair's Third Way in Britain in the late 1990s. The political success of such measures consequently facilitated the Hartz IV reforms that introduced workfare and imposed more stringent regulations, as I discuss in Chapter 5. Whether such measures are going to work for homeless people with their diminishing human capital remains questionable. I have discussed how the homeless in Los Angeles may find low-income jobs more easily yet remain impoverished and subject to immediate layoffs once the local economy contracts again, and how Berlin's own experiences in the aftermath of unification provided the empirical basis for this study. Throughout most of the 1990s, the local welfare state was simply unprepared for the onslaught of demand for homeless services and consequently provided the insufficient or substandard service that underlies sociospatial exclusion.

Access to housing markets, on the other hand, was generally more successful; much of this success can be attributed to self-initiative and social networks, thereby providing a link to the important welfare dimension of family.

The Family: Social Networks and Social Capital

It is telling that respondents who were able to maintain their social capital (kinship support and other social networks) were more likely to find housing. Shelter and service exclusion, most notably the omnipresent practice of "warehousing" homeless people into low-quality shelters, is one important reason why many older respondents with regular life courses and preexisting social networks in their home districts experienced a deterioration in such relations or decided, out of shame, to discontinue their contact with family, friends, and acquaintances. For those respondents who either maintained or created new relations, such social networks often proved instrumental in the quest for acceptable housing solutions. In a few cases, social connections to previous employers also allowed for temporary employment opportunities. Ultimately, however, welfare state deficiencies—most notably substandard shelter and service provision—became a feature of sociospatial exclusion in Berlin, albeit within a more-developed welfare system.

The State: Facilitator of or Barrier to Exiting Homelessness?

A coherent synthesis of the state's impact on homeless people's immediate life circumstances, their quest to generate income and obtain shelter, and their long-term objectives to find housing and employment reveals mixed results. If we apply the parameters of successful welfare state intervention commonly used in comparative social policy analyses, we find support for the assumption about the superiority of the conservative/corporatist German system (Goodin et al. 1999; Huber and Stephens 2001). Yet when looking at the experiences of homeless people on the ground, we notice substantial welfare state deficiencies at the local scale that often reinforce sociospatial exclusion.

To begin making sense of this contradiction, let us consider the apparent advantages of the German system, which, de jure, provides homeless people with the same social rights as any resident with documented need, resulting in substantially greater coverage and more-extensive benefits when compared with the options for homeless people in Los Angeles. Every respondent in the Berlin study (with delays in the case of some migrants) gained access to the local welfare state and received services that are prescribed by Germany's extensive federal welfare legislation. First, all respondents were issued cash assistance, which was, despite lower overall costs of living in Berlin, almost double the commonly available welfare payment in Los Angeles. Second, all respondents were quickly referred to shelters, and most were able to continue accessing previous medical care or to make new arrangements. Third, in accordance with Germany's welfare principle of subsidiarity, the local welfare administration delegated most of the actual service and shelter provision to nonprofit organizations and, if need arises, to commercial providers. The key difference from U.S. cities is that the local government provides almost all the funding for such projects. Finally, through labor and welfare offices (since 2005 consolidated into job centers), homeless welfare recipients had access to a range of referral services and educational and job training opportunities.

In that light, it is even more surprising that the German welfare system—exemplified by its new capital, Berlin—appeared so ineffective in helping homeless people move out of homelessness throughout the 1990s and during a time of economic transition. This investigation shows clearly that, all legal parameters of welfare notwithstanding, there were quantitative and qualitative deficiencies in the provision of services to homeless people, especially service provided directly by the welfare state. Virtually all respondents felt that they were merely processed and poorly served by local authorities; over time, this perception reconfirmed their own beliefs that welfare system efforts were a waste of time and they had no chance of exiting homelessness, thus diminishing their self-initiative and hope. The local welfare state, especially the public sector, was therefore largely complicit in the sociospatial exclusion of the respondents, with effects on their short-term life circumstances and their long-term chances to find housing and jobs.

So although the German welfare system may, after all, provide its citizens with more social rights and services, it is simply not doing enough; worse, it might even exacerbate homeless people's personal circumstances in that insufficient cash assistance might lead to legal exclusion, ineffective and futile job referrals might reinforce market exclusion, and warehousing might help cause the destruction of vital social contacts and thus, indirectly, adversely affect the dimension of family so important to the welfare regime. The quest to decommodify and defamilialize people with multiple social vulnerabilities is therefore only partially successful and not as successful as for welfare recipients without housing problems (see Leisering and Leibfried 1999).

Whether a move further away from the regulatory welfare state toward a more U.S.-style neoliberal policy orientation is going to help or hurt homeless people must be a subject for further research. But if the experiences of homeless people in Los Angeles over the past three decades and the twenty-eight respondents in Berlin during times of economic transition during the 1990s are any indication, the prospects are not good. Los Angeles is most certainly a good test case for the neoliberal approach to homeless and poverty management. True to the welfare regime postulation about the liberal welfare state's putting a prime emphasis on the market, the local welfare state in Los Angeles (and arguably in most other U.S. cities) has moved away from providing direct services to delegating much of the provision to nonprofits, who, by competing for federal, state, and local grants and other private and philanthropic resources, ought to provide accountable, effective, and longitudinal service provisions. Economic reintegration occurs primarily through direct, largely unassisted labor market access, which under positive economic circumstances (the case in late 1990s) allows almost one-quarter of homeless people to rely on wage labor as their primary income. The obvious problem is that such income is often too low for people to afford increasingly expensive (because it is unregulated) urban rental housing. A tremendous gap remains between minimum wages and urban living expenses, which explains why so many working poor are just a paycheck away from homelessness. Worse, by earning incomes slightly above the federal poverty line, such working poor do not even qualify for most rudimentary public assistance programs. And such programs are largely inaccessible to homeless people, because stringent requirements often exclude people without fixed residences from receiving benefits (Wolch and Dinh 2001; DeVertueil 2006; Tepper 2004).

Because such neoliberal welfare state restructuring and its implications for homeless service and shelter delivery are primarily viewed negatively by most commentators, it is only prudent to caution that similar neoliberal inroads in the European context ought to be viewed with skepticism (Wolch and Sommer 1997). And, as I suggest in the previous chapter, the verdict is still out regarding the neoliberal Hartz IV regulations' long-term effects on urban homelessness, but the overall prospects remain better for Germany's homeless vis-à-vis their U.S. counterparts. After all, it must be remembered that any neoliberal inroads in Germany are occurring on the foundation of a comprehensive and tightly woven social safety net, a luxury the United States has never had. The potentially negative ramifications of workfare and the foreseeable lack of success many homeless and formerly homeless people are likely to experience will still be mitigated by a fairly comprehensive system of public and nonprofit service and shelter providers who, unlike their U.S. counterparts, can link individual service provision to a relatively broad catalogue of public policy options and mainstream welfare support. Despite substantial problems and deficiencies in the actual provision of services at the local level, the German system remains, true to welfare regime theory, superior to the U.S. rather residual and highly commodified approach.

Still, with the state largely ineffective, the market largely inaccessible, and family and social network options increasingly depleted, homeless people often have no choice but to resign themselves to their fates and live, often disillusioned, bored, and depressed, in the few places they are allowed to remain, increasingly relying on shadow work to deal with the growing addiction problems fed by the discouraging ambience of shelters and day centers. Urban geography thus becomes another major determinant of homeless people's immediate life circumstances and long-term prospects for overcoming homelessness.

Sociospatial Exclusion and Urban Geography

One clear finding of the Berlin study is that the geographic processes that underlie sociospatial exclusion are similar in German and U.S. cities, although, as I argue, they are not as pronounced in Berlin as in Los Angeles. The example of Berlin shows how, as in the United States, homeless people's daily and periodic activity patterns are affected by different geographies underlying each trajectory of exclusion, which, if overlaid, culminate in sociospatial exclusion, as Figure 6.3 shows. Specifically, the geographies of legal exclusion (shown by arrows that vary in thickness, depending on the number of permanent bans issued in a particular place) show how homeless people are deliberately excluded from the central city and other prime urban spaces while being contained in service agglomerations right outside the urban center (illustrated by circles that indicate either service/shelter agglomerations or the location of large day centers). Such geographies of shelter and service distribution clearly correspond with the geographies of market exclusion (darker shades in background color indicate lower social indices and higher extents of market exclusion). It is consequently perhaps not surprising that Berlin's four second-order service agglomerations are all located within the 10 (out of 338) spatial statistical units with the lowest social indices (Hermann, Imme, and Meinlschmidt 1998).

The finding that homeless people's exit chances are largely determined by multiple overlapping and interrelated geographies has important theoretical implications. Most important, perhaps, it warrants attention to processes of exclusion beyond the current academic preoccupation with legal exclusion and, more broadly, the "right to the city" debates that have come to dominate the discourse. As Geoffrey DeVerteuil, Jon May, and I (2009) have argued elsewhere, it is imperative to expand the focus of exclusion beyond criminalization and displacement. After all, most of my respondents indicated that harassment by the police and the occasional displacement was, all things considered and despite the frequent harshness and illegality of such measures, one of their lesser problems. Much more important to them was their ongoing lack of success in the marketplace and, for older respondents, their warehousing into dilapidated facilities with all their detrimental social effects.

And although, undoubtedly, the geographies of sociospatial exclusion are configured similarly in Berlin and U.S. cities in that homeless people find themselves excluded from prime urban spaces, contained in service ghettos, and excluded from market opportunities, a number of important differences exist, most notably that even the most deprived urban quarters in Berlin do not resemble North American ghettos, being less affected by extreme poverty, hypersegregation, disinvestment, and neglect (Veith and Sambale 1999).

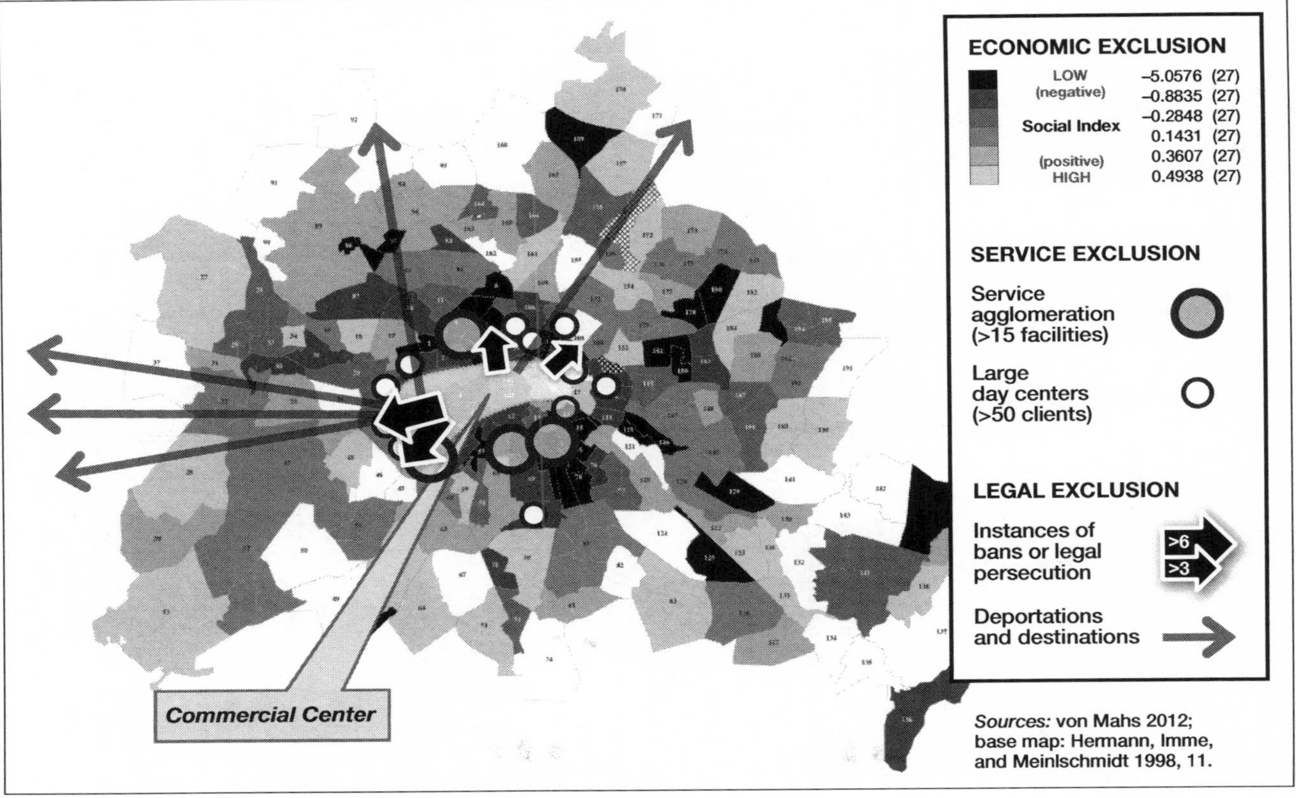

FIGURE 6.3 Sociospatial Exclusion in Berlin

A second difference is that, despite evidence of inequitable urban shelter and service distributions, such exclusion in Berlin is less the result of exclusionary community attitudes and NIMBYism than of rather simple cost calculations—the need to find locations with affordable rents. This is a clear difference from Los Angeles, where NIMBY battles to exclude homeless service facilities are raging fiercely; in Berlin, I found very little if any evidence for deliberate attempts by communities to prevent the location of homeless service facilities in their neighborhoods (Dear 1992; Dear and von Mahs 1995; Sambale and Veith 1998).

A third difference relates to access to urban spaces. Berlin has a tremendous advantage over the United States and even some other European cities: one of the most extensive public-transit systems, making even the most deprived neighborhood in Berlin easily accessible. The existence of public transit also works to mitigate the effects of spatial mismatch between the location of shelter or service and that of potential housing and job opportunities. Although Los Angeles and most other sprawling U.S. Sun Belt cities (and to a lesser extent, East Coast and Rust Belt cities) are hampered by the lack of effective public transit, Berlin's homeless face few obstacles in reaching urban destinations pertinent to job and housing searches.

Although the geography reinforces the multiple structural and institutional constraints and thus serves as a justification for exclusion, the experience of such exclusion and of the spaces associated with it (for example, locations of displacements, the community context of a shelter), and the impact they have on individuals and their life chances, are subject to great variations. What may be an extremely deprived, exclusionary, and constricting place for some people may, in fact, be quite agreeable to others. One particularly insightful way to differentiate such experiences is to look at people's life courses and examine from that viewpoint how policy and service provision affects outcomes.

Sociospatial Exclusion and the Life Course

How sociospatial exclusion and lack of success are ultimately "experienced" is, as I show, likely to be related to people's life-course trajectories and their inherent differences. Although it is clear that only twenty-eight cases cannot reveal replicable patterns, we see that the extent of regularity in one's life, represented by higher amounts of human and social capital, generally implies less experience of sociospatial exclusion but more daunting consequences of certain aspects of exclusion, most notably service and market exclusion. Conversely, some of the younger people and people with a lesser extent of "regularity" and greater isolation and social problems tended to experience sociospatial exclusion (especially legal exclusion) more frequently, yet they often remained less affected by such exclusion in psychological terms.

The life course consequently also matters when it comes to the impact of public policy intervention on homeless people's life chances. Respondents with more-regular life courses experienced legal exclusion less frequently and were more often able to overcome market exclusion than people with comparatively less-regular life courses, especially younger respondents with deviant and transient life courses. The latter were more likely to be underserved and, as the severity of social problems escalated, increasingly entrenched.

One factor that seemed to have a particular effect on older homeless people with regular life courses and preexisting social networks was service exclusion. Regardless of the quality provided, those respondents were most likely to perceive the situation as unacceptable and degrading, which, as I explain in Chapter 4, resulted in self-isolation and the gradual demise of their nonhomeless social networks. People without preexisting social networks and with less social capital, and thus lacking the same kind of reference point, were less affected by service exclusion; in these cases, the extent of exclusion depended on the type of shelter. Although high- and mid-level shelters (e.g., Wohnheim Trachenbergring) were viewed as rather agreeable interim housing solutions, low-quality shelters—the majority of shelter offerings in the late 1990s—were unanimously viewed as unacceptable shelter options that, if anything, exacerbated people's personal problems.

Ultimately, homeless people with transient and with deviant life courses are, as we have suspected, the groups most likely to experience all three trajectories at the same time. They are more likely to have exacerbating problems, less likely to possess local social capital, more likely to have low human capital, and, predictably perhaps, least likely to succeed.

An awareness of people's life courses and paying attention to their individually quite distinct needs and expectations consequently ought to be a guiding principle in the provision of effective, ideally proactive policy and service intervention. The Berlin study, without a doubt, shows that case-based, individualized interventions and collaboratively developed and individually tailored service plans are key for most successful respondents. Three out of four cases of optimized poverty management and more than half the respondents who at least stabilized their situations owed their success to such service interventions. Conversely, overly regimented, bureaucratic, and rigid approaches often practiced by mainstream social welfare agencies failed to directly facilitate homeless people's exits. The key to successful service intervention, therefore, is attention to the individual person in need of shelter, employment, and a range of other services. The upcoming discussion of policy intervention starts with the premise that the local welfare state, regardless of the extent of intervention, fails to effectively use the most important resources to end homelessness—the homeless themselves.

Overcoming Sociospatial Exclusion

Overcoming sociospatial exclusion is a considerable challenge, in large part because it involves the complicated interplay between individuals and their distinct problems and myriad public, voluntary, and private entities that, more often than not, operate independently from one another and pursue different objectives. So aside from the aforementioned centrality of homeless people's agency, a main challenge involves the more-timely use of case management, service and policy coordination, and communication among all these entities.

In this context, German homeless people have a distinct advantage, because provisions in federal welfare law promote the use of case-based interventions and more interventionist services (according to §72 BSHG). More recent changes contained in the much-contested Hartz IV reforms may actually increase the use of more-individualized assistance in the newly consolidated job centers, where case managers assist their clients with reentering housing and labor markets in more collaborative fashion by creating individualized service plans. Whether such change in rhetoric and practice will really materialize, resulting in better chances for homeless recipients of the new and largely insufficient Unemployment Assistance II payments, remains an open question. Because of the uncertainty, it is crucial that innovative grassroots organizations continue to serve as messengers to help overcome the stigma that often contributes to poor service provision and prevents homeless people's integration. In this area, much can be learned from the United States, where, out of necessity perhaps, more grassroots efforts challenge the status quo in an attempt to improve the public image of homeless people and their struggles.

The Three Cs of Reform: Case Management, Communication, and Coordination

Although comprehensive solutions, including increasing benefit levels and funding for better shelter and service facilities, are certainly desirable, reform in both countries has obvious limits. Any broader reform consideration, especially local solutions, must be prefaced with a sobering reality: Under current political and particularly fiscal circumstances, it is unlikely—unfeasible, even—that social welfare spending and funding for homeless services will substantially increase anytime soon. Berlin, Los Angeles, and, for that matter, most large German and U.S. cities have acquired substantial public debt and are facing perennial budget woes. Under such fiscal conditions, it is simply unlikely that service catering to an already highly stigmatized group could garner the local political and business support necessary to increase service provision, cash assistance, or other benefits, which the homeless already perceived as too low during the 1990s. Consequently, it is imperative to develop pragmatic and cost-effective solutions that involve the clients themselves early in the decision-making process.

There is no doubt that the main policy implication of the study—advocating for better case management, including case-based, concerted social work intervention and collaborative approaches—is not new. In fact, dozens of studies call for more-individualized assistance and dozens of evaluative reports emphasize and recommend client-based solutions. Such collaborative solutions are more likely to be successful simply because they involve the homeless themselves, allowing them to describe their problems and state their needs and goals. Social workers, especially those trained for and experienced in working with such stigmatized groups, can then use their knowledge and creativity to develop feasible plans with their clients that ideally prevent homelessness or, should that fail, at least facilitate rapid reentry before personal circumstances can deteriorate any further.

To promote more-effective case management, it is necessary—through communication—to coordinate and consolidate service options so they can be tailored to each homeless person individually. Perhaps the biggest challenge that caseworkers dealing with the homeless face in most countries pertains to the lack of coordination among the various entities involved in the actual service provision and the tremendous costs and delays associated with administrative fragmentation. Caseworkers and service providers in Germany, the United States, and arguably any industrialized nation-state have experienced the difficulty of facilitating cross-agency collaboration and communication when several public administrative and nonprofit entities are involved (Abgeordnetenhaus von Berlin 1999). One promising method for improving communication among different agencies is through the use of information technology. Some U.S. municipalities may in fact be leading the charge, having made great strides in either piloting or implementing Homeless Service Management Information Systems (HSMIS; for New York City and Philadelphia, see Culhane and Smith 1997). The idea behind HSMIS is to create a user-friendly computer interface that allows caseworkers and other authorized people involved in the provision of services to access a variety of data and information sources pertinent to helping homeless people. Such systems provide instantaneous access to housing and labor market data, service and shelter options, income support, and other relevant social programs. Access to such information allows caseworkers and homeless people to immediately explore up-to-date service options and tailor individualized service plans. In such fashion, the typical information deficits and delays are quickly surmounted, information can be readily shared, and a coherent, comprehensive, and chronological client data file and service record can be created over time and shared among relevant entities. The latter may additionally serve the purpose of research and evaluation of service options. Although complicated legal issues surrounding privacy and social control must be carefully addressed, this step alone would correct a number of welfare state deficiencies that the respondents identified during my investigations, including bureaucratic fragmentation, lack of individualized assistance and choice, and lack of referral capabilities.

Perhaps the most immediate reform objective and a prerequisite for the success of other policy and reform proposals is to continue working on destigmatizing homelessness by communicating with and informing the public about this persistent social problem and by clearing up many of the misconceptions that underlie the public image of homeless people. As long as the homeless are commonly perceived as some amorphous group of people who have brought this predicament on themselves by their own choices, politicians will find reason to pursue minimalist interventions and increasingly punitive approaches. After all, if the homeless themselves are to blame, why increase assistance when such funds might be better used to serve other, more deserving groups? Likewise, why should culpable people who choose to engage in detrimental behaviors be permitted in commercially important places?

By portraying homeless people as knowledgeable agents, this study—like many that have come before it—provides ample evidence that homeless people cannot simply be blamed for their situations and that, lacking alternatives, they must perform all private functions under constant public scrutiny; rather, they find themselves surrounded by broader structural and institutional constraints over which they have little or no control. They also cannot be blamed for having to use public and semipublic spaces to make ends meet and get through their days. The concept of sociospatial exclusion allows us to understand and conceptualize this broader context of homeless people's experiences with legal and service exclusion and their difficulties, through market exclusion, achieving reentry into mainstream society. Such understanding of the complicated nature of homeless people's problems and the barriers they face may help show homeless people as they really are: impoverished citizens down on their luck, with more-complex social problems than most people.

Setting the record straight about homeless people and the adverse circumstances that surround their lives, however, cannot be accomplished through academic studies alone. In the United States, to a much greater extent than in Germany and Berlin, we find numerous highly innovative grassroots organizations whose purpose is to inform, advocate, and mobilize. Local grassroots organizations and their advocacy allies at any level work tirelessly to change stereotypical notions of homelessness and homeless people. In my years living and working in Los Angeles, Philadelphia, and New York, I have had the pleasure of working with a number of these organizations, learning about a range of innovative approaches (Dear and von Mahs 1997; von Mahs 2012). Given the success of many of these organizations and the ability of some to grow into multiservice agencies, I believe that German homeless people and their advocates could learn a great deal from the last thirty years of activism in the United States. Although the Mob e.V. is a notable exception with its advocacy and support for homeless vendors, we generally find little in the way of creative, independent grassroots activism that is largely directed and organized by the homeless themselves.

Considering that completely different structural and institutional frameworks are in place in Germany and in the United States, as well as different attitudes toward social welfare and social justice, I separately address the feasibility of implementing these broader changes for Berlin and for Los Angeles as potentially exemplary for both countries. In this cursory outlook, I also consider preexisting institutional and policy frameworks, highlighting particularly successful approaches.

Berlin: Market Inclusion in the Corporatist Welfare Regime

Some of the general improvements noticed in Berlin since 2000, including declining numbers of poor and homeless people and more-favorable market conditions, can be directly attributed to proactive welfare state intervention, which, all things considered, remains much more extensive than in the United States. Germany's recent inroads toward neoliberal practice inherent in the 2005 Hartz IV regulations do address some key concerns of the respondents of this and other studies, as I suggest in Chapter 5. Some of the innovations of these reforms may be advantageous to recipients, most notably the simplification in process and procedure and the consolidation of previously separate, albeit related, entities of labor and welfare administration. Also positive is the reorientation in service philosophy that elevates the client from mere recipient of one-sided service provision to partner in the decision-making process (Stumberger 2005). In addition, a number of local approaches have contributed to declining homeless numbers of late, including the "protected market segment" policy that I discuss in Chapter 5, which has allowed more than nine thousand individuals to either avoid or overcome homelessness and, assisted by other welfare measures, to remain stably housed (Mühlich-Klinger 2010).

Another positive local change that may have assisted many homeless to exit is associated with better shelter provision, as I suggest in Chapter 4. Abetted by declining numbers and the aforementioned slackening of urban rental housing markets in Berlin, administrators were able to increase the proportion of more promising mid-level shelters while discontinuing funding for exploitative commercial-shelter providers (Abgeordnetenhaus von Berlin 1999, 2008). Although no conclusive quantitative data are available regarding the actual effect of better shelter provisions, the experiences of the Berlin respondents suggest that higher-quality shelters provide substantially better exit chances than multiple-occupancy, low-quality shelter facilities that offer no social services and thus, at best, contain people without offering any realistic chances for improvement.

Although the aforementioned steps may have had a positive impact on homeless people's chances to (re)access urban rental housing in Berlin, the prospects of helping homeless people with often low and declining human capital access local labor markets remain relatively grim. Instead, most homeless people will continue to be dependent on welfare payments, especially if they wish to avoid performing informal and often illegal material survival strategies that involve more frequent encounters with legal exclusion. One promising way to facilitate homeless people's labor market access, as my study suggests, is the use of active labor market policies (ALMP) that provide employers with assistance in hiring and paying for new employees. Given homeless people's competitive disadvantage in the local economy (despite substantial declines, unemployment still hovers around 14 percent in Berlin), subsidized work may in fact be one of the few ways to help people reenter the local economy. Yet the fact that two of the three respondents who enjoyed access to such programs lost their jobs again after one year is discouraging. Similarly discouraging is the fact that only two out of the eight younger respondents in need of job training received it. Moreover, none of the older respondents who would have benefited from retraining and other educational programs were offered a chance to participate.

As long as the local welfare administration is just maintaining homeless people without enhancing their human capital, it is unlikely that recent workfare policies in the Hartz IV reforms are going to improve homeless people's chances in the marketplace. Berlin's and Germany's homeless, just like their U.S. counterparts, may now find jobs more easily because of the softening of labor standards, but such low-income, part-time, or other precarious work is unlikely to generate the living wages and income stability necessary for consistent payment of rent and thus may expose German homeless people to more cyclical forms of homelessness. Although Germany's more-comprehensive welfare system will mitigate against the extreme manifestations of cyclical homelessness experienced in the United States (according to Burt et al. 2001, more than one-third of U.S. homeless people have experienced more than three bouts of homelessness over their lifetimes), it is conceivable that people will fall in and out of homelessness more easily if forced to live at the economic margins that the increasingly less-regulated urban labor market is contributing to. To better understand the potential long-term impact of neoliberal policies on homelessness, it is imperative, as suggested throughout this book, to look at the first country to experiment with neoliberal policy and the subsequent privatization, dismantling, and defunding of the welfare state—the United States and its exemplar, Los Angeles.

Los Angeles: Neoliberalism and Its Discontents

The challenges local welfare systems face in the United States are much more profound than those in Germany (Simpson and Tepper 2004). After all, the United States operates without a comprehensive, all-encompassing welfare system based on mass participation and extensive social rights. Under current political and ideological circumstances, it is highly unfeasible that the United States would, in any state or any city, undergo the fundamental changes necessary to implement anything resembling a European-style comprehensive welfare system. Given the limited prospects of institutional change, the U.S. residual welfare system and its locally varied approaches will continue to rely on nonprofits and, increasingly, the for-profit sector to fill the void left by government.

It is important to point out that not all local approaches in the United States are bad. For one thing, the competitive nature of grant applications has resulted in programmatic changes that have vastly improved services for clients. Fierce competition brings out particularly innovative approaches, because nonprofit organizations need to set themselves apart from other organizations applying for the same pool of resources. With such approaches and with ongoing local, state, and national attempts to inform and advocate best practices, substantial qualitative improvements have occurred. Competition has also facilitated better evaluative practice, because organizations are held accountable and must showcase their "success" to win funding (Alexander and Weiner 1998).

Such improvements in the United States, however, have occurred primarily in services for those with needs seen as particularly pressing (for example, homeless people with HIV/AIDS or severe mental illnesses) or for the groups seen as most "deserving" (e.g., families, women, children). Most single men remain underserved, with very little attention given to preventive strategies. The sad truth is that most U.S. homeless—the homeless of Los Angeles are a good example—do not even have access to mainstream welfare services, being categorically excluded or ineligible (see Wolch and Dear 1993); they are denied an entire spectrum of services that people in need are entitled to and, more often than not, utilize. Coverage therefore is and will likely continue to be much lower, which in itself adversely affects their chances for short-term economic stability and long-term upward mobility.

The biggest obstacle for any reform in the United States may very well be political and ideological. Specifically, conservative and increasingly faith-based politics continue to wield substantial influence, making a strong ideological case against any government intervention. The fact that the U.S. government had tremendous difficulties even implementing commonsense health-care reforms bodes poorly for any prospect of increasing government funding for what many perceive to be a lost cause, one that results from personal failure and bad choices. If anything, the privatization of social service provision will only proliferate, which will make self-organization and advocacy the most important drivers of social service improvements. Whether the third sector will ultimately be able to fill the void left by declining government intervention is doubtful. Rather, it is likely that the United States and Los Angeles will continue to pursue a patchwork approach that may serve some fortunate clients quite well but will leave many others permanently outside.

Therefore, it is imperative that German lawmakers carefully assess the U.S. situation to be mindful of the perils of neoliberalism and punitive approaches. Although it is surely tempting to toy with politically successful, highly simplified neoliberal rhetoric, the actual implementation is flat-out dangerous, putting citizens at risk of being exposed to social misfortunes without a safety net. Fortunately for Germany, neither conservatives nor social democrats have fully bought into the argument that privatization at all costs is the solution to social problems, such as homelessness. Moreover, the German electorate—which is highly integrated into the mainstream welfare system—is showing little inclination to move away from the principle behind a regulatory welfare state. This, clearly, is a major advantage over the United States, where the target-specific nature of social programs (with the exception of Social Security) includes only a small percentage of the population, who, due to its marginality, lacks the political clout to mobilize and lobby the political process. Although several nonprofit advocacy organizations at various administrative levels seek to create awareness and political support, they simply do not possess the power to influence the political process as do other, more financially powerful interests. In such fashion, the tens of thousands of dedicated, hard-working, and often highly creative administrators, caseworkers, facility operators, activists, and homeless people themselves will continue to fight an uphill battle with little prospect of really solving the U.S. homelessness crisis—which, under current (2012) economic circumstances and soaring poverty levels, is only likely to get worse.

Conclusion

I began my study of homelessness in Berlin and Los Angeles with the objective of explaining some contradictions: Why did the numbers of homeless people in Berlin and Germany increase to U.S. levels, and why was the extent of long-term homelessness almost double that of the United States, despite Germany's more coherent and encompassing social safety net? And why did the number of homeless then decline in Germany, despite the implementation of neoliberal policies that have been attributed to increasing homelessness in the United States?

My findings demonstrate that sociospatial exclusion helps explain these developments, as it is often the confluence of different forms of exclusion that determines why, how, and under which circumstances some homeless succeed while others remain unsuccessful. Market exclusion, in particular, played a major role in the proliferation and persistence of homelessness in Berlin during the 1990s and its decline thereafter. Here, the ultimate weakness of the conservative/corporatist welfare regime came to light in that "outsiders" to the system, including long-term unemployed and homeless people, have difficulties breaking into labor and housing markets, especially during profound economic restructuring periods, such as the first decade following unification. The high demand for services beyond the state's ability to deliver them reinforced the service exclusion and, over time, increased the legal exclusion of homeless people with more irregular life courses, who often had no choice but to engage in shadow work or congregate with other homeless people.

My research shows that local welfare state deficiencies play an important role in all these trajectories of exclusion, despite the fact that Berlin and Germany, in line with welfare regime theory, provide a much more comprehensive set of services, including cash assistance and shelter. Qualitative problems of service delivery at the local level reinforced sociospatial exclusion, involving insufficient cash assistance (leading to legal exclusion), containment and warehousing (service exclusion), and inadequate referrals to labor and housing market opportunities (market exclusion). Yet rather than providing evidence for the neoliberal case against government intervention by showcasing its ineffectiveness, this research is a call for *more*—and more precisely, *better*—welfare intervention. Berlin has a distinct advantage over any U.S. city simply because of its greater extent of social rights, guarantee of services, and demonstrably effective policy instruments, such as ALMP or the protected market segment. Path dependence and the ability to rely on a more tightly woven social safety net prevent Germany's homeless from experiencing sociospatial exclusion as harshly as American homeless people do.

Workfare and neoliberal inroads, it turns out, have not yet had the same adverse consequences as in the United States, because Germany's reforms have been enacted on top of a comprehensive system that remains largely unchanged and, if anything, has experienced noticeable improvements. Whether these improvements will last remains to be seen. If Los Angeles and most U.S. cities are any indication, the prospects are rather grim, because it is conceivable that the newly reformed and slimmed-down German system, once again, will be unprepared for the onslaught of demand that the economy's next cyclical downturn will bring.

Considering that substantial risks remain pertaining to a future resurgence of homelessness, it is imperative to be proactive and use, within given constraints, existing resources more effectively, with particular emphasis on case management, communication, and coordination and their potential to break down the barriers inherent in sociospatial exclusion. The ultimate key to any reform remains communication to help break the stereotypes that still surround the public and political image of homelessness and reveal it as a condition that could conceivably happen to any of us. With this in mind, we can better help homeless people with quick, proactive, and sustained assistance, taking sociospatial exclusion into consideration and thus understanding more clearly the multiple barriers they face. Only in that way can we help our fellow citizens overcome this traumatic social condition for good.

Postscript

I often think back to the sunny Saturday morning in October 1993 when I first ventured into Skid Row with my classmates. In fact, to this day I use a virtual field trip to downtown Los Angeles in some of my classes, roughly following the path Professor Jennifer Wolch took that day, with the goal of generating a similar response in my classroom. It works every time, for one reason—homelessness *should* shock us. It should make us uncomfortable. It should make us feel guilty.

The research described in this book, like many ethnographic studies before it, demonstrates very clearly that it would be much too easy to blame homelessness solely on those who experience it. Personal circumstances, behaviors, and people's life courses undoubtedly matter, but none of these lived experiences occurs in a vacuum. Societal forces—most notably market barriers, institutional obstacles and welfare state deficiencies, social stigmatization, and legal constraints—all surround homeless people's lives, in surprisingly similar fashion whether in Berlin or in Los Angeles. Yet this study also documents that a more comprehensive welfare system can make a difference, and it is therefore important that Germany continue its path-dependent ways and not only maintain but expand its social safety net. The critiques of the welfare system in this volume, therefore, do not support the antigovernment arguments so commonly employed in the United States—quite the contrary. Unfortunately, the prospects of any productive social reform or even welfare state expansion in the United States remain grim. Bipartisan gridlock and seemingly insurmountable ideological differences will, if anything, continue to provide the basis for further neoliberal welfare state restructuring and scapegoating. To make matters worse, such restructuring occurs on the base of an already poorly developed, fragmented, selective, and underfunded system. The concurrent privatization and devolution to the private and nonprofit sector may, at times, result in excellent services but at the expense of coverage, leaving the most vulnerable and economically disenfranchised permanently on the outside (market exclusion) and contained in service-dependent ghettos (service exclusion) while being simultaneously and systematically driven out of commercially important or more affluent urban areas (legal exclusion). Sociospatial exclusion, then, will continue to be a major feature of the American approach to homelessness and thus, I argue, remains relevant.

The relevance and applicability of the concept of sociospatial exclusion has also found its expression in my teaching and my anticipated future research. For one thing, the concept has been quite a useful heuristic tool in classes on homelessness that I have taught, as it allows me to coherently discuss the trajectories of exclusion in separate class sections leading up to a comprehensive understanding of how such exclusions intersect to foreclose opportunities. I have also employed the concept in a course on immigration and found it useful there as well, suggesting that this conceptualization might be applied to social problems beyond homelessness. Next, I will be using the concept in new empirical longitudinal research on policy effects on homeless people in New York City, which I will be starting in 2013. In using sociospatial exclusion as a heuristic device to study policy effects over time and thus to expose the multiple trajectories of exclusion, I hope to be able to provide a more-nuanced understanding of how homeless people in New York City attempt to break the vicious cycles associated with the social condition of homelessness and their consequent inability to afford housing on their own. In expanding the empirical base by also focusing on homeless families, women, and children, I intend to test the utility of sociospatial exclusion with the goal of helping formulate local policies that more effectively address the problem.

My research has also provided invaluable insight into the use of appropriate methods for a multiperspectival approach. I was, in hindsight, satisfied with the choice of methods that underlay this research and found, like others before me, the ethnographic approach to be particularly useful for understanding homeless people's lives and their experiences. In my new research, I will consequently maintain a strong ethnographic component by developing—with the help of student researchers—a multiyear, qualitative database of individual homeless people and their families' experiences over time. I intend to subsequently triangulate such information with existing quantitative data that the New York Department of Homeless Services collects on a regular basis. My insistence on continuing to rely heavily on ethnographic research is based on my conclusion that qualitative research is a promising way to build the trust necessary to make in-depth observations and connections possible. Although my choice of qualitative methods in Berlin did cause a host of ethical and practical dilemmas (see von Mahs 2012 for more detail), the approach satisfied my criteria for data collection, thus allowing me to develop a very rich set of information on each respondent. At the same time, it was also a very humbling experience, affecting me at a much-deeper, emotional level.

The implications of this research for me personally were therefore more profound. Studying homelessness and the tremendous misfortune that often surrounds homeless people's lives has shown me how incredibly lucky I am. Not only that, I might very well owe my respondents my professional path and success. I remember clearly how Bob, one of my respondents, consoled me upon my confessing my doubts and ethical dilemmas about living in the shelter and feeling like a voyeur:

> Look, man. We actually talked about you. We appreciate what you are doing here. At least you are trying to see things from our perspective. The damn politicians certainly don't. And if we can help you get a dissertation out of this, why not? Good for you! (Bob, age 24, shelter resident, younger regular life course, interview, February 26, 1998)

This generosity of spirit did, in the end, work out for me. I got my dissertation done, became an academic, and wrote this book. Whether I have lived up to my end of the bargain—setting the record straight about homeless people and enhancing our understanding from a comparative perspective—remains to be seen. Although the situation for homeless people in Berlin and in Germany has certainly improved, it remains problematic, and if the United States and its advanced stage of neoliberalism is any indication, the prognosis is not good.

It is all the more important, then, to continue to educate and mobilize to help our fellow citizens prevent or more rapidly address homelessness and thus reduce its tremendous social and economic costs. Germany and the United States most certainly have the resources to do so, so it is time that we use them more effectively.

APPENDIX 1

Biographical Sketches of Respondents in Berlin

Older Homeless People with "Regular" Life Courses

Respondent: Sachse, age 35
Place of birth: Dresden, GDR
Interviewed: February 17, 1998, Trachenbergring
Follow-ups: Four contacts
Final status: Exited from homelessness (after 32 months homeless)

Sachse was born in Dresden, East Germany, where he had a relatively inconspicuous childhood, graduated from high school,[1] completed an apprenticeship in the construction business, and subsequently worked for many years. In 1990, he lost his job, moved to Berlin, found work in the booming construction business, worked continuously for five years, and lived in a one-bedroom apartment in eastern Berlin. After again becoming unemployed, he was unable to pay his rent and was evicted.

Respondent: Helmut, age 37
Place of birth: West Berlin
Interviewed: February 23, 1998, Trachenbergring
Follow-ups: Six contacts
Final status: Homeless (duration 30 months as of March 1999)

Helmut was raised in West Berlin as the third son of a business owner, had a "normal" childhood, graduated from high school, and completed an apprenticeship in food and consumer retail. He was employed at a supermarket chain, where he eventually became a store manager while maintaining an apartment. He married in 1990, yet following his job loss in 1994 and subsequent increasing alcohol abuse, his wife left him in 1995. One year later, he was evicted because of past-due rent.

Respondent: Kalle, age 44
Place of birth: West Berlin
Interviewed: February 28, 1998, Trachenbergring
Follow-ups: Five contacts
Final status: Exited from homelessness (after 36 months homeless)

Kalle was born in West Berlin and raised in a foster-care institution following the death of his single mother when he was three years old. He graduated from high school, completed an apprenticeship as a painter, and subsequently worked as a painter for a number of companies, which allowed him to maintain an apartment. In 1994, he lost his job due to physical problems and his increasing dependency on alcohol. Soon after, he lost his apartment because of past-due rent.

Respondent: Hanno, age 35
Place of birth: East Berlin
Interviewed: March 6, 1998, Trachenbergring
Follow-ups: Five contacts
Final status: Exited from homelessness (after 42 months homeless)

Hanno was born and raised in East Berlin as the second son of industrial workers, graduated from high school, completed job training as an electrician, and subsequently worked for a construction company doing manual labor until the company went out of business in 1995. Increasing debts as a result of his problem managing finances resulted in his failure to pay rent and subsequent eviction.

Respondent: Det, age 49
Place of birth: East Berlin
Interviewed: March 6, 1998, Trachenbergring
Follow-ups: Four contacts
Final status: Homeless (duration 32 months as of March 1999)

Det was born and raised in East Berlin, completed high school and an apprenticeship as an electrician, joined the East German police force, and remained a police officer until 1983. Afterward, he worked as a security officer for Berlin's public-transportation authority before and after unification. He was married twice and has two adult daughters. When his second marriage fell apart in 1996, he had an alcohol-induced nervous breakdown, left his family's residence, did not show up for work for two weeks, and was subsequently fired, leaving him homeless.

Respondent: Hans, age 50
Place of birth: West Berlin
Interviewed: March 9, 1998, Warmer Otto
Follow-ups: Three contacts
Final status: Exited from homelessness (after 276 months homeless)

Hans, the only child of a working-class family, completed high school and an apprenticeship as a varnisher and subsequently worked for ten years in his field for the same company. He married in 1966 and lived in a two-bedroom apartment in West Berlin. After the marriage ended in divorce in 1975 and he lost his job, he decided to begin an independent life on the streets free of any material obligations and pressures, alternating between shelter life, life on the streets, and the correctional system.

Respondent: Bernie, age 40
Place of birth: Dortmund, FRG
Interviewed: March 9, 1998, Warmer Otto
Follow-ups: Three contacts
Final status: Homeless (duration 12 months as of March 1999)

Bernie was born and raised in Dortmund as the first child of miners, completed high school and an apprenticeship as a miner, and worked in the mining industry in Castrop-Rauxel until the mine closed in 1992. He is married and has two sons. Since he became unemployed, he underwent retraining yet remained unsuccessful in finding employment in the Ruhr Conurbation. He came to Berlin in 1997 to search for work while his family continued to live in Dortmund on public assistance.

Respondent: Maria, age 42
Place of birth: Palermo, Italy
Interviewed: March 10, 1998, Warmer Otto
Follow-ups: Two contacts
Final status: Exited from homelessness (after 5 months homeless)

Maria was born and raised in a small village in Sicily as the fourth of seven children. She received basic education, married at the age of seventeen, and moved with her husband to Berlin in 1976. There, the childless couple managed to build a middle-class existence, yet the relationship, accompanied by increasing alcohol consumption by both, worsened, often resulting in domestic violence. Upon becoming unemployed in 1993, her husband began borrowing money and left her unaware of their financial situation. The marital problems, alcohol consumption, and domestic violence escalated, causing Maria to escape to a domestic-violence shelter. When she returned home, she discovered that her husband had left. She found an eviction notice for failure to pay rent and became homeless.

Younger Homeless People with "Regular" Life Courses

Respondent: Mario, age 26
Place of birth: West Berlin
Interviewed: February 22, 1998, Trachenbergring
Follow-ups: Eight contacts
Final status: Exited from homelessness (after 10 months homeless)

Mario, the only child of civil servants, completed high school and began but did not complete an apprenticeship as an automobile mechanic while living with his parents. In his late teenage years, conflicts with his parents began due to his self-admitted lack of discipline and failure to complete the apprenticeship. Ultimately, his parents threw him out and cut off their financial assistance in 1997.

Respondent: Bob, age 24
Place of birth: West Berlin
Interviewed: February 25, 1998, Trachenbergring
Follow-ups: Nine contacts
Final status: Exited from homelessness (after 17 months homeless)

Bob, the second child of a German entrepreneur and his Jamaican wife, spent his early childhood years in the United States, Canada, and Spain, where his father owned restaurants.

His parents eventually relocated to Berlin, where his father opened a restaurant. Bob took ballet and dance lessons and appeared in numerous TV shows as a child dancer while furthering his education in a prestigious private school. His parents divorced while he was in school, and he subsequently lived with his mother while still maintaining close contact with his father, for whom he worked in his Spanish and German franchises. After a fight with his father over alleged drug use (which Bob denies), his father fired him and withdrew his financial support. Unemployed, and with his mother unable to support him financially following her own unemployment, he found himself homeless.

Respondent: Radek, age 23
Place of birth: Danzig, Poland
Interviewed: March 6, 1998, Trachenbergring
Follow-ups: Six contacts
Final status: Exited from homelessness (after 13 months homeless)

Radek was born and raised in Danzig, Poland, by his single mother. In 1989, his mother lost her job and decided to move to West Germany, where they lived in a number of cities, relying primarily on welfare payments. In 1993, they moved to Berlin, where his mother found employment as a secretary and Radek continued his education, quickly making friends and playing guitar in a hard-rock band. In 1996, Radek graduated from high school and started an apprenticeship as an industrial mechanic. In October 1997, Radek moved out of his mother's apartment following an argument and became homeless.

Respondent: Markus, age 21
Place of birth: West Berlin
Interviewed: March 12, 1998, Trachenbergring
Follow-ups: Five contacts
Final status: Exited from homelessness (after 24 months homeless)

Markus grew up in Berlin-Tempelhof as the second child of middle-class parents with whom he had a good relationship during his childhood. He did poorly in school and barely graduated from the nine-year system. While in school, he began to experiment with drugs (cannabis and inhalants) and became increasingly alienated from his parents. He began an apprenticeship as a baker in 1992 yet terminated it after one year. Due to his drug use and his lack of initiative to find job-training opportunities, he had repeated arguments with his father, who eventually threw him out in early 1996.

Homeless Migrants with "Transient" Life Courses

Respondent: Tobias, age 32
Place of birth: West Berlin
Interviewed: March 11, 1998, Warmer Otto
Follow-ups: Four contacts
Final status: Homeless (duration 11 months as of March 1999)

Tobias was raised in foster-care institutions in West Berlin following his parents' death in a car accident. After successfully graduating from higher-tier high school in 1980, he began yet terminated an apprenticeship as a cook and subsequently held a number of jobs in the restaurant business. In 1982, he inherited a significant amount of money after a former boyfriend died of AIDS, which allowed him and his current partner to move to South Africa in 1984, where they bought a piece of property outside Durban and started a pottery business. In 1996, however, Tobias was deported by the South African Immigration Authority due to overstaying his visa and was sent back to Germany, where he became homeless upon arrival.

Respondent: Dan, age 52
Place of birth: Pittsburgh, Pennsylvania, USA
Interviewed: March 10, 1998, Trachenbergring
Follow-ups: Four contacts
Final status: Homeless (duration 20 months as of March 1999)

Dan, a U.S. citizen, grew up in Pittsburgh as the oldest son of a wealthy steel-mill owner. Defying the wishes of his father to take over the family business, Dan enrolled at the American University in Washington, D.C., where he received a B.A. in German history in 1965. Because of his language skills, he fulfilled his mandatory U.S. military service in Germany, where he worked as an interpreter for military intelligence. Upon receiving an honorable discharge in 1972, he resumed his studies and earned an M.A. in German literature at Indiana University in 1976. He then moved back to West Berlin, where he lived for eight years working as a civilian employee for the U.S. Army. In 1985, he moved back to the United States to work as an interpreter. He was fired because of an alcohol problem. He maintained a number of odd jobs over the years and had temporary experiences with homelessness, living in cars. In 1995, he took a lucrative job as an English teacher in Seoul, South Korea, where he stayed for two years. Feeling isolated, he decided to move back to Berlin, which he considered his "home," hoping to find a job as an interpreter or teacher. Once he arrived in Berlin in mid-1997, he found himself unable to find work and quickly depleted his savings. He consequently became homeless in early 1998.

Respondent: Schlöter, age 52
Place of birth: Konstanz, FRG
Interviewed: February 26, 1998, Trachenbergring
Follow-ups: Six contacts
Final status: Homeless (duration 36 months as of March 1999)

Schlöter, whose mother was too poor to take care of her five children during the post-WWII era, was raised in a foster-care institution near Konstanz, graduated from high school, and completed an apprenticeship as a painter. He attributes his desire to maintain a transient lifestyle to his negative experiences in foster care. He moved from one German city to the next, living in hotels and supporting himself through day labor as a painter. In the winter months, he would typically apply for and receive seasonal unemployment compensation specifically designed for construction workers. Although he drank alcohol excessively throughout his life, his alcoholism never posed a problem to finding short-term employment. In 1991, he moved to Berlin and worked in the booming post-unification construction business, which allowed him to maintain an apartment for the first time in his life. In 1997, however, he lost his job due to increasing health and alcohol problems and eventually became homeless.

Respondent: Harri, age 48
Place of birth: Duisburg, FRG
Interviewed: March 12, 1998, Strassenfeger
Follow-ups: Eight contacts
Final status: Exited from homelessness (after 120 months homeless)

Harri was born and raised in Duisburg as the only child of a working-class family. He completed an apprenticeship as an automobile mechanic in 1970. Over the next fifteen years, he worked as a traveling assembly worker at large construction sites in a number of West German cities, primarily living in hotels. Throughout his travels, he developed a substantial drinking habit, which eventually caused him to lose his job. He lived in a small apartment while relying on unemployment compensation for a number of years. In 1990, with increasing debts and continuing alcohol problems, he was evicted and decided to move back to Duisburg, where he subsequently became homeless. For the next two years, he lived on the streets in a number of cities in the Ruhr Conurbation. In 1992, he bought a train ticket to Berlin after he heard from other homeless people that the service infrastructure was better.

Respondent: Matze, age 35
Place of birth: Wuppertal, FRG
Interviewed: March 9, 1998, Strassenfeger
Follow-ups: Three contacts
Final status: Homeless (duration 132 months as of March 1999)

Matze, the second child of upper-middle-class parents, was born and raised in Wuppertal. He did poorly in school, barely graduated, and began but interrupted an apprenticeship as a painter. After working for a chemical company for a couple of years, he had to quit his job due to health problems. During this time, he became politically active in the peace and anti–nuclear power movement and left his parents to join other anti–nuclear power activists protesting the construction of a nuclear-waste reprocessing facility in Wackersdorf, Bavaria. After the activist encampment was forcibly dismantled by the police in 1986, he became homeless and lived in homeless encampments in a number of German cities, including Hamburg, Berlin, and Saarbrücken. In 1997, he moved to Berlin, where he continued to be homeless.

Respondent: Marty, age 30
Place of birth: West Berlin
Interviewed: March 7, 1998, Strassenfeger
Follow-ups: Three contacts
Final status: Homeless (duration 30 months as of March 1999)

Marty was born and was raised by his grandparents in West Berlin, where he graduated from high school and began, yet failed to complete, an apprenticeship as a painter. In 1992, following the death of one of his grandparents, he moved to Uelzen, West Germany, where he lived in a dormitory for migrant workers and held a number of publicly subsidized jobs over the years. In 1994, he moved to a farm in rural Lower Saxony, where he lived on social assistance, subsidizing his welfare income working as a farmhand in exchange for room and board. In 1996, he moved back to Berlin to find regular employment yet remained unsuccessful and homeless.

Respondent: Leo, age 32
Place of birth: Rostock, GDR
Interviewed: February 23, 1998, Trachenbergring
Follow-ups: Five contacts
Final status: Unknown

Leo, the second of three children of industrial workers, successfully graduated from high school, completed an apprenticeship as a construction worker, and worked continuously for seven years in Rostock. In 1989, a few months before the Berlin Wall fell, he fled East Germany and settled in a small town in West Germany. Unable to find a job and without any resources (his parents had died, and both of his brothers were unemployed), he became homeless in 1991 and lived in a communal shelter. In 1993, he moved to Berlin, hoping for better economic opportunities, and immediately found employment at a private security company. He lived in a one-bedroom apartment. In 1997, he had to quit his job due to increasing orthopedic problems and shortly thereafter lost his apartment because of past-due rent as a result of his gambling addiction.

Respondent: Jens, age 27
Place of birth: Cottbus, GDR
Interviewed: March 24, 1998, Trachenbergring
Follow-ups: Seven contacts
Final status: Homeless (duration 36 months as of March 1999)

Jens, the second child of industrial workers from Trettschau, had a rather lonely childhood, barely graduated from the high school system, and began yet interrupted an apprenticeship in the construction business. In 1990, he left his parents' home and moved to Berlin to find work yet became homeless immediately upon arrival, causing him to return to his parents after one year of homelessness. He was unable to find work and lived at his parents' home until 1996, when he moved out following his parents' own unemployment. He returned to Berlin and became homeless again upon arrival.

Homeless People with "Deviant" Life Courses

Respondent: FTW, age 26
Place of birth: West Berlin
Interviewed: March 3, 1998, Trachenbergring
Follow-ups: Ten contacts
Final status: Homeless (duration 36 months as of March 1999)

FTW, the only child of a single mother, experienced severe abuse as a child. Public child services removed him when he was five years old and placed him into foster care. Because he displayed disruptive and aggressive behaviors, he was frequently moved between different foster-care institutions in Berlin, where he acquired only minimal reading and writing skills. At the age of fourteen, he ran away and began taking heroin and other drugs, financing his consumption through drug dealing and other criminal activities. He had multiple encounters with law enforcement and cycled in and out of juvenile detention centers, living on the streets, in abandoned buildings, in squatter communities, or in railroad stations when not in jail. In 1992, he was sentenced to four years in jail for aggravated assault. While in jail, he successfully overcame his heroin addiction, yet he immediately became homeless upon his release from prison.

Respondent: Oliver, age 26
Place of birth: West Berlin
Interviewed: March 10, 1998, Trachenbergring
Follow-ups: Four contacts
Final status: Exited from homelessness (after 16 months homeless)

Oliver, the youngest of seven children of an impoverished German family, was raised first by foster parents and then in a Catholic foster-care institution. He successfully graduated from high school and began yet interrupted an apprenticeship as a locksmith after he became dependent on heroin. During this time, he alternated between squatting and sleeping rough and was once arrested for drug dealing, spending six months in juvenile detention. In 1992, he temporarily moved in with his older brother and managed to overcome his addiction "cold turkey"; he has remained off drugs since then. He held a number of odd jobs over the years in the construction business, fulfilled his mandatory military service, and, over the years, managed to maintain an apartment in Berlin-Köpenik. Following a break-up with his girlfriend, he attempted to commit suicide. While recovering in a hospital, he was unable to pay his rent and was consequently evicted in absentia.

Respondent: Sioux, age 31
Place of birth: Erlangen, FRG
Interviewed: March 8, 1998, Strassenfeger
Follow-ups: Twelve contacts
Final status: Exited from homelessness (after 13 months homeless)

As the second of five children of a poor family in Erlangen, Sioux repeatedly experienced child abuse in his youth, barely graduated from high school, and eventually moved out of his parents' home at the age of sixteen. He became a member of Erlangen's punk scene, got heavily involved with drugs, and lived primarily on the streets and occasionally at friends' places. In 1986, he was arrested on drug-related charges and spent eighteen months in jail. Upon release, he got married, worked for a professional cleaning company, and lived with his wife in a two-bedroom apartment in Erlangen, where they had two children. In 1991, the couple divorced, and Sioux moved out; shortly afterward, he moved in with his new girlfriend, married her, and fathered another child. In 1992, he was involved in a brawl and was sentenced to three and a half years in jail for aggravated assault. During his incarceration, his second marriage fell apart, and upon release, he moved away from Erlangen to leave his past behind. Between 1995 and 1996, he lived at a halfway house in Kulmbach and worked as an upholsterer. In 1996, having fulfilled his parole obligations, he decided to move to Berlin to start over and became homeless upon arrival.

Respondent: Marita, age 19
Place of birth: Halle, GDR
Interviewed: April 28, 1998, Treberhilfe
Follow-ups: Four contacts
Final status: Homeless (duration 60 months as of March 1999)

Marita, who lived with her mother and her stepfather, was repeatedly sexually molested from the time she was two years old. Afraid of her abusive husband, her mother placed Marita in a foster-care institution when she was five years old. When she was thirteen, she managed to run away and hitchhiked to Berlin. Once in Berlin, she was unable to find a place to stay and quickly got involved in Berlin's drug scene. She soon began taking heroin and has remained addicted and more or less homeless since then. She has attempted to overcome her addiction numerous times, with and without assistance, only to resume using shortly thereafter. To finance her addiction, she had to generate up to DM 300 ($167) per day, and prostitution became her only option. Since she began prostituting herself, she has been raped, beaten, and cheated out of her compensation numerous times. She has also had a number of encounters with law enforcement and spent months in juvenile detention yet was always forced to return into the same milieu.

Homeless People with "Disabilities"

Respondent: Andrea, age 54
Place of birth: Kaliningrad, Russia
Interviewed: March 10, 1998, Warmer Otto
Follow-ups: Three contacts
Final status: Exited from homelessness (after 12 months homeless)

Andrea, a mentally disabled woman, was born in Kaliningrad (then Königsberg) shortly before the Russian Army occupied the city, forcing her widowed mother to join the desperate trek of millions of refugees moving west to flee the approaching army. Andrea suspects that her mental disability was the result of malnutrition during this treacherous march. She and her mother lived for a few years at a camp for displaced persons in West Germany and then moved to Berlin. Her mother devoted her life to raising Andrea, home-schooling her (she has minimal writing and reading skills) and completely sheltering her daughter from the outside world. Andrea recalls having had no friends and spending her entire life with her mother. Her mother received a very modest war-widow pension and worked part-time in a public library. In 1987, her mother unexpectedly died of a heart attack without having made any arrangements for Andrea. Devastated by her mother's passing, Andrea stayed in their small rental apartment and ate canned food until she was formally evicted for past-due rent and found herself, unaware of any options, homeless and wandering the streets of Berlin.

Respondent: Monika, age 34
Place of birth: West Berlin
Interviewed: March 8, 1998, Strassenfeger
Follow-ups: Eight contacts
Final status: Exited from homelessness (after 108 months homeless)

Monika, the only child of a wealthy German family, was born with an incurable visual impairment (she has very limited peripheral vision). She recalls a miserable childhood characterized by emotional abuse by both parents and feeling isolated, unloved, depressed, and bored. During that time, she attended a school for visually impaired children and graduated successfully. At the age of eighteen, she finally managed to leave her parents' home, taking a train to Hamburg, West Germany. Once she arrived in Hamburg, and lacking any alternatives, she began to prostitute herself and was quickly caught in the treacherous world of prostitution, violence, and abuse. Most attempts to escape the "red-light district" resulted in severe beatings by the pimps who capitalized on the fact that her visual impairment limited her options and mobility. She managed to escape twice, moving to other West German cities, only to end up in the same type of environment. In 1996, she moved back to Berlin, only to find herself homeless again.

Respondent: Biker, age 38
Place of birth: West Berlin
Interviewed: March 9, 1998, Trachenbergring
Follow-ups: Ten contacts
Final status: Exited from homelessness (after 120 months homeless)

Biker was born in Berlin and grew up in Cologne after his parents moved following the construction of the Berlin Wall in 1961. He recalls a worry-free childhood. He successfully graduated from higher-tier high school and completed an apprenticeship in window repairs, specializing in historic and art window restorations. From 1976 to 1983, he worked in a number of West German cities until he decided to move to Berlin in 1983, where he continued working in his field, making very good money. In 1985, he met his future wife, with whom he had two daughters. In the late 1980s, the marriage began falling apart, and in 1989, after losing his job, he left his family. Shortly thereafter, he had a severe motorcycle accident in which he almost lost his right leg. The injuries rendered him disabled and incapable of working in his field. After recuperating from surgery and a brief stay at a shelter, he became homeless in 1989, living primarily in cars and minivans for the next nine years.

Respondent: Paule, age 37
Place of birth: West Berlin
Interviewed: February 22, 1998, Trachenbergring
Follow-ups: Five contacts
Final status: Homeless (duration 48 months as of March 1999)

Paule grew up in West Berlin as the only child of a marginalized family, frequently experiencing abuse from his father. Upon graduating from high school, he completed an apprenticeship as a bricklayer in 1980 and subsequently worked for the same company for fifteen years, until the company went bankrupt. He married in 1985, but the relationship worsened over time and was accompanied by alcohol abuse by him and his wife. In 1994, he lost his job and has remained unable to regain employment. He says that for some years, he suspected that something was wrong with him, because he experienced increasingly severe mood swings, which he attributed to his miserable life and his abusive relationship at the time, not mental illness. Following a particularly deep depression in 1995, he attempted suicide and was consequently committed to a mental health clinic, where he stayed for three weeks and was diagnosed as having bipolar disorder. Upon release and on the recommendation of his doctors, he filed for divorce and moved out of the marital apartment. He ended up homeless.

APPENDIX 2

Key Informants

Key Informants Interviewed in Berlin

Informant: Klaus Breitfeld
Title/function: Social Worker
Organization: Wärmestube Warmer Otto (day center)
Interviewed: March 11, 1998

Informant: Helga Burkert
Title/function: Administrator, Head of Division
Organization: Senatsverwaltung für Gesundheit und Soziales, Grundsatzplanung und Konzeption zum Thema Wohnungslosenpolitik (Senate Administration for Health and Social Affairs, office of general planning on homeless policy)
Interviewed: April 24, 1998

Informant: Sigi Deiß
Title/function: Social Worker, Pastor
Organization: Foyer an der Gedächtniskirche (religious organization; nonprofit)
Interviewed: March 4, 1998

Informant: Jürgen Demmer
Title/function: Social Worker, Administrator
Organization: Bezirksamt Charlottenburg, Abteilung Soziale Wohnhilfe (one of twenty-three local welfare agencies within Berlin's Department of Social Housing Assistance)
Interviewed: March 11, 1998

Informant: Ralf Gruber
Title/function: Social Worker, Street Worker
Organization: Bezirksamt Charlottenburg, Abteilung Soziale Wohnhilfe (one of twenty-three local welfare agencies within Berlin's Department of Social Housing Assistance)
Interviewed: March 6, 1998; December 10, 1998

Informant: Michael Haberkorn
Title/function: Representative, State Parliament; Social Political Speaker
Organization: Fraktion Bündnis 90/Die Grünen (political party)
Interviewed: March 6, 1998

Informant: Karlheinz Kramer
Title/function: Social Worker
Organization: Beratungsstelle für Wohnungslose in der Lewetzowstrasse (referral center; nonprofit)
Interviewed: March 5, 1998

Informant: Anneliese Leps
Title/function: Head Nurse
Organization: Deutsches Rotes Kreuz (DRK), Obdachlosenbetreuung im Bahnhof Lichtenberg (German Red Cross, health services facility for the homeless located in a railroad station; nonprofit)
Interviewed: March 6, 1998

Informant: Sybille Paetow-Spinosa
Title/function: Administrator, Social Worker
Organization: Senatsverwaltung für Schule, Jugend und Sport, Landeskommission Berlin gegen Gewalt (Senate Administration for Education, Youth and Sports, Berlin State Commission against Violence)
Interviewed: March 12, 1998

Informant: Stefan Schneider
Title/function: Chairman, Activist
Organization: MOB e.V. (Strassenfeger) (advocacy project; nonprofit)
Interviewed: April 27, 1998

Informant: Matthias Schulz
Title/function: Administrator, Planner
Organization: Senatsverwaltung für Gesundheit und Soziales, Sachbearbeiter ZEKO, Geschütztes Marktsegment (Senate Administration for Health and Social Affairs, office of the case manager for the protected market segment)
Interviewed: February 27, 1998

Informant: Uwe Spacek
Title/function: Editor
Organization: Mob e.V. (Strassenfeger) (advocacy project; nonprofit)
Interviewed: December 10, 1998

Informant: Uta Sternal
Title/function: Shelter Manager, Social Worker
Organization: Internationaler Bund, Wohnheim Trachenbergring (national service organization, transitional shelter; nonprofit)
Interviewed: February 10, 1998; December 8, 1998

Informant: Ingo Thederan
Title/function: Assistant Director
Organization: UB U-Bahn, Fahrgastsicherheit, Berliner Verkehrsgemeinschaft (subway security)
Interviewed: December 9, 1998

Informant: Carola von Braun
Title/function: Administrator
Organization: Senatsverwaltung für Arbeit, Berufsbildung und Frauen (Senate Adminstration for Labor, Job Training and Women)
Interviewed: April 27, 1998

Informant: Reiner Wild
Title/function: Managing Director
Organization: Berliner Mieterverein (rental association; nonprofit)
Interviewed: April 22, 1998

Key Informants Interviewed in Los Angeles

Informant: Harrold Adams
Title/function: Executive Director
Organization: Los Angeles Homeless Services Authority (LAHSA)
Interviewed: September 16, 1997

Informant: Richard E. Bonneau
Title/function: Captain, Commanding Officer
Organization: Los Angeles Police Department (LAPD), Central Area
Interviewed: September 22, 1997

Informant: Mark Casanova
Title/function: Executive Director
Organization: Health Care for the Homeless
Interviewed: September 23, 1997

Informant: Deborah Davenport
Title/function: Clinical Nursing Director
Organization: Community Health Services
Interviewed: September 22, 1997

Informant: Maya Dunne
Title/function: Policy Director
Organization: Los Angeles Homeless Services Authority (LAHSA)
Interviewed: September 16, 1997

Informant: Merryl Edelstein
Title/function: Senior City Planner
Organization: Los Angeles City Planning Department
Interviewed: September 18, 1997

Informant: Bob Erlenbusch
Title/function: Executive Director
Organization: Los Angeles Coalition to End Hunger and Homelessness
Interviewed: September 23, 1997

Informant: Ted Hayes
Title/function: Servant Director, Activist
Organization: Genesis I, Dome Village
Interviewed: September 25, 1997

Informant: Arthur Jones
Title/function: Lawyer, Homeless Resident
Organization: Genesis I, Dome Village
Interviewed: September 25, 1997

Informant: Gregg Kawczynski
Title/function: Manager
Organization: Community Development Commission, Housing Development and Preservation
Interviewed: September 17, 1997

Informant: Dale Lowery
Title/function: Database and Communication Specialist
Organization: Los Angeles Coalition to End Hunger and Homelessness
Interviewed: September 23, 1997

Informant: George Malone
Title/function: Supervising Regional Planner
Organization: Los Angeles County Department of Regional Planning
Interviewed: September 17, 1997

Informant: Ruth Schwarz
Title/function: Executive Director
Organization: Shelter Partnership, Inc.
Interviewed: September 11, 1997; September 24, 1997

Informant: Judy Weddle
Title/function: Human Services Administrator I
Organization: Department of Public and Social Services (DPSS), Office of Welfare Reform Strategy
Interviewed: September 24, 1997

Key Informants Interviewed in Washington, D.C.

Informant: Steven Berg
Title/function: Senior Policy Analyst
Organization: Center on Budget and Policy Priorities (CBPP)
Interviewed: August 26, 1997

Informant: Laura DeKoven-Waxman
Title/function: Assistant Executive Director
Organization: United States Conference of Mayors
Interviewed: October 3, 1997

Informant: Barbara Duffield
Title/function: Director Information Exchange
Organization: National Coalition for the Homeless (NCH)
Interviewed: August 26, 1997

Informant: John Heinberg
Title/function: Program Analyst
Organization: Job Evaluation for the Homeless Demonstration Program, U.S. Department of Labor
Interviewed: September 5, 1997

Informant: Kirsten T. Johnson
Title/function: Professional Staff
Organization: U.S. Congress, House of Representatives, Banking Committee, Congressman Bruce Vento (D-Minnesota)
Interviewed: October 3, 1997

Informant: Dr. Fred Karnas Jr.
Title/function: Deputy Assistant Secretary
Organization: Office of Community Planning and Development/Interagency Council for Homelessness, U.S. Department of Housing and Urban Development (HUD)
Interviewed: September 3, 1997

Informant: Tanesha P. Hembrey
Title/function: Program Analyst
Organization: Office of Elementary and Secondary Education, Title I and Homeless, U.S. Department of Education
Interviewed: September 5, 1997

Informant: Dr. Marsha Martin
Title/function: Special Assistant to the Secretary
Organization: U.S. Department of Health and Human Services (HHS)
Interviewed: September 3, 1997

Informant: Shawn A. Mussington
Title/function: Education Program Officer
Organization: Office of Elementary and Secondary Education, Title I and Homeless, U.S. Department of Education
Interviewed: September 5, 1997

Informant: Nan Roman
Title/function: Vice President
Organization: National Alliance to End Homelessness
Interviewed: August 25, 1997

Informant: Laurel Weir
Title/function: Policy Director
Organization: National Law Center on Homelessness and Poverty
Interviewed: October 2, 1997

Notes

CHAPTER 1

1. Virtually any study on homelessness in American cities to date—too many to list here—provides evidence for public policy failures. Most notably, mainstream cash assistance and housing programs remain largely inaccessible, and the emerging nonprofit sector simply lacks the means and infrastructure to provide all people in housing crisis with adequate and ideally preventive service.

2. For information on numbers of homeless in Germany, see BAG Wohnungslosenhilfe 2010. For recent numbers in the United States, including a discussion of variations, see U.S. Department of Housing and Urban Development 2010.

3. Almost all surveys of homeless people in Los Angeles indicate that their duration of homelessness is shorter than that of homeless people in Berlin (Burnam and Koegel 1988; Flaming and Drayse 1997b; Husick and Wolch 1990; Shelter Partnership 1994; Takahashi, Dear, and Neely 1989). The only exception is Cousineau's 1993 survey of 134 primarily older male street encampment residents in downtown Los Angeles, which reveals that 65.6 percent of his respondents have been homeless for more than one year at the time of the interview (16).

4. The term "workfarist" refers to the welfare-to-work programs that undergird the U.S. welfare reforms of 1996 (for discussion, see Handler 2004).

5. Between 1987 and 1993, the Los Angeles Homelessness Project (LAHP) conducted an interdisciplinary study of different aspects of homelessness in Los Angeles, producing fifty-eight working papers as well as twenty-six publications. This research is summarized in Wolch and Dear's 1993 book, *Malign Neglect: Homelessness in an American City*. Furthermore, a longitudinal and quantitative survey, the Course of Homelessness Study (1991–1993), provides further information on homeless people's exit chances (for an overview, see Koegel 2004). Additionally, Burns, Flaming, and Haydamack (2004) provide data on the long-term economic prospects of homeless people by following a cohort of more than twelve hundred participants in a job-training program over a period of nine years. Tepper (2004) provides a coherent overview of studies on homelessness in Los Angeles that shows the comprehensive nature of research that has been conducted over the past two decades. For Berlin, I found no studies that explicitly focus on exit and long-term chances, but I have drawn on insightful studies provided by Eick (1996), Neubarth

(1997), Schenk (2004), Schneider (1998), and Gerull, Merckens, and Dubrow (2009). This research does not address the exit chances of homeless people.

6. Unlike U.S. cities that enforce specifically formulated antihomeless ordinances, European cities, including Berlin, use broader, preexisting public order and safety ordinances to remove homeless people (Busch-Geertsema 2008; Belina 2003). Moreover, impoverished urban quarters by no means resemble North American ghettos (for a discussion, see Veith and Sambale 1999).

7. Very few international comparative studies on homelessness are available to date. A number of studies directly compare countries in the European Union but do not include the United States (Avramov 1995, 1999; Edgar, Doherty, and Mina-Coull 1999; Edgar, Doherty, and Meert 2003). Other research uses case studies from the United States and other countries but does not provide a thorough comparative analysis (G. Daly 1996; Greenhalgh et al. 2004; Heilman and Dear 1988; Huth and Wright 1997; Toro 2007; Shinn 2010; von Mahs and Mitchell 2011). The only study that addresses homelessness in more comprehensive comparative fashion is Helvie and Kunstmann's (1999) publication on homelessness in ten industrialized countries. Like most other studies, however, their report remains largely descriptive, providing accounts for each country but not a clear comparative analysis.

8. The following studies provide clear evidence that the German "conservative" welfare regime, despite weaknesses, provides its residents with a greater range of social rights, coverage, and benefits than does the "liberal" U.S. type: Esping-Andersen 1996, 1999; Goodin et al. 1999; Huber and Stephens 2001; Leisering and Leibfried 1999; Lewis 1992; Mishra 1999.

9. Although geographic processes, especially processes of exclusion and displacement, have been studied extensively by geographers in the United States, to my knowledge only two studies on homelessness in Germany have been published by geographers: Hundhammer 1979 and Pape 1996.

10. Wright's (1996) unpublished dissertation on "Pathways Off the Streets" draws on results from the Oakland sample, which he complemented by conducting qualitative interviews (between five and thirty minutes in length) with 101 of the 397 respondents of the third wave to gain a better understanding of success or failure in finding housing (103).

11. A large body of literature in the United States and Europe critically discusses the implications of properly defining this phenomenon and how the politicized nature of terminology alone affects the "numbers game" (for excellent discussions, see Busch-Geertsema 2010; Corday and Pion 1997). Accordingly, government agencies are interested in low numbers to avoid being put on the spot, whereas advocacy organizations and service providers need high numbers to justify their existence. Several attempts have been made to streamline and universalize definitions to achieve more consistency and allocate resources more effectively. In the United States, for matters of expediency, most researchers accept the official government definition used in the McKinney Act and define a homeless person as someone who "lacks a fixed, regular, and adequate night-time residence and . . . has a primary night-time residence that is: (A) a supervised publicly or privately operated shelter designed to provide temporary living accommodations . . . , (B) an institution that provides a temporary residence for individuals intended to be institutionalized, or (C) a public or private place not designed for, or ordinarily used as, a regular sleeping accommodation for human beings" (quoted in NCH 1997). This definition is broad enough to encompass and correspond with commonly used definitions in Germany.

12. For monetary figures reported throughout, I use the prevailing exchange rate during the period of the study, $1.00 = DM 1.80. This rate remained relatively stable during the late 1990s and prior to the introduction of the euro in 2001.

13. According to data provided by the Beratungsstelle (1996, 24), 36.3 percent of their homeless clients were foreign nationals, whereas estimates of ethnic/racial minorities among the homeless in Los Angeles ranged between 51 percent (Flaming and Drayse 1997a, 2) and 93.3 percent (Cousineau 1993, 11).

14. For more information on the role of social networks and social capital in becoming homeless, in the condition of homelessness, and as facilitators of or barriers to exit, see Conley 1996; Husick and Wolch 1990, 22; Wolf et al. 2001, 393; B. Wright 1996; Zlotnick, Robertson, and Lhiff 1999.

15. For discussions of economic factors associated with homelessness from a comparative European perspective, see Avramov 1995, 50; 1999, 27–142; M. Daly 1999, 319–327; Edgar, Doherty, and Mina-Coull 1999, 18–21; Helvie and Kunstmann 1999, 229–233. For a discussion of the German situation, see Busch-Geertsema 2004; Vranken 1999, 337–340. For the U.S. situation, see Wolch and Dear 1993, 1–49; Tepper and Simpson 2003.

16. Using the data from a longitudinal study of 1,250 homeless job seekers in downtown Los Angeles over nine years (1992–2001), Burns, Flaming, and Haydamack (2004) demonstrate that only one-sixth of the homeless respondents found living-wage jobs, overcame homelessness, escaped poverty, and significantly improved their socioeconomic circumstances (50–51). Eighty percent of all successful job seekers, on the other hand, experienced either marginal socioeconomic improvements, stagnation, or even further decline (47–53).

17. Among the more sobering results from U.S. studies was that few of the respondents who exited from homelessness in either the Course of Homelessness Study in Los Angeles or the STAR study in Northern California were able to maintain their housing. Among those who exited in Los Angeles, for instance, 72 percent became homeless again after having stayed housed for at least thirty days, and 50 percent became homeless again at least twice within the fourteen months following the initial interviews (Koegel 2004, 17; Wong 1997, 63).

18. Although homelessness in the former East Germany is growing at a faster rate than in the west, less than 10 percent of the nation's homeless resided in eastern Germany, compared with 22 percent of the overall population (BAG Wohnungslosenhilfe 2010, 3; Busch-Geertsema 2003). Similarly, more than three-quarters of the homeless people in Berlin were registered in and had their last official residences before becoming homeless in western districts, compared with 60 percent of the overall population (Abgeordnetenhaus von Berlin 1995, 5). Moreover, homelessness was already a significant problem in West Berlin before unification, as close to six thousand people were registered as homeless in 1988 (3). So although unification and the resulting economic and social consequences undoubtedly contributed to the rise of homelessness and to barriers out of it, homelessness cannot be interpreted entirely as a transitional phenomenon resulting from German unification.

19. For further evidence of service delivery problems in Los Angeles, see DeVerteuil 2003a, 2003b; Wolch and Dear 1993. For nationwide discussions, see Burt et al. 2001; J. Wright, Rubin, and Devine 1998; Baumohl 1996.

20. Greater coverage and higher public expenditures also translate into more comprehensive shelter provision and thus better client-shelter ratios. For instance, 8,687 people in Berlin used the publicly funded shelter system in 1997 (Senatsverwaltung

für Gesundheit und Soziales 1997, 41–43). As a result, the client-shelter ratio in Berlin (approximately 2:1) is certainly much more favorable than that in Los Angeles (Shelter Partnership 1994, 15; see also LAHSA 2011).

CHAPTER 2

1. This may explain why to date so few researchers have dared to tread the empirically thin ice of international comparisons, as they are easily questioned about their accuracy. Consequently, we find only a few studies that make transatlantic comparisons (exception: Helvie and Kunstmann 1999) alongside a few collections of essays in books (Huth and Wright 1997) and special journal editions (Toro 2007; von Mahs and Mitchell 2011). Rather, most comparative studies pertain to the European Union, where the European Observatory on Homelessness (FEANTSA) and other agencies have succeeded in standardizing definitions and thus developing a language and criteria for comparisons (see FEANTSA's Web site, www.feantsa.org/code/en/hp.asp, for an overview of comparative multicountry studies on data and policy).

2. Snow and Anderson's (1993) fascinating multiyear study examines the material survival strategies of homeless street people in Austin, Texas, and includes interviews with 168 homeless street people, participant observation, and key-informant interviews. To link such local experience with broader data, the authors triangulate their qualitative data with survey research that tracks a random sample of 767 service users through a number of core institutions.

3. Although many scholars have employed ethnographic research methods to examine homelessness, a number of studies stand out for their depth, clarity, and ability to persuasively link lived experiences to the broader societal and spatial context. They include Bauer's (1980) study of life circumstances of homeless people in Marioth, Germany; Knowles's (1999) analysis of mentally ill homeless people in Montreal, Canada; Ruddick's (1996) study of homeless youth in Hollywood, California; Schneider's (1998) investigation of homeless street people in Berlin, Germany; Snow and Anderson's (1993) examination of street people in Austin, Texas; Desjarlais's insights into shelter life in Boston, Massachusetts (1997); and Wright's (1997) analysis of homeless grassroots resistance in Chicago, Illinois, and San José, California. Although none of these studies focuses explicitly on exit from homelessness, each demonstrates the utility of ethnographic research methods for gaining insights into the lives and daily struggles of homeless people.

4. Bennett's (1999) nursing Ph.D. thesis, titled "Crossing the Line: Experiences of the Formerly Homeless Living Past Homelessness," remains disappointingly brief and sketchy, dedicating only four pages to actual exit from homelessness and including the experiences of only four people in her analysis.

5. Existing administrative data on homelessness in Berlin, compiled by the Senate Administration for Health and Social Affairs' research department, provides only relatively general information on the characteristics of homeless people and overall durations of homelessness and does not reveal exit destinations, any reasons for how people accomplished exit from homelessness, or explanations for why they did not. (See quarterly reports by the Senatsverwaltung für Gesundheit und Soziales, available online at www.wohnungslos-in-berlin.de/material/zahlen.htm, and analysis of such data in publications of Berlin's parliament, e.g., Abgeordnetenhaus von Berlin 1995 and 1999.)

6. The facility, a large two-winged housing complex initially built in the 1950s to accommodate migrant workers, also provided housing for approximately 160 Bosnian

war refugees and 20 single homeless women. I inquired whether I could also talk with the female residents, but the manager declined, arguing that most women had severe problems and experiences with domestic abuse and should not be subjected to inquiries. I respectfully obliged.

7. In the mid- to late 1990s, more than three-quarters of all shelter facilities in Berlin were either drop-in emergency shelters or so-called low-level transitional shelters, both of which consisted of multiple-occupancy rooms and were reputed to be characterized by dismal social and hygienic conditions, offering little or no additional social services (see Neubarth 1997; Schneider 1998; Abgeordentenhaus von Berlin 1999).

8. Elsewhere, I have discussed the ethical and practical problems I encountered during my close ethnographic work with homeless people, along with some solutions I found to overcome those problems (von Mahs 2012). One of the unexpected challenges I experienced was difficulty approaching people and starting conversations. I felt guilty about my intrusion and, during the first few days or visits, at least, I could not shed the feeling that residents perceived me with some suspicion. With time, allowing for relationships to develop naturally, I was able to break the silence and engage some people in conversation and, through them, reach out to other potential respondents.

9. Three part-time social workers assisted visitors with a number of tasks, including administrative matters, personal problems, referrals, and job and housing searches. Once a week, a doctor and a lawyer visited the facility on a pro bono basis and provided medical and legal advice and referrals. Moreover, visitors could receive fresh clothes and use the bathroom to change their clothes, wash up, and shave. The social workers also organized social events, such as local day trips (hiking, sightseeing, and cinema), holiday parties, and sporting events (soccer and ping-pong tournaments). I talked to facility operator Klaus Breitfeld and informed him about my research, and he permitted me to conduct interviews if visitors gave their consent.

10. Dr. Stefan Schneider, chairman of the Mob e.V., provided me with some initial information about street-newspaper vendors that suggested the importance of including this group in the study. First, many vendors sell street newspapers because they either have no access to welfare and shelter or actively choose not to take advantage of public welfare, a choice that I wanted to explore. Second, street-newspaper vendors serve as examples of homeless people who use self-initiative in their attempts to exit homelessness, therefore demonstrating alternatives to welfare. Third, vendors tend to be younger than the average homeless population yet tend to experience a greater extent of exacerbating social problems, including substance abuse and mental and physical health problems (especially HIV/AIDS), legal problems, and difficulties associated with decarceration, which allowed me to explore the role of supportive social services and the problems with accessing such services.

11. One of the primary features of the German welfare system is the principle of "subsidiarity," which entails that the actual provision of services at the local level ought to be performed by nonprofit organizations, which are, in contrast to U.S. policy, almost exclusively funded by the government. Over the decades, five leading religious and secular national welfare associations have emerged that provide more than 80 percent of all social services (Leisering 2001).

12. The general idea behind the concept is that vendors borrow an initial set of newspapers, sell them to the public for DM 2 ($1.10), receive a new set of papers after having paid off the first set for DM 1 ($0.55) per issue, and then sell the new set for DM 2 ($1.10). They keep all the profits and any tips received.

13. I use illustrative quotations throughout the text. Except for my interview with Dan (in English; he is American), all interviews were conducted in German, and I have translated them to convey meaning and equivalency rather than word-for-word conversions. More information about the person who provided the quotation can be found in Appendix 1, in which I provide a biographical sketch of each respondent.

14. Indigenous homeless are defined as people who have lived in the city for at least four years.

15. It is well documented that such social problems disproportionately exist among homeless people, and the present group of homeless people is no exception (BAG Wohnungslosenhilfe 1997; Baumohl and Huebner 1991; Burt et al. 2001; Flaming and Drayse 1997b).

16. Although most of the twelve younger homeless respondents did not engage in excessive alcohol consumption, nine of them regularly smoked cannabis. Whether and to what extent such drug consumption might have contributed to homelessness or may impede exit potential is so far a virtually unexamined topic.

CHAPTER 3

1. For excellent academic contributions, see Amster 2008; Mitchell 2003. For discussion of antihomeless measures in Los Angeles, see DeVerteuil 2006; Reese, DeVerteuil, and Thach 2010. For the most recent national report, see NLCHP 2011.

2. The list of contributors to academic debates around the exclusion of homeless people reads like a who's who in urban studies, including Marcuse (1988), Davis (1990), Hopper (2003), Smith (1996, 1998), Mitchell (1997, 2003), Wolch and Dear (1993), and J. Wright, Rubin, and Devine (1998), just to name a few. Such literature draws insights from geography, legal studies, anthropology, and urban sociology and shows clearly how capital interests, scale, and exclusion intersect to deliberately exclude the homeless from vital urban spaces. Such literature, in turn, has spawned substantial research in other cities around the globe, suggesting that a backlash against homeless people is occurring in other areas, too (for an overview, see Doherty et al. 2008; von Mahs 2011b).

3. An increasing number of scholars counter that these exclusionary measures and their underlying philosophy are characteristic of "revanchism" (Smith 1996) and thus struggles over capital, space, and access in a globalizing city. Smith, and subsequently a range of scholars, provides persuasive arguments that capitalist interests and their influence determine the course of action by selectively redeveloping, gentrifying, and upscaling central city areas. Gentrification is perhaps the most visible consequence of the process of displacing original, often marginalized, residents. To make these places attractive—the concept of "ambience" comes to mind—gentrifying areas begin "cleaning up" the neighborhood and demand action on the part of local government to address crime and vandalism (Thorn 2011).

4. Please note that although courts often side with the homeless when it comes to directives to remove them directly, other court-related matters, such as NIMBY battles, reveal that courts also side with business interests and wealthy residential communities (Dear and von Mahs 1995).

5. The fourth vendor, Matze, preferred selling his papers at a regular spot outside a department store. He reached a modus vivendi with store security by obliging their request that he move his spot a few yards away from the main entrance. He later developed cordial relations with store security and staff members, who occasionally provided him with food or drink.

CHAPTER 4

1. To examine the geography of shelter and service provision in Berlin, I performed a spatial analysis of the geographic distribution and locational characteristics of 139 homeless services in Berlin. Specifically, I looked at the geographic patterns of distribution of different service types, including 47 day centers, 11 soup kitchens, 23 emergency shelters, and 58 transitional shelters and housing facilities. For each facility, I determined the basic characteristics (size, location, organizational features, service options, etc.) and the locational attributes (social index and socioeconomic characteristics of the immediate surrounding community, distance to public transit, distance to undesirable land-use forms). I then located the facilities on a map and produced separate maps for each service type. I eventually overlaid the maps to show distributional patterns and to determine the existence of service agglomerations.

2. The former GDR did not have a substantial homelessness problem and thus no need to build a homeless service infrastructure, because there was, de jure, a right to housing, and the government went to great lengths to provide affordable housing. The fact that such housing still exists may explain why eastern districts have substantially less homelessness than western districts, which had already experienced housing shortages and thus a substantial rise in homelessness prior to unification. This does not mean, however, that homelessness did not exist in the GDR. Rather, people who "refused" housing were persecuted as "antisocial deviants" (Busch-Geertsema and Ruhstrat 1997; Pape 1996).

3. Such apartment complexes are referred to as rental barracks (*Mietskasernen*) and were first commissioned by Emperor Wilhelm II in the boroughs surrounding the immediate city center after the economic boom following the founding of the German Reich in 1871. Most of these rental barracks were rebuilt after sustaining substantial damage from Allied bombing raids in World War II and were somewhat upgraded in terms of apartment sizes and amenities. Still, most barracks contain unattractive, small, dark apartments.

4. Service facilities that used to exist inside the commercial center prior to unification and the gentrification of downtown have almost all ceased operations because of rent increases. The highly acclaimed medical clinic at the Hauptbahnhof, for instance, had to relocate because of rent increases on the premises of the now-privatized German railroad, the refusal of the railroad management to renew the lease, and subsequent renovations at the facility without provisions for the homeless. The clinic relocated to Lichtenberg, four subway stops farther east.

5. In addition, I relied on field observations and a systematic examination of the vicinity of the case studies. I informally talked with neighbors, local store owners, and pedestrians about the facilities and their clients and detected no noteworthy opposition. In the vicinity of the Wohnheim Trachenbergring, I conducted a survey of 136 neighbors within a five-hundred-meter radius to examine potential community resistance yet found hardly any.

6. A social index is a statistical value that comprises the correlation of twenty demographic economic, social, and health variables (for explanation of methods, see Hermann, Imme, and Meinlschmidt 1998, 6–13). These authors determined the social indices of Berlin's 338 traffic cells, indicated in a seven-tier hierarchy from 1 (highest, positive social index) to 7 (lowest, negative social index) and have published their findings in Berlin's "Social Structure Atlas" (1998 and 2004). The study has been criticized for using "foreign nationals" as a potentially negative variable.

7. Upon sign-in, respondents would, on average, wait for up to two and a half hours in line. Once in the office, the welfare recipients would see the caseworker for typically no

more than ten minutes. Following standard procedures, the caseworker would put the applicant through an intake and verification process (especially for transient homeless), inquire about basic needs, typically issue cash assistance, and quickly refer people to a shelter. People were rarely given the opportunity to state their problems and to inquire about options. Decisions were basically made for them by caseworkers, who for the most part were unfamiliar with the multifaceted nature of homelessness.

8. "Night cafés" usually have strict alcohol prohibitions and hygienic entry requirements (which Matze and Bernie, as nonalcoholics with inconspicuous appearances, did not mind), forcing street homeless or people with alcohol problems to rely on other, more-accepting, communal and voluntary emergency shelters—which are characterized by terrible conditions.

9. "Housing prostitution" is a not-uncommon informal housing strategy used by homeless women, who in doing so often venture from a bad situation (sleeping rough) to an even worse one (abusive relationship), as Sybille Paetow-Spinosa, spokesperson for the Berlin State Commission Against Violence, told me in an interview on March 12, 1998.

10. Sioux is founding member of the *Bundesbetroffeneninitiative* (BI), a federal advocacy group founded and organized by homeless people themselves. The BI is affiliated with a number of street-newspaper agencies and the Federal Task Force on Homelessness (BAG Wohnungslosenhilfe).

11. Winkelby and White's (1992) medical study is aptly subtitled "Onset of Morbidity over Time," showing that substance abuse and medical problems in general increase exponentially over the course of homelessness. For support of the argument that alcohol and drug consumption increased in Berlin, see Podschus and Dufeu 1995.

12. No clear guidelines explain how to determine excessive drug consumption or alcoholism, as personal circumstances and tolerances vary. I defined "excessive use" on the basis of the amount of alcohol and/or drugs consumed and the frequency of use (i.e., if a person had more than three drinks a day more than three times a week). To find out about people's consumption, I used self-reporting as well as personal observations while living in the shelter and having contact with the respondents. In addition, I used my training as an assistant psychiatric nurse to detect common symptoms of alcohol dependence.

13. For further discussion of the relationship between shelter and alcohol or controlled substance (ab)use in Germany, see Bauer 1980; Giesbrecht 1987; Schmid 1990; Schneider 1998. For the United States, see Glaser 1994; Desjarlais 1997; Snow and Anderson 1993; Wolch and Dear 1993.

14. It is important to remember that recreational alcohol or drug consumption in mainstream society is also widespread. Because people are doing this either in the sanctuary of their private homes or in designated spaces (i.e., bars, restaurants where alcohol can be purchased), such use does not come under the same public scrutiny as alcohol or drug use among homeless people.

15. Unfortunately, Kalle did eventually relapse. Interestingly, the relapse occurred after Kalle found an apartment and a job yet resumed drinking out of loneliness and boredom. After six years of independent living, he ended up in the Wohnheim Trachenbergring again, where he plans on staying for the foreseeable future (Uta Sternal, shelter manager, conversation, July 23, 2008).

16. The demise of social connections to nonhomeless people and the increasing reliance on peer networks throughout the course of homelessness has been discussed in more detail in Desjarlais 1997; Rowe and Wolch 1990; Schneider 1998; Snow and Anderson 1993; Wolch and Dear 1993.

17. The ability to maintain important external social networks with nonhomeless

family, neighbors, and acquaintances has been positively correlated to homeless people's chances of overcoming homelessness in a number of U.S. studies (Koegel 1994; Schoeni and Koegel 1998; B. Wright 1996; Zlotnick, Robertson, and Lhiff 1999).

18. FTW's and Marita's extensive contacts with Berlin's heroin scene, for instance, were obviously not facilitators of exit. In Marita's case, such networks may have occasionally led to temporary shelter yet kept her entrapped in the heroin scene that nourished and exploited her addiction.

19. The term "*Kiez*" should not be confused with the commercial entertainment stretch that is branded as a "*Kiez*" in tourist guides. Regardless of how small it is, any urban center (*Stadtteil*) with at least a few bars constitutes a *Kiez* for old-timers—and relatively quickly for newcomers also.

20. The *Strassenfeger* printed an article about homeless people's sex life. Tellingly, the article consisted of an empty page (Sioux, interview, March 8, 1998). Sioux's and Sachse's newfound relationships eventually allowed them to move in with their partners and thus overcome homelessness.

21. Los Angeles (DeVerteuil 2003a, 2003b; Wolch and Dear 1993; Stoner 2002), New York (Hopper 2003), and Austin (Snow and Anderson 1993).

22. Berlin's most impoverished communities, host to most of the service agglomerations, have lesser extents of poverty (40 vs. 60 percent) and extreme poverty (10 vs. 35 percent) than Los Angeles. Ethnic minorities, most notably Turks, make up to 40 percent of the population in impoverished communities, compared to a minority population of 85 percent in marginalized communities in Los Angeles. Despite the omnipresent poverty in Berlin, signs of economic vitality and commercial activity are emerging, and there is an unmistakable presence of thriving Turkish businesses. Occasional tourists are drawn to the seediness yet safety of the place and, especially at night, its vibrancy. For discussion, see Veith and Sambale 1999.

23. Skid Row is home to some eleven thousand homeless people who live within a five-by-seven-block area just east of the city's central business district (Burns, Flaming, and Haydamack 2004). A vast array of nonprofit organizations creates a patchwork of services with, in parts, exemplary service for "deserving" homeless at the expense of presumably "undeserving" clients, such as able-bodied single adults. The community characteristics reveal that such agglomerations are clearly located in the most socioeconomically deprived communities of the entire metropolitan area (DeVerteuil 2003; Wolch and Dear 1993). Only downtown, Southeast L.A., and Long Beach have such concentrations, all of which serve primarily African American homeless people.

24. According to key informants and a newspaper archive search, NIMBYism was evident in only one instance. In the early to mid-1990s, a number of informal homeless encampments (*Wagenburgen*) had to relocate after their previous locations along the Berlin Wall became prime real estate. Their attempts to find sites in more peripheral residential communities were met with severe community resistance and a vicious media campaign, resulting in only two successful relocations (Sambale and Veith 1998). Otherwise, shelters and service facilities seem to coexist peacefully with their host communities. My own investigations in the neighborhood surrounding the Wohnheim Trachenbergring, the Warmer Otto, and the Strassenfeger revealed indifference or relative support rather than rejection. Few neighbors had contact with residents or clients, and if they did, they were typically positive.

25. Personal conversations with Uta Sternal (AK Wohnungsnot), Stefan Schneider (Mob e.V.), and Susanne Gerul (ASK Fachhochschule) during a Germany visit sponsored by the Andrew Mellon Foundation travel grant.

CHAPTER 5

1. As described in Chapter 3, six respondents with regular life courses received direct cash assistance—unemployment compensation—from such offices yet saw their eligibility expire (after three years of unemployment insurance and compensation receipt, one year after the Hartz IV reforms in 2005) and subsequently joined the pool of social-assistance recipients.

APPENDIX 1

1. To ensure consistency and to properly translate attendance in the lower tiers of the German education system, including Hauptschule (nine-year education) and Realschule (eleven-year education) in West Germany, and the Polytechnische Oberschule (ten-year education) in East Germany, I use the English term "high school." To describe attendance in the higher tier of German education, commonly referred to as Gymnasium (thirteen-year education), I use the term "higher-tier high school."

References

Abgeordnetenhaus von Berlin. 1995. *Mitteilung—zur Kenntnisnahme: Über Obdachlosenplan* [Announcement—FYI: Homelessness action plan]. Drs. Nr. 12/494, II.B.33.b. Schlußbericht. Berlin: Kulturbuch Verlag.

———. 1996. *Besprechung gemäß § 21 Abs. 5 GO Abghs über Vertreibung von Obdachlosen aus den Bahnhöfen und rechtswidriges Verbringen von Personen an den Stadtrand von Berlin durch die Polizei* [Hearing of Berlin's State Parliament pertaining to paragraph 22, section 5 of public order law regarding the displacement of homeless people from railroad stations and the unlawful deportation of people to the urban fringe through the police]. Wortprotokoll des Auschuß für Soziales, 7. Sitzung am 3.06.96, Soz 13/7. Berlin: Kulturbuch Verlag.

———. 1999. *Mitteilung—zur Kenntnisnahme: Leitlinien und Maßnahmen -bzw. Handlungsplan der Wohnungslosenhilfe und -politik in Berlin. Schlußbericht* [Announcement—FYI: Guidelines and measures or action plan of homeless assistance and policy in Berlin. Final report]. Drs. Nr. 13/4095. Berlin: Kulturbuch Verlag.

———. 2008. *Kleine Anfrage des Abgeordenten Gregor Hoffman (CDU) Fortschreibung der Leitlinien zur Wohnungslosenpolitik* [Hearing request by Rep. Gregor Hoffmann (CDU) from 05.22.2008 about continuation of guidelines for homeless people]. Drucksache 16/12 170. Berlin: Kulturbuch Verlag.

Acosta, O., and P. Toro. 2000. Let's ask the homeless people themselves: A needs assessment based on a probability sample of adults. *American Journal of Community Psychology* 28 (3): 343–366.

AK Wohnungsnot. 1996. *Denn sie wissen, was sie tun. Thesenpapier zur Aktionswoche vom 28.10.96–07.11.96.* Berlin: AK Wohnungsnot. Available at http://ak-wohnungsnot.de/home.

———. 2007. *Statements des Arbeitskreises Wohnungsnot zur Überarbeitung der Leitlinien,* July. Available at http://ak-wohnungsnot.de/home/.

Albrecht, U. 1994. Los Angeles und New York—eine Metropolenperspektive für Berlin? In *Hauptstadt Berlin, Band 1: Nationale Hauptstadt europäische Metropole,* ed. Süß, 248–263. W. Berlin: Berlin Verlag.

Alcock, P., and G. Craig, eds. 2001. *International social policy: Welfare regimes in the developed world.* Houndmills, Basingstoke, UK: Palgrave.

Alexander, J., and B. Weiner. 1998. The adoption of the corporate governance model by nonprofit organizations. *Nonprofit Management and Leadership* 8 (3): 233–242.

Amster, R. 2008. *Lost in space: The criminalization, globalization, and urban ecology of homelessness.* New York: LFB Scholarly Publishing.

Amt für Statistik Berlin-Brandenburg. 2011. *Regionaler Sozialbericht Berlin und Brandenburg.* Potsdam: Amt für Statistik Berlin-Brandenburg.

Avramov, D., ed. 1995. *Homelessness in the European Union: Social and legal context of housing exclusion in the 1990s.* Brussels: FEANTSA.

———. 1999. *Coping with homelessness: Issues to be tackled and best practices in Europe.* Aldershot, UK: Ashgate.

BAG Wohnungslosenhilfe. 2001. *Für eine bürger- und gemeindenahe Wohnungslosenhilfe: Grundsatzprogramm der Bundesarbeitsgemeinschaft Wohnungslosenhilfe e.V.* Bielefeld, Germany: BAG Wohnungslosenhilfe.

———. 2009. *BAG Informationen: Zahl der Wohnungslosen* [BAG Information: Numbers of homeless people]. Bielefeld, Germany: BAG Wohnungslosenhilfe.

———. 2010. *BAG Informationen: Zahl der Wohnungslosen* [BAG Information: Numbers of homeless people]. Bielefeld, Germany: BAG Wohnungslosenhilfe.

———. 1997. Obdachlosigkeit—eine gesamtgesellschaftliche Herausforderung: Beschlußempfehlung und Bericht des Ausschusses für Raumordnung, Bauwesen und Städtebau zu dem Bericht der Bundesregierung über Maßnahmen zur Bekämpfung der Obdachlosigkeit [Homelessness—a challenge for society: Recommendations and report of the committees for spatial order, construction, and urban development on the report of the federal government on measures to combat homelessness]. *Wohnungslos* 3 (97): 125–128.

Baker, S. 1994. Gender, ethnicity, and homelessness. *American Behavioral Scientist* 37 (4): 476–504.

Bauer, R. 1980. *Obdachlos in Marioth: Von der Notunterkunft zum "modernen Asyl."* Weinheim, Germany: Belz Verlag.

Baumohl, J., ed. 1996. *Homelessness in America.* Phoenix: Oryx Press.

Baumohl, J., and R. Huebner. 1991. Alcohol and other drug problems among the homeless: Research, practice and future directions. *Housing Policy Debate* 2 (3): 837–866.

Belina, B. 2003. Evicting the undesirables: The idealism of public space and the materialism of the bourgeois state. *Belgeo* 3 (2): 47–62.

———. 2007. From disciplining to dislocation: Area bans in recent urban policing in Germany. *European Urban and Regional Studies* 14 (4): 321–336.

Bennett, S. 1999. Crossing the line: Experiences of the formerly homeless living past homelessness. Ph.D. diss., University of San Diego.

Beratungsstelle für Wohnungslose. 1996. *Jahresbericht 1996. Beratungsstelle für Wohnungslose, Lewetzowstrasse.* Berlin: Caritasverband.

Berthold, M., ed. 1998. *Wege aus dem Ghetto. . . . In der Krise des Sozialstaates muss sich die Wohnungslosenhilfe neu orientieren: Dokumentation der Bundestagung 1997 der BAG Wohnungslosenhilfe.* Bielefeld, Germany: Verlag Soziale Hilfe.

Blair, T., and G. Schröder. 1999. *Europe: The third way/Die neue Mitte.* Available at http://www.labour.org.uk/views/items/00000053.html.

Blasi, G., and F. Stuart. 2008. *Has the Safer Cities Initiative in Skid Row reduced serious crime?* Los Angeles: UCLA School of Law.

Blum, E., ed. 1996. *Wem gehört die Stadt? Armut und Obdachlosigkeit in Metropolen* [Who owns the city? Poverty and homelessness in metropolitan areas]. Basel, Switzerland: Lenos.

Brenner, N. 2004. Urban governance and the production of new state spaces in western Europe, 1960–2000. *Review of International Political Economy* 11 (3): 447–488.

Brenner, N., and N. Theodore. 2002. Cities and geographies of actually existing neoliberalism. *Antipode* 34 (3): 349–379.

Bundesagentur für Arbeit. 2010a. *Arbeitsmarkt in Deutschland: Zeitreihen bis 2009* [The German labor market: Time series until 2009]. Nuremberg: Bundesagentur für Arbeit, Statistik Datenzentrum.

———. 2010b. *Formulare für Arbeitslosengeld II.* Available at http://www.arbeitsagentur.de/nn_26642/Navigation/zentral/Formulare/Buerger/Arbeitslosengeld-II/Arbeitslosengeld-II-Nav.html.

Burnam, A., and P. Koegel. 1988. Methodology for obtaining a representative sample of homeless persons: The Skid Row study. *Evaluation Review* 12 (2): 117–152.

Burns, P., D. Flaming, and B. Haydamack. 2004. Homeless in L.A.: A working paper for the 10-year plan to end homelessness in Los Angeles County. Los Angeles: Economic Roundtable. Available at http://www.economicrt.org.

Burt, M. 2008. *Evaluation of LA's HOPE: Ending chronic homelessness through employment and housing: Final report.* Washington, DC: Urban Institute.

Burt, M., L. Aron, E. Lee, and J. Valente. 2001. *Helping America's homeless: Emergency shelter or affordable housing.* Washington, DC: Urban Institute.

Busch-Geertsema, V. 2002. When homeless people are allowed to decide by themselves: Rehousing homeless people in Germany. *European Journal of Social Work* 5 (1): 5–19.

———. 2003. *The changing role of the state in housing and social policy.* Thematic Paper for the European Observatory on Homelessness. Bremen: FEANTSA.

———. 2005. Does rehousing lead to reintegration? Follow-up studies of re-housed homeless people. *Innovation: The European Journal of Social Science Research* 18 (2): 205–226.

———. 2006. Hartz IV: Folgen und Risiken für das Wohnen einkommensschwacher und sozial ausgegrenzter Bürgerinnen und Bürger [Hartz IV: Consequences and risks for housing poor and excluded citizens]. In *Integration statt Ausgrenzung—Gerechtigkeit statt Almosen: Herausforderungen für eine bürger- und gemeindenahe Wohnungslosenhilfe.* Heft 58, *Reihe Materialien zur Wohnungslosenhilfe* [Integration instead of exclusion—justice instead of handouts: Challenges for community and citizenship-based homeless assistance], Working Paper 58, ed. W. Rosenke, 88–102. Bielefeld, Germany: BAG Wohnungslosenhilfe.

———. 2008. Urban governance, homelessness and exclusion: Homelessness and access to space in Germany. In *In my caravan, I feel like Superman: Essays in honour of Henk Meert, 1963–2006,* ed. J. Doherty and B. Edgar, 31–48. Brussels: FEANTSA.

———. 2010. Defining and measuring homelessness. In *Homelessness research in Europe: Festschrift for Bill Edgar and Joe Doherty,* ed. E. O'Sullivan, V. Busch-Geertsema, D. Quilgars, and N. Pleace, 19–39. Brussels: FEANTSA.

Busch-Geertsema, V., and J. Evers. 2006. *Auswirkungen der Hartz-Gesetzgebung auf die Hilfe in Wohnungsnotfällen in Schleswig-Holstein: Ergebnisse der ersten Erhebungswelle (Winter 2005–2006)* [The impact of Hartz legislation on housing emergency assistance in Schleswig-Holstein: Results of the first wave, winter 2005–2006]. Bremen: Gesellschaft für innovatives Sozialforschung und Sozialplanung.

Busch-Geertsema, V., J. Evers, and E.-U. Ruhstrat. 2005. *Wirksamkeit persönlicher und wirtschaftlicher Hilfe by der Prävention von Wohnungslosigkeit* [Effectiveness of personal and economic assistance in the prevention of homelessness]. Bremen: Gesellschaft für innovatives Sozialforschung und Sozialplanung.

Busch-Geertsema, V., and S. Fitzpatrick. 2009. Effective homelessness prevention? Explaining reductions in homelessness in Germany and England. *European Journal of Homelessness* 2:69–96.

Busch-Geertsema, V., and E.-U. Ruhstrat. 1997. Wohnungslosigkeit in Ostdeutschland: Ergebnisse eines Forschungsprojektes in Sachsen-Anhalt. *Nachrichtendienst des Deutschen Vereins,* Heft 11/1997.

Cameron, A. 2007. Geographies of welfare and exclusion: Reconstituting the "public." *Progress in Human Geography* 31:519–526.

Claasen, J., ed. 1999. *Comparative social policy: Concepts, theories and methods.* Oxford, UK: Blackwell.

Claasen, J., and R. Freeman, eds. 1994. *Social policy in Germany.* New York: Harvester Wheatsheaf.

Clarke, J., and F. F. Piven. 2001. United States: An American welfare state? In *International social policy: Welfare regimes in the developed world,* ed. P. Alcock and G. Craig, 26–44. Houndmills, Basingstoke, UK: Palgrave.

Conley, D. 1996. Getting it together: Social and institutional obstacles to getting off the streets. *Sociological Forum* 11 (1): 25–40.

Continuum of Care. 1996. *A report on the new federal policy to address homelessness: Summary of findings.* Gaithersburg, MD: Community Connections.

Corday, D., and G. Pion. 1997. What's behind the numbers? Definitional issues in counting the homeless. In *Understanding homelessness: New policy and research perspectives,* ed. D. Culhane and S. Hornburg, 69–99. Washington, DC: Fannie Mae Foundation.

Cousineau, M. 1993. *A profile of urban encampments in central Los Angeles.* Los Angeles: Los Angeles Coalition to End Homelessness.

Culhane, D., and S. Metraux. 1997. Where to from here: A policy research agenda based on the analysis of administrative data. In *Understanding homelessness: New policy and research perspectives,* ed. D. Culhane and S. Hornburg, 341–360. Washington, DC: Fannie Mae Foundation.

Culhane, D., and K. Smith. 1997. The anchor system for homeless services: An information system for the continuum of case information and service implementation resource guide. Philadelphia: University of Pennsylvania Press.

Dalet, D. 2012. Germany > Berlin: Boundaries, districts, names. D-Maps.com. Available at http://d-maps.com/carte.php?num_car=6155&lang=en.

Daly, G. 1996. *Homeless: Policies, strategies, and lives on the street.* London: Routledge.

Daly, M. 1999. Regimes of social policy in Europe and the patterning of homelessness. In *Coping with homelessness: Issues to be tackled and best practices in Europe,* ed. D. Avramov, 309–330. Aldershot, UK: Ashgate.

Davis, M. 1990. *City of Quartz.* London: Verso.

Dear, M. 1992. Understanding and overcoming the NIMBY syndrome. *Journal of the American Planning Association* 58:288–300.

Dear, M., and L. Takahashi. 1992. Health and homelessness. In *Community, environment, and health: Geographic perspectives,* ed. M. Hayes, L. Foster, and H. Foster, 112–145. Victoria, BC, Canada: University of Victoria.

Dear, M., and J. von Mahs. 1995. *Case studies of successful and unsuccessful siting strategies: A guide for providers, planners, advocates and activists—interim report #4.* Santa Monica, CA: Campaign for New Community.

———. 1997. Housing for the homeless, by the homeless, and of the homeless. In *The Architecture of Fear,* ed. N. Ellin, 187–200. Princeton, NJ: Princeton University Press.

Dear, M., and J. Wolch. 1987. *Landscapes of despair.* Princeton, NJ: Princeton University Press.

Del Casino, V., and C. Jocoy. 2008. Neoliberal subjectivities, the "new" homelessness, and struggles over spaces of/in the city. *Antipode* 40:192–199.

Department of Public Social Services (DPSS). 2009. *Cash aid.* Los Angeles: Los Angeles County Department of Public Social Services. Available at http://dpss.lacounty.gov/new_portal/dpss_cashaid.cfm.

Der Paritätische Gesamtverband. 2009. *Armutsatlas Berlin.* Available at http://www.forschung.paritaet.org/index.php?id=1468.

Desjarlais, R. 1997. *Shelter blues: Sanity and selfhood among the homeless.* Philadelphia: University of Pennsylvania Press.

Deutscher Gewerkschaftsbund (DGB). 2010. 5 Jahre Hartz IV—keine Erfolgsstory [5 years of Hartz IV—no success story]. *Arbeitsmarkt Aktuell* (January): 1–10.

DeVerteuil, G. 2003a. Homeless mobility, institutional settings, and the new poverty management. *Environment and Planning A* 35 (2): 361–379.

———. 2003b. Welfare reform, institutional practices and service delivery settings. *Urban Geography* 24 (6): 529–550.

———. 2004. Systematic inquiry into barriers to researcher access: Evidence from a homeless shelter. *Professional Geographer* 56 (3): 372–380.

———. 2005. The relationship between government assistance and housing outcomes among extremely low-income individuals: A qualitative inquiry in Los Angeles. *Housing Studies* 20 (3): 383–399.

———. 2006. The local state and homeless shelters: Beyond revanchism? *Cities* 23 (2): 109–120.

DeVerteuil, G., W. Lee, and J. Wolch. 2002. New spaces for the local welfare state? The case of general relief in Los Angeles County. *Journal of Social and Cultural Geography* 3 (3): 229–246.

DeVerteuil, G., M. Marr, and D. Snow. 2009. Any space left? Homeless resistance by place-type in Los Angeles County. *Urban Geography* 30 (6): 633–651.

DeVerteuil, G., J. May, and J. von Mahs. 2009. Complexity, not collapse: Recasting geographies of homelessness in a punitive age. *Progress in Human Geography* 33 (5): 646–666.

Doherty, J., V. Busch-Geertsema, V. Karpuskiene, J. Korhonen, E. O'Sullivan, I. Sahlin, A. Tosi, A. Petrillo, and A. Wygnańska. 2008. Homelessness and exclusion: Regulating public space in European cities. *Surveillance and Society* 5 (3): 290–314.

Duneier, M. 1999. *Sidewalk.* New York: Farrar, Straus and Giroux.

Edgar, B., J. Doherty, and H. Meert. 2003. *Review on statistics on homelessness in Europe.* Brussels: FEANTSA.

Edgar, B., J. Doherty, and A. Mina-Coull. 1999. *Services for the homeless: Innovation and change in the European Union.* Bristol, UK: Policy Press.

Eick, V. 1996. *Mein ist die Stadt . . . : Das Berliner Sicherheitssystem und die Zugangsbedingungen der Stadt für Ihre Bewohner* [The city is mine . . . : Berlin's security system and access to the city for its residents]. Master's thesis, Otto-Suhr-Institut FU Berlin.

———. 1998. Neue Sicherheitsstrukturen im Neuen Berlin: "Warehousing" öffentlichen Raumes und staatlicher Gewalt [New safety structures in the New Berlin: The "Warehousing" of public space and state power]. *PROKLA* 28 (1): 95–118.

———. 2008. Verlängertes Gewaltmonopol? Der kommerzielle Teil der "neuen Sicherheitsarchitektur" [Extended monopoly of power? The commercial aspect of the "new security architecture"]. *Bürgerrechte und Polizei/CILIP* 91:61–68.

Eick, V., M. Mayer, and J. Sambale, eds. 2003. *From welfare to work: Nonprofits and the workfare state in Berlin and Los Angeles.* Berlin: JFK Institute, Freie Universität Berlin.

Einbinder, S., D. Flaming, Y. Hasenfeld, J. Henly, and J. Wolch. 1995. *Jobs, welfare, and homelessness.* Los Angeles: Southern California Inter-University Consortium on Homelessness and Poverty.

Esping-Andersen, G. 1990. *Three worlds of welfare capitalism.* Cambridge, UK: Polity Press.

———. 1996. *Welfare states in transition: National adaptations in global economies.* London: Sage Publications.

———. 1999. *Social foundations of postindustrial societies.* Oxford, UK: Oxford University Press.

Fernandez, H., S. Harrington, D. Lowery, and B. Erlenbush. 2000. *Welfare to worse: The effects of welfare reform in Los Angeles County 1998–2000.* Los Angeles Coalition to End Hunger and Homelessness. Available at http://www.peoplesguide.org/lacehh/welfare%20to%20worse.htm.

Ferrera, M., and A. C. Hemerijck. 2003. Recalibrating Europe's welfare regimes. In *Governing work and welfare in a new economy—European and American experiments,* ed. J. Zeitlin, M. David, and D. M. Trubek, 88–128. Oxford, UK: Oxford University Press.

Flaming, D., ed. 1995. *Jobs, welfare and homelessness.* Los Angeles: Southern California Inter-University Consortium on Homelessness and Poverty.

Flaming, D., and M. Drayse. 1997a. *Homeless workers: A labor market analysis.* Los Angeles: Economic Roundtable.

———. 1997b. *Identifying individuals at risk of homelessness.* Los Angeles: Economic Roundtable.

Foscarinis, M. 1996. The federal response: The Stuart B. McKinney Homeless Assistance Act. In *Homelessness in America,* ed. J. Baumohl, 160–171. Washington, DC: National Coalition for the Homeless.

Gallup Organization. 1995. *Homeless but not hopeless: A Los Angeles mission report on what Americans believe about homeless people, their problems and possible solutions.* Princeton, NJ: Gallup Organization.

Geiger, M., and E. Steinert. 1992. *Alleinstehende Frauen ohne Wohnung: Soziale Hintergründe, Lebensmilieus, Bewältigungsstrategien, Hilfeangebote.* Stuttgart: Schriftenreihe des Bundesministers für Frauen und Jugend, Bd. 5.

Gerull, S. 2003. *Behördliche Maßnahmen bei drohendem Wohnungsverlust durch Mietschulden.* Berlin: KBW-Fachbuchverlag.

Gerull, S., M. Merckens, and C. Dubrow. 2009. Qualitative Stude zu "Erfolg" in der Hilfe nach Par. 67ff SGB XII [Qualitative study about the "success" of assistance on basis of Par. 67ff SGB XII]. Berlin: Alice Salomon Hochschule.

Giesbrecht, A. 1987. *Wohnungslos—Arbeitslos—Mittellos: Lebensläufe und aktuelle Situationen Nichtseßhafter.* Opladen, Germany: Leske und Budrich.

Girtler, R. 1990. *Vagabunden in der Großstadt: Teilnehmende Beobachtung in der Lebenswelt der Sandler* [Vagabonds in the big city: Participant observation in the life world of homeless people]. Vienna: Universität Wien.

Glasser, I. 1994. Homelessness in global perspective. Boston: G. K. Hall.

Goodin, R., B. Headey, R. Muffels, and H. J. Dirven. 1999. *The real worlds of welfare capitalism.* Cambridge, UK: Cambridge University Press.

Greenberg, M., and J. Baumohl. 1996. Income maintenance: Little help now and less on the way. In *Homelessness in America,* ed. J. Baumohl, 63–78. Washington, DC: National Coalition for the Homeless.

Greenhalgh, E., A. Miller, E. Mead, K. Jerome, and J. Minnery. 2004. *Recent international and national approaches to homelessness: Final report to the National SAAP Coordination and Development Committee.* Queensland, Australia: Australian Housing and Urban Research Institute Queensland Research Centre.

Haber, M., and P. A. Toro. 2004. Homelessness among families, children and adolescents: An ecological developmental perspective. *Clinical Child and Family Psychology Review* 7:123–164.

Handler, J. 2004. *Social citizenship and workfare in the United States and western Europe: The paradox of inclusion.* Cambridge, UK: Cambridge University Press.

Hardin, B. 1996. Why the road off the road is not paved with jobs. In *Homelessness in America,* ed. J. Baumohl, 46–62. Washington, DC: National Coalition for the Homeless.

Häußermann, H. 1997–1998. Amerikanisierung der deutschen Städte—Divergenz und Konvergenz [Americanization of German cities? Divergences and convergences]. *CENTRUM. Jahrbuch für Architektur und Stadt* (1997–1998): 92–96.

Häußerman, H., and D. Förste. 2009. *Monitoring Soziale Stadtentwicklung 2008: Kurzfassung* [Monitoring urban social development 2008: Short version]. Available at http://www.stadtentwicklung.berlin.de/planen/basisdaten_stadtentwicklung/monitoring/download/2008/Kurzfassung-Monitoring2008.pdf.

Hecker, W. 2002. Der öffentliche Raum in der Bundesrepublik Deutschland—Bettel- und Alkoholkonsumverbote, Aufenthaltsverbote, Privatisierung: Zum Stand der Entwicklung [Public space in Germany—anti-panhandling laws and alcohol bans through privatization: Current status]. In *Wohnungslosenhilfe: Verbindlich verbunden! Kooperationen—Verbundsysteme—Bündnisse* (Issue 51 of Materialien zur Wohnungslosenhilfe), ed. M. Berthold, 221–230. Bielefeld, Germany: Verlag Soziale Hilfe.

Heilman, J., and M. Dear. 1988. *Homelessness: A comparison of national experiences.* Working Paper 5, Los Angeles Homelessness Project.

Helvie, C., and W. Kunstmann, eds. 1999. *Homelessness in the United States, Europe, and Russia: A comparative perspective.* Westport, CT: Bergin and Garvey.

Hermann, S., U. Imme, and G. Meinlschmidt. 1998. *Sozialstrukturatlas Berlin 1997: Eine Disaggregierte statistische Sozialraumanalyse* [Atlas of Berlin's social structure 1997: A disaggregated statistical socio-spatial analysis]. Senatsverwaltung für Gesundheit, Referat Gesundheitsstatistik, Gesundheitsberichterstattung, Informations- und Kommunikationstechnik, Datenschutz. Berlin: Verlagsdruckerei.

Holzner, C. 2006. Hartz IV fördert Minijobs und krankt an undgenügenden Durchsetzbarkeit der Zumutbarkeitsregeln [Hartz IV proliferates mini-jobs and is ailing from insufficient implementation of acceptability rules]. *Ifo Dresden Berichtet* 13 (2): 5–10.

Hopper, K. 2003. *Reckoning with homelessness.* Ithaca, NY: Cornell University Press.

Huber, E., and J. Stephens. 2001. *Development and crisis of the welfare state: Parties and policies in global markets.* Chicago: University of Chicago Press.

Hundhammer, F. 1979. *Räumliche Aspekte des Randgruppenproblems: Sozialgeographische Studien zur Situation von Obdachlosen und Sozialhilfeempfängern im städtischen Bereich.* Neusäss/Augsburg, Germany: Paul Kieser Verlag.

Husick, T., and J. Wolch. 1990. *On the edge? An analysis of homed and homeless applicants for general relief in Los Angeles County.* Working Paper 29, Los Angeles Homeless Project.

Huth, M., and T. Wright, eds. 1997. *International Critical Perspectives on Homelessness.* Westport, CT: Praeger.

Interagency Council on the Homeless. 1994. *Priority home! The federal plan to break the cycle of homelessness.* Washington, DC: Interagency Council on the Homeless.

Jocoy, C. L., and V. J. Del Casino Jr. 2010. Homelessness, travel behavior, and the politics of transportation mobilities in Long Beach, California. *Environment and Planning A* 42 (8): 1943–1963.

Kennett, P., ed. 2004. *A handbook of comparative social policy.* Cheltenham, UK: Edward Elgar.

Klodawsky, F. 2006. Landscapes on the margins: gender and homelessness. *Gender Place and Culture* 13 (4): 365–381.

Knecht, M. 1999. *Die andre Seite der Stadt: Armut und Ausgrenzung in Berlin* [The other side of the city: Poverty and exclusion in Berlin]. Cologne: Böhlau Verlag.

Knowles, C. 1999. *Bedlam on the streets.* London: Routledge.

Koegel, P. 2004. The course of homelessness. In *Encyclopedia of homelessness,* ed. D. Levinson, 247–263. Thousand Oaks, CA: Sage Publications.

Krätke, S. 2001. Berlin toward a global city? *Urban Studies* 38 (10): 1777–1799.

Law, R. 2001. "Not in my city": Local governments and homelessness policies in the Los Angeles Metropolitan Region. *Environment and Planning C* 19:791–815.

Lee, B., B. Link, and P. A. Toro. 1991. Images of homelessness: Public opinion and media portrayals. *Housing Policy Debate* 2 (3): 3–36.

Leisering, L. 2001. Germany: Reform from within. In *International social policy: Welfare regimes in the developed world,* ed. P. Alcock and G. Craig, 161–182. Houndmills, Basingstoke, UK: Palgrave.

Leisering, L., and S. Leibfried. 1999. *Time and poverty in western welfare states: United Germany in perspective.* Cambridge, UK: Cambridge University Press.

Leitner, S., and S. Lessenich. 2003. Assessing welfare state change: The German social insurance state between reciprocity and solidarity. *Journal of Public Policy* 23:325–347.

Levinson, D., ed. 2004. *Encyclopedia of homelessness.* Thousand Oaks, CA: Sage Publications.

Lewis, J., 1992. Gender and the development of welfare regimes. *Journal of European Social Policy* 2 (3): 159–173.

Linde, C. 2003. Wohnungsmarkt bleibt geteilt: Halbherzige Korrekturen der verfehlten Wohnungsbauförderung. *Mieterschutz* 1/2003. Available at http://www.wohnungslos-in-berlin.de/texte/ms0301a.htm.

Link, B. G., S. Schwartz, R. Moore, J. Phelan, E. Struening, A. Stueve, and M. E. Colten. 1995. Public knowledge, attitudes, and beliefs about homeless people: Evidence for compassion fatigue? *American Journal of Community Psychology* 23 (4): 533–555.

Los Angeles Coalition to End Hunger and Homelessness (LACEHH). 1997. Special welfare reform issue. *The Bottom Line: LACEHH Quarterly Newspaper* (September).

———. 2004. Homelessness, hunger, poverty and housing in Los Angeles: Fact sheet. Available at http://www.lacehh.org.

Los Angeles Homeless Services Authority (LAHSA). 2011. Homeless: Greater Los Angeles homeless count report. Los Angeles: Shelter Partnership. Available at http://www.lahsa.org/homelessness_data/reports.asp.

Ludwig, R., and J. Neumeyer, eds. 1991. *Die narkotisierte Gesellschaft? Neue Wege in der Drogenpolitik und akzeptierende Drogenarbeit* [The narcotic society? New pathways in drug policy and accepting drug treatment]. Marburg: Schüren-Verlag.

Lyon-Callo, V. 2001. Making sense of NIMBY: Poverty, power, and community opposition to homeless shelters. *City and Society* 13:183–209.

Marcuse, P. 1988. Neutralizing homelessness. *Socialist Review* 18:69–86.

Marr, M. D., G. DeVerteuil, and D. Snow. 2009. Towards a contextual approach to the place–homeless survival nexus: An exploratory case study of Los Angeles County. *Cities* 26 (6): 633–651.

May, J. 2004. 12 things wrong with the revanchist city thesis. Paper presented at the annual meeting of the Association of American Geographers, Philadelphia.

———. 2008. Of nomads and vagrants: Single homelessness and narratives of home as place. In *The Cultural Geography Reader*, ed. T. S. Oakes and P. L. Price, 334–342. London: Routledge.

Mayer, M. 1995. Los Angeles und Berlin im Vergleich [Los Angeles and Berlin in comparison]. In *Los Angeles–Berlin: Stadt der Zukunft, Zukunft der Stadt*, ed. F. Sträter, 98–105. Stuttgart: Context.

———. 1997. Berlin–Los Angeles: Berlin auf dem Weg zur "Global City"? [Berlin–Los Angeles: Berlin on the way toward a "global city"?]. *PROKLA* 27 (4): 519–544.

Meinlschmidt, G. 2004. *Sozialstrukturatlas Berlin 2003: Ein Instrument der quantitativen, interregionalen, intertemporalen Sozialraumanalyse und Planung* [Atlas of Berlin's social structure 2003: An instrument of quantitative, interregional, intertemporal socio-spatial analysis and planning]. Senatsverwaltung für Gesundheit, Referat Gesundheitsstatistik, Gesundheitsberichterstattung, Informations- und Kommunikationstechnik, Datenschutz. Berlin: Verlagsdruckerei.

Mitchell, D. 1997. The annihilation of space by law: The roots and implications of anti-homeless laws in the United States. *Antipode* 29:303–335.

———. 1998a. Anti-homeless laws and public space I: Begging and the First Amendment. *Urban Geography* 19:6–11.

———. 1998b. Anti-homeless laws and public space II: Further constitutional issues. *Urban Geography* 19:98–104.

———. 2003. *The right to the city: Social justice and the fight for public space.* New York: Guilford Press.

———. 2011. Homelessness—American style. *Urban Geography* 32 (7): 933–957.

Mitchell, D., and N. Heynen. 2009. The geography of survival and the right to the city: Speculations on surveillance, legal innovation, and the criminalization of intervention. *Urban Geography* 30:611–632.

Mishra, R. 1999. *Globalization and the welfare state.* Cheltenham, UK: Edgar Elgar.

Mühlich-Klinger, I. 2010. *Fallstudie "Geschütztes Marktsegment" in Berlin: Konzept, Umsetzung, Ergebnisse und Erfahrungen* [Case study "Protected Market Segment" in Berlin: Concept, implementation, results, and experiences]. Darmstadt, Germany: Institute Wohnen und Umwelt.

National Center for Children in Poverty (NCCP). 2009. California: Temporary Assistance for Needy Families (TANF) cash assistance. Available at http://www.nccp.org/profiles/CA_profile_36.html.

National Coalition for the Homeless (NCH). 1997. *Homelessness in America: Unabated and increasing—a 10-year perspective.* Washington, DC: National Coalition for the Homeless.

———. 2009. How many people experience homelessness? Washington, DC: National Coalition for the Homeless. Available at http://www.nationalhomeless.org/factsheets/How_Many.html.

National Law Center on Homelessness and Poverty (NLCHP). 1999. *Out of sight—out of mind? A report on anti-homeless laws, litigation, and alternatives in 50 United States cities: 1998.* Washington, DC: National Law Center on Homelessness and Poverty.

———. 2011. *Criminalizing crisis: The criminalization of homelessness in U.S. cities.* Washington, DC: National Law Center on Homelessness and Poverty.

Neale, J. 2001. Homelessness among drug users: A double jeopardy explored. *International Journal of Drug Policy* 12:353–69.

Neubarth, J. 1997. *Struktur der Hilfen für wohnungslose Menschen in Berlin: Gegebenheiten und Visionen* [The structure of homeless assistance in Berlin: Realities and reform]. Master's thesis, Free University, Berlin.

Neubeck, K., and N. Cazenave. 2001. *Welfare racism: Playing the race card against America's poor.* London: Routledge.

Pape, M. 1996. Obdachlosigkeit in Ost- und Westdeutschland im Vergleich: Dargestellt am Beispiel der Städte Nordhausen und Northeim. *Praxis Kultur- und Sozialgeographie* 14:105.

Passaro, J. 1996. *The unequal homeless: Men on the street, women in their place.* New York: Routledge.

Peck, J. 2001. *Workfare states.* New York: Guilford Press.

Pierson, P., ed. 2001. *The new politics of the welfare state.* Oxford, UK: Oxford University Press.

Piven, F. F., and J. Clark. 2001. The United States: A welfare state? In *International social policy: Welfare regimes in the developed world,* ed. P. Alcock and G. Craig, 161–182. Houndmills, Basingstoke, UK: Palgrave.

Piven, F. F., and R. Cloward. 1993. *Regulating the poor: The functions of public welfare,* 2nd ed. New York: Vintage Books.

Podschus, J., and P. Dufeu. 1995. Alcohol dependence among homeless men in Berlin. *Sucht* 41 (5): 348–354.

Proksch, J. 2011. *Soziale Mindestsicherung in Deutschland 2009* [Basic social support in Germany]. Wiesbaden, Germany: Statistisches Bundesamt.

Quadagno, J. 1994. *The color of welfare: How racism undermined the war on poverty.* New York: Oxford University Press.

Rahimian, A., P. Koegel, and J. Wolch. 1992. A model of homeless migration: Homeless men in Skid Row, Los Angeles. *Environment and Planning A* 24:1317–1336.

Reese, E., G. DeVerteuil, and L. Thach. 2010. "Weak center" gentrification and the contradictions of containment: Deconcentrating poverty in downtown Los Angeles. *International Journal of Urban and Regional Research* 34 (2): 310–327.

Robe, C. 1999. Und Raus bist Du! Wie soziale Probleme in der Berliner Innenstadt ausgegrenzt werden [And you are out! How social problems are excluded in Berlin's inner city]. In *Die Andere Seite der Stadt: Armut und Ausgrenzung in Berlin* [The other side of the city: Poverty and exclusion in Berlin], ed. M. Knecht, 30–42. Cologne: Böhlau Verlag.

Rosenke, W. 1996. Weibliche Wohnungsnot: Ausmaß—Ursachen—Hilfsangebote. *Wohnungslos* (March): 77–80.

———, ed. 2006. *Integration statt Ausgrenzung—Gerechtigkeit statt Almosen: Herausforderungen für eine bürger- und gemeindenahe Wohnungslosenhilfe.* Heft 58, *Reihe Materialien zur Wohnungslosenhilfe* [Integration instead of exclusion—justice instead of handouts: Challenges for community and citizenship-based homeless assistance. Working Paper 58, 88–102. Bielefeld, Germany: BAG Wohnungslosenhilfe.

Rowe, S., and J. Wolch. 1990. Social networks in time and space: Homeless women in Skid Row, Los Angeles. *Annals of the Association of American Geographers* 80 (2): 184–204.

Ruddick, S. 1996. *Young and homeless in Hollywood: Mapping social identities.* New York: Routledge.

Sambale, J., and D. Veith. 1998. Berliner Wagenburgen: Transformation peripherer Räume, Stigmatisierung sozialer Gruppen und die Abwehr von Marginalisierung [Berlin's Trailer Communities: Transformation of peripheral spaces, stigmatization of social groups, and the repulsion of marginality]. In *PROKLA* 28 (100): 67–93.

Sard, D. 2009. Number of homeless families climbing due to recession: Recovery package should include new housing vouchers and other measures to prevent homelessness. Washington, DC: Center on Budget and Policy Priorities.

Schenk, L. 2004. Auf dem Weg zum ewigen Wanderer? Wohnungslose und ihre Institutionen [Down-and-out without an end?]. Ph.D. diss., Free University, Berlin. Available at http://www.diss.fu-berlin.de/2004/146/indexe.html.

Schmid, C., 1990. *Die Randgruppe der Stadtstreicher: Im Teufelskreis der Nichtseßhaftigkeit.* Vienna: Böhlau Verlag.

Schneider, S. 1998. Wohnungslosigkeit und Subjektentwicklung: Biographien, Lebenslagen und Perspektiven Wohnungsloser in Berlin [Homelessness and the social construction of subjects: Biographies, life circumstances and perspectives of homeless people in Berlin]. Ph.D. diss., Free University, Berlin. Available at http://userpage.fu-berlin.de/zosch/diss/index.html.

Schnur, O. 1999. Wohnungsmarkt und Wohnungspolitik in Berlin seit 1990 [Housing market and housing policy in Berlin since 1990]. In *Märkte und Strukturen im Wandel* (VI. Konferenz Amsterdam-Berlin), *Berliner Geographische Arbeiten* 86, ed. M. Schulz and O. Gewand, 1–14. Berlin: Humboldt Universität zu Berlin.

Schoeni, R., and P. Koegel. 1998. Economic resources of the homeless: Evidence from Los Angeles. *Contemporary Economic Policy* 16:295–308.

Senatsverwaltung für Gesundheit, Soziales und Verbraucherschutz. 2002. *Armut und Soziale Ungleichheit in Berlin* [Poverty and social inequality in Berlin]. Berlin: Verlagsdruckerei.

Senatsverwaltung für Gesundheit und Soziales. 1997. *Empfänger und Leistungen im Bereich Soziales: II. Quartal 1997* [Recipients and services in the area of social policy: 2nd quarter of 1997]. Berlin: Referat Gesundheits- und Sozialstatistik, Gesundheitsbereichterstattung, Epidemiologie, Gesundheitsinformationssysteme.

———. 2004. *Empfänger und Leistungen im Bereich Soziales: I. Quartal 2004* [Recipients and services in the area of social policy: 1st quarter of 2004]. Berlin: Referat Gesundheits- und Sozialstatistik, Gesundheitsbereichterstattung, Epidemiologie, Gesundheitsinformationssysteme.

Senatsverwaltung für Integration, Arbeit und Soziales. 2010. *Leistungsbeschreibungen für den Personenkreis nach Par. 67 SGB XII.* Berlin: Verlagsdruckerei.

Senatsverwaltung für Stadtentwicklung. 2003. Der Berliner Wohnungsmarkt: Ein Bericht. Available at http://www.stadtentwicklung.berlin.de/wohnen/wohnungsmarktbericht/pdf/wohnungdmarkt_bericht.pdf.

———. 2004. Berliner Mietspiegel: Abfrageservice [Berlin's rental statistics: Instant data]. Available at http://www.stadtentwicklung.berlin.de/wohnen/mietspiegel/.

Shelter Partnership. 1994. *A report of implementation plans for the Los Angeles area homeless initiative.* Los Angeles: Shelter Partnership.

———. 1995. *The number of homeless people in Los Angeles City and County: July 1993 to June 1994.* Los Angeles: Shelter Partnership.

———. 2001. *A survey of general relief recipients: Housing, utilization of systems of care, and employability status.* Los Angeles: Shelter Partnership.

Shinn, M. 2007. International homelessness: Policy, socio-cultural, and individual perspectives. *Journal of Social Issues* 63:659–679.

———. 2009. *Ending homelessness for families: The evidence for affordable housing.* Washington, DC: National Alliance to End Homelessness.

———. 2010. Homelessness, poverty, and social exclusion in the United States and Europe. *European Journal of Homelessness* 4:19–44.

Shinn, M., and S. N. Fischer. 2004. Research on homelessness: Overview. In *Encyclopedia of Homelessness,* 475–482. Thousand Oaks, CA: Sage Publications.

Shinn, M., B. C. Weitzman, D. Stojanovic, J. R. Knickman, L. Jiménez, L. Duchon, S. James, and D. H. Krantz. 1998. Predictors of homelessness among families in New York City: From shelter request to housing stability. *American Journal of Public Health* 88 (11): 1651–1657.

Shipler, D. 2004. *The working poor: Invisible in America.* New York: Alfred A. Knopf.

Simpson, J., and P. Tepper. 2004. Can the United States end homelessness in ten years? Los Angeles joins the municipal planning movement. *Homeless in Europe: The Newsletter of FEANTSA* (Spring): 8–11.

Smith, N. 1996. *The new urban frontier: Gentrification and the revanchist city.* London: Routledge.

———. 1998. Giuliani Time: The revanchist 1990s. *Social Texts* 57 (18): 1–20.

Snow, D., and L. Anderson. 1993. *Down on their luck: A study of homeless street people.* Berkeley: University of California Press.

Spars, G., P. Jacob, and A. M. Werner. 2009. *Der Berliner Wohnungsmarkt: Ein Standortvorteil* [Berlin's rental market: A locational advantage?]. Wuppertal, Germany: Quaestio Forschung und Beratung.

Statistisches Landesamt Berlin. 2000. Ten years of unity in Berlin—a narrative and statistical analysis of the unification. *Statistische Monatsschrift* 1–6 (2000): 1–164.

Stoner, M. 2002. Globalization and urban homelessness. In *From Chicago to Los Angeles: Making sense of urban theory,* ed. M. Dear, 213–234. Thousand Oaks, CA: Sage Publications.

Sträter, F. 1995. *Los Angeles–Berlin: Stadt der Zukunft, Zukunft der Stadt.* Stuttgart: Context.

Stuart, F. 2011. Race, space, and the regulation of surplus labor: Policing African Americans in Los Angeles's Skid Row. *Souls* 13 (2): 197–212.

Stumberger, R. 2005. *Hartz IV—der Ratgeber* [Hartz IV—the guide]. Vienna: Linde Verlag.

Takahashi, L. 1996. A decade of understanding homelessness in the USA: From characterization to representation. *Progress in Human Geography* 20 (3): 291–310.

Takahashi, L., M. Dear, and M. Neely. 1989. *Characteristics of the homeless population in Downtown Los Angeles, 1988–1989.* Working Paper 23, Los Angeles Homelessness Project.

Tepper, P. 2004. *Homelessness in Los Angeles: A summary of recent research.* Los Angeles: Institute for the Study of Homelessness and Poverty at the Weingart Center. Available at http://www.weingart.org/institute/research/other/pdf/homelessness_in_los_angeles-a_summary_of_recent_research.pdf.

Tepper, P., and J. Simpson. 2003. *The puzzle of the Los Angeles economy: A look at the last 30 years.* Los Angeles: Institute for the Study of Homelessness and Poverty at the Weingart Center. Available at http://www.weingart.org/institute/research/other/pdf/PuzzleLAEconomy.pdf.

Theodore, N. 1998. *On parallel paths: The Clinton/Blair agenda on the new geopolitics of workfare.* Paper presented at the Royal Geographical Society/Institute of British Geographers annual conference, University of Surrey, UK.

Thorn, C. 2011. Soft policies of exclusion: Entrepreneurial strategies of ambience and control of public space in Gothenburg, Sweden. *Urban Geography* 32 (7): 989–1008.

Torck, D. 2001. Voices of homeless people in street newspapers: A cross-cultural exploration. *Discourse Society* 12 (3): 371–392.

Toro, P. A., ed. 2007. International perspectives on homelessness in developed nations: Special edition. *Journal of Social Issues* 63 (3): 461–677.

Toro, P. A., C. J. Tompsett, S. Lombardo, P. Philippot, H. Nachtergael, B. Galand, N. Schlienz, N. Stammel, Y. Yabar, M. Blume, L. MacKay, and K. Harvey. 2007. Homelessness in Europe and the United States: A comparison of prevalence and public opinion. *Journal of Social Issues* 63 (3): 505–524.

United Way of Greater Los Angeles. 1997. *State of the county databook Los Angeles 1996–97.* Los Angeles: Community Development Commission.

U.S. Conference of Mayors. 1998. *A status report on hunger and homelessness in America's cities: A 29-city survey December 1997.* Washington, DC: U.S. Conference of Mayors.

———. 2006. *A status report on hunger and homelessness in the American cities.* Washington, DC: U.S. Conference of Mayors.

———. 2011. *Hunger and homelessness survey: A status report on hunger and homelessness in the American cities: A 29-city survey.* Washington, DC: U.S. Conference of Mayors.

U.S. Department of Housing and Urban Development (HUD). 2001. *Affordable housing shortage in Metro Los Angeles, California.* Rockville, MD: HUD.

———. 2010. *The 2010 annual homeless assessment report to Congress.* Washington, DC: HUD.

van Kersbergen, K. 1995. *Social capitalism: A study of Christian democracy and the welfare state.* London: Routledge.

Veith, D., and J. Sambale. 1999. Wer drinnen ist, ist draußen: Warum auch in Berlin neuerdings über "Ghettos" debattiert wird [Who isn't in stays out: Why there is a recent debate about "ghettos" in Berlin]. In *Die Andre Seite der Stadt: Armut und Ausgrenzung in Berlin,* ed. M. Knecht, 42–59. Cologne: Böhlau Verlag.

Vitale, A. S. 2010. The Safer Cities Initiative and the removal of the homeless. *Criminology and Public Policy* 9:867–873.

von Mahs, J. 2005a. The socio-spatial exclusion of homeless people in Berlin and Los Angeles. *American Behavioral Scientist* 48 (4): 926–960.

———. 2005b. Different welfare regimes, similar outcomes? The impact of social policy on homeless people's life courses and exit chances in Berlin and Los Angeles. Ph.D. diss., University of Southampton.

———. 2011a. Introduction—an Americanization of homelessness in post-industrial societies. *Urban Geography* 32 (7): 923–932.

———. 2011b. Homelessness in Berlin: Between Americanization and path dependence. *Urban Geography* 32 (7): 1023–1043.

———. 2012. A "buddy researcher"? Prospects, limitations, and ethical considerations in ethnographic research on homeless people in Berlin. In *Professional lives, personal struggles: Ethics and advocacy in research on homeless people,* ed. Martha Trenna Valado and Randall Amster. Lanham, MD: Lexington Books: 75–88.

von Mahs, J., and D. Mitchell, eds. 2011. The Americanization of homelessness: Special issue. *Urban Geography* 32 (7): 923–1043.

Vranken, J. 1999. Different policy approaches to homelessness. In *Coping with homelessness: Issues to be tackled and best practices in Europe,* ed. D. Avramov, 331–355. Aldershot, UK: Ashgate.

Wilson, J., and G. Kelling. 1982. Broken windows: The police and neighborhood safety. *Atlantic Monthly* (March): 29–38.

Winkelby, M., and R. White. 1992. Homeless adults without apparent medical and psychiatric impairment: Onset of morbidity over time. *Hospital and Community Psychiatry* 43 (10): 1017–1023.

Wolch, J. 1998. America's new urban policy: Welfare reform and the fate of American cities. *Journal of the American Planning Association* 64:8–11.

Wolch, J., and M. Dear. 1987. *Landscapes of despair: From deinstitutionalization to homelessness.* Princeton, NJ: Princeton University Press.

———. 1993. *Malign neglect: Homelessness in an American city.* San Francisco: Jossey-Bass.

Wolch, J., and G. DeVerteuil. 2001. New landscapes of urban poverty management. In *TimeSpace: Geographies of temporality,* ed. J. May and N. Thrift, 149–168. London: Routledge.

Wolch, J., and S. Dinh. 2001. The new poor laws: Welfare reform and the localization of help. *Urban Geography* 22 (5): 482–489.

Wolch, J., A. Rahimian, and P. Koegel. 1993. Daily and periodic mobility patterns of the urban homeless. *Professional Geographer* 45:159–169.

Wolch, J., and H. Sommer. 1997. *Los Angeles in an era of welfare reform: Implications for poor people and community well-being.* Los Angeles: Southern California Inter-University Consortium on Homelessness and Poverty.

Wolf, J., A., Burnam, P. Koegel, G. Sullivan, and S. Morton. 2001. Changes in subjective quality of life among homeless adults who obtain housing: A prospective evaluation. *Social Psychiatry and Psychiatric Epidemiology* 36:391–398.

Wong, I. 1997. Patterns of homelessness: A review of longitudinal studies. In *Understanding homelessness: New policy and research perspectives,* ed. D. Culhane and S. Hornburg, 135–164. Washington, DC: Fannie Mae Foundation.

Wong, I., and I. Pilavin. 1997. A dynamic analysis of homeless-domicile transitions. *Social Problems* 44 (3): 408–423.

Wright, B. 1996. *Pathways off the streets: Homeless people and their use of resources.* Ph.D. diss., University of Wisconsin–Madison.

Wright, J., and A. Donley. 2008. Shelter life for homeless men: Risk or respite. In *Homelessness in America,* vol. 1, *Faces of Homelessness,* ed. R. McNamara, 43–60. Westport, CT: Praeger.

Wright, J., B. Rubin, and J. Devine. 1998. *Beside the golden door: Policy, politics, and the homeless.* New York: Aldine De Gruyter.

Wright, T. 1997. *Out of place: Homeless mobilizations, subcities, and contested landscapes.* Albany: State University of New York Press.

Zlotnick, C., M. Robertson, and M. Lhiff. 1999. Getting off the streets: Economic resources and residential exits from homelessness. *Journal of Community Psychology* 27 (2): 209–224.

Index

Page numbers followed by the letter t *or* f *refer to tables or figures.*

Jürgen von Mahs is Associate Professor of Urban Studies at The New School in New York City.